The Narcs' Game

The Narcs' Game
Organizational and Informational Limits on Drug Law Enforcement

Peter K. Manning

The MIT Press
Cambridge, Massachusetts, and
London, England

This book was set in VIP Helvetica by Trade Composition, Inc., and printed and bound by The Al-
pine Press Inc. in the United States of America

Research on which this book is based was supported in part by a grant from the National Institute
of Law Enforcement and Criminal Justice, Law Enforcement Assistance Administration, U.S. Department of Justice in the form of a Visiting Fellowship
in 1974–1975 (No. 74-NI-99-0029). Points of view or
opinions expressed in this document are those of
the author and do not necessarily reflect the official
position or policies of the United States Department
of Justice.

Library of Congress Cataloging in Publication Data

Manning, Peter K
    The narcs' game.

    Bibliography: p.
    Includes index.
    1. Narcotics, Control of. 2. Narcotics, Control
of—United States. I. Title.
HV8079.N3M36   363.4′5   79-24620
ISBN 0-262-13154-4

For Pat, Tamara, Elizabeth, and Vykkie
Schiebel and in memory of Joseph Schiebel

Contents

Preface

Underlying formal plans, tables of organization, and statements of goals and objectives are deep understandings that from time to time are made visible, their import made known. There is a form of dialectic between personal experience and organizational plan, between formal goals and agendas and subjectively intended meanings, yet it is difficult to trace these sources of order in organizational analysis. When a fieldworker enters organizations, a similar tension is set to work. While it is rather easy to elicit and lay out clearly the organizational plan and intent as enunciated by executives and administrators, it is rather more difficult to read what they mean and how meanings associated with the formal plans and with different positions in the social structure of the organization coalesce, fuse, divide, and embed the formal plans. Thus experience, feelings, observations, snatches of conversation, a wink, an averted head, a touch, interplay with written documents, annual reports, memos, and ad hoc advisos. In an important sense, although there are other constraints, implicit meanings and deeply structured feelings, along with personal goals, intentions, and self-maximizations are set off against organizational plans, rules, and strategies. This book, based on my field experience as well as interviews and document analysis, examines closely on a day-to-day basis the limitations and constraints on drug policing as it is claimed to be organized and mobilized.

In gathering this information and developing themes that were introduced in *Police Work* (The MIT Press, 1977) I came into close association with a large number of officers and spent a great deal of time with them, in and out of occupational roles. We developed, I think, a good understanding on several levels: Although I was viewed as a marginal participant, I was in some sense a part of the work, even as I maintained a degree of personal and intellectual distance. I value the experiences I shared with these officers. Many fleeting encounters when we shared a dry sandwich, quickly gulped several beers, or engaged in an awkward, touching conversation were and still are warm, significant moments for me. They were human moments, suffused with the problematics of drug policing. I liked many of the people, respected their courage and conviction, but became profoundly more pessimistic about gathering convincing evidence of the positive effects and consequences of the work of drug policing. Even the significant question of whether the task itself was essential in this society, or was properly a police function, came increasingly to demand my attention. This somewhat self-protective dualism, affection linked with doubt, remained with me for a considerable period after I physically left the field. One can easily adopt the view that the persons one studies are appealing and understandable, while the organizational mandate itself is questionable. Consistency requires that one see properly the extent to which officers are free to choose and are committed to the organizational project, and how this tension creates an important organizational dialectic.

An appreciation of this dialectic and my ambivalence are manifested in this book. One sort of ambivalence is symbolized by the title of the book.

When I first walked into the Metro Department in the spring of 1974, I noted the slightly foreboding nature of the place, the grime around the edges, the shadowy halls and frosted glass panes in the office doors, I began to ask myself, "What *do* you expect to see and hear, feel and touch here?" Who are these people? Although I had spent considerable time as a fieldworker in police departments, I realized, almost as I reached the door of the administrator I was to interview to make the first contacts for initiating the study, that I was quite ignorant of the patterns and processes of drug law enforcement and specifically of the role of the drug officer.

I seized on the title early in my project, before I knew very much about the work or about what officers call themselves. Police officers who work with narcotics do not call themselves "narcs" (although in California I have heard police refer to the "narco unit"). The "narc" label is sometimes employed by drug users to refer to officers in a deprecating fashion. In calling the book *The Narcs' Game*, I do not mean to connote that it is a frivolous or silly job, for although there are some game-like features to the work, not all officers view themselves as cynically as do the users. Adopting the metaphor allows me to work it a bit. In working it, it may appear at times that the metaphor is stretched beyond recognition. The reader should not be misled because I adopt or try to articulate the game-like rational view of enforcement, for it is taken as a lightly held point of departure, soon to be slightly modified, smudged and discredited, and turned over to see what lies under the metaphor. The game metaphor is a misleading one that conceals more than it reveals about what the police officer who works in a drug unit does. What lies under or around a metaphor, the fringe meanings that are conveyed, may provide fruitful sources of insights. My view of the officer's work, or the narcs' game, is colored by considerable ambivalence.

In *Police Work* I argued that the dramatic concentration and repetition of certain messages within a sacred context serves to maintain a public image of the police. By adducing and organizing ethnographic materials that incorporated close observation of everyday practices and procedures within an organization, I tried to demonstrate how these images and "blindness" are produced. These images of police work were contradicted by observations of the behavior and practices of policing and changing historical ideologies. The public's attention, focused in one way, is focused away from other facts. A systematic blindness is created. In the argument presented here, I have drawn on the perspective developed in *Police Work* and attempted to refine it for the analysis of drug law enforcement as I observed it in two units in a large metropolitan area of the Southeastern United States. I was a participant observer in these two units and was involved in the full range of activities in each: surveillance, interrogation, arrest, search warrant ("raids") and arrest warrant servings, meetings and planning sessions, and informal interactions on and off the job. Over a period of months in 1975, I observed, interviewed, questioned, and worked closely with officers in these two units.

In doing this work over the course of months, I was converted from one sort of blindness to another; I believe I learned to "think like a good police officer" and have been able to describe and criticize that frame of mind. Many of the more "obvious" aims and purposes of drug law enforcement became less obvious to me, and I saw that the organizations were rarely able to achieve what they formally claimed or even described as their aims. They were protected from public scrutiny by public trust, by their own statements, misleading news releases and descriptions of their work (they rationalize these distortions as ways of

protecting informants and their operations), and by their own secrecy.
The autonomy they enjoy is both created by their obfuscation of their
aims and by the general public concern for "the drug problem."

Clearly these organizations and their participants maintain considerable autonomy in defining, shaping, and executing their collectively
defined activity. The symbols, myths, and publicly constraining collective representations of drug policing, partially created by police organizations themselves, cloak their activities. Officers are inclined not to
see how the individualistic, craft-like nature of their work determines
the rather narrow, temporally isolated effects of police work on drug
markets. Neither the specific rationality nor the long-run consequences
of their activities are frequently mentioned; they are not fully understood and seldom even considered. To state that the action of officers
was not seen in terms of long-range rationality does not mean that they
do not have long-range effects. The selective enactment of social values implicit in every choice, as Goffman (1959:35) reminds us, makes
something of a ceremony of such activity. Drug law enforcement is a
selective and arbitrary declamation of certain legitimated social values. It communicates to various audiences not only a set of instrumental messages, but it also expresses selves, an organizational line or
rhetoric, a set of strategies and subjective meanings that audiences
attach to drug policing. These ceremonial aspects of what officers do,
that is by their actions they assert socially valued symbols and beliefs,
do not lessen the small holocausts strewn in their wake.

The names used in this volume are pseudonymns. I have also attempted to conceal the site and settings of this research. The facts en-
compassed in any event are described as I observed them or as they
were told to me, but occasionally I made slight modifications in descriptions of the personal characteristics of officers.

I have described my ambivalence about the term "narc" and
"narcs"; like other terms used, it is meant to produce a slightly harsh
effect or to evoke a mood or style of interaction. I frequently use the
words of my informants when summarizing an example to add verisi-
militude to the story and to capture some of the vocabulary, style, and
sensibilities of the officers. The reader should appreciate that the long
narrative examples are taken from my field notes, which are drawn

either from brief notes made at the time or my recollections of conversations and events recorded as soon as possible after the event took place. I have tried to provide parenthetical definitions of the jargon or argot of the officers and the drug world the first time the word is used. Examples are "buy-bust," "burn," "fronting the money," "snitch," "made," "getting over (on some one)," "dope." These words indicate the range of sensibilities of the officers. The reader reading them in another time, in another place, and in another social milieu perhaps, may find them offensive or de trop. I want to retain some sense of what was said as well as to preserve and communicate the content.

The implications of this book for drug law enforcement can be drawn by the reader from the results reported here. The criticism one finds in this book derives from my willingness to take police claims, rhetorics, publicity, and accomplishments as seriously as do the police themselves. This book is an attempt to describe, on the basis of observations, the informational and organizational constraints upon drug policing, which are not included in official claims. What follows should show precisely why these claims are false and misleading.

The book is organized in a somewhat dialectic fashion. Just as there is a dialectic process resulting from the tension between organizational requirements, constraints, and commitments and individual choice, there is also a dialectical process resulting from the tension between an organizational mandate and the environment in which it operates.

The study thus examines and outlines a conception of organizational action, only to see that police organizations neither describe their actions in this way nor act as they claim they do. They do, however, act in the ways that individual agents define as being consistent with their aims and purposes. In this sense the perspective of the individual agent is the most significant locus of power, authority, and control over the allocation of organizational resources. The targeting metaphor, taken from systems theory and the engineering language of the Pentagon, is used as a means of ordering the ways in which agents receive or obtain cases. Insofar as the targeting metaphor most accurately describes what individual agents decide to do and least accurately describes the other forms of resource allocation and designation of targets, it is a front or a rhetoric designed for administrative self-assurance and public relations. But it is inaccurate as a description of what police drug control units can do or are now doing.

Acknowledgments

I would like to acknowledge the support of Michigan State University, especially the College Scholars program, and the National Institute of Law Enforcement and Criminal Justice, which granted me a Fellowship in 1974–1975. I am also indebted to the two unnamed departments who were helpful and tolerant of me during the course of my inquiries. A great many people, in Washington, D.C., and elsewhere, assisted me in the course of gaining access, in shaping the research design and objectives, and in pointing out potential problems and the limitations of my research. I would like to thank in particular John Van Maanen, Larry Redlinger, Jay Williams, and Bill McDonald. I could not have written this book without the love and support of several people, including Victoria, Kerry, Sean Peter, and Merry Kathleen Manning, and Pat, Tammy, Vykkie, and Elizabeth Schiebel and John Van Maanen and Colleen McCallion. Contributions of a varied but essential sort were made by Judy Flositz, Michele Carrier, Mary Quinn Guenther, ABL Associates, Ella Schrader, Felicia Pettygrue, Jim Thomas, and Harry Mika. I thank them, for all in their own way contributed to the book, and I am very grateful both for what they did and who they are.

I Background

1 The Organizational Attempt to Control Drug Markets

The tradition of organizational analysis that is reviewed in this chapter, growing from the work of Max Weber, has always seen the organization in relation to its environment. Whether that environment is seen as fixed and objective, subjective and irrational, or solely a social construction created and maintained by organizational members, the organization is seen as a rational tool by which that environment is to some greater or lesser extent controlled. For a number of historic reasons, the United States has attempted to control the markets in certain drugs by legal means and by police enforcement of laws limiting the access to drugs, their use, possession and/or sale. Clearly in some fashion this environment of drug markets shapes and constrains the organization of a police drug law enforcement unit. But how does this shaping take place? To what degree is the tradition of organizational analysis in the social sciences a means by which we can understand the structure and function of these units? What necessary modifications in organizational analysis will have to be made prior to undertaking a study of drug law enforcement? Whatever else organizational theory does, it does posit the centrality of information in identifying goals and objectives, providing feedback to align organizational actions and resource allocation with the stipulated priorities, and evaluating the degree to which individuals are able to carry out their functions adequately.

In the absence of information, organizations will act, and these actions will nevertheless be seen as predicated on information because it is assumed that information is the basis of all organizational action. Drama and instrumental actions merge in that sense, for the organizational "outputs" are indistinguishable. In the same fashion, individual agents are constrained to act and constrained by information. But in the absence of information, they act in any case. It is this acting out of preferences, collectively and individually, that creates the dramatic fiction that the police engage in concerted and effective organizational action.

In order to understand how these actions are produced by organizational processes, and how the environment and organization interact in drug enforcement units, several kinds of information are required. The first is a sketch of the historical background of the attempt to regulate drug use by the police and legal means. The second is an overview of sociological research in the general area of drugs and drug control. Most of the work has been subjective and social-psychological, focusing on the subculture of use or the user rather than the organizational problem of enforcement and control. The perspective on organizational action that undergirds the book is also outlined; it is as much a statement of the current lack of knowledge as it is a promise for fulfillment.

Social Attempts to Control Drug Markets

Although all societies attempt to control the production, distribution, and use of "feel-good" substances such as coffee, tea, tobacco, alcohol, marijuana, and opiates and the like, the means employed to exercise this control vary (Brown, 1974, 1975). In preliterate societies, and even to some extent in literate ones, religious, ceremonial, or mystical means of control are commonly used. An aura of the powerful or dangerous is associated with the substance, and its use may be limited to specially designated persons, places, times, or occasions. In societies with a more developed socioeconomic base, sacred control diminishes in both prevalence and power, and secularized means are developed. In industrialized nations the law, still having something of a sacred quality about it, is the preeminent means of asserting society's interest in circumscribing these substances. In the United States, the attempt to control opiates began in the early part of the twentieth century and a legal and quasi-police mandate was shaped. In order to understand what the police are meant to do with respect to drug control, one must look at the development of the law regulating opiates, the present control structure, and social science attempts to understand organizational action in the drug law enforcement field and elsewhere.

Opiate use in the United States, prior to the early part of this century, was fairly widespread and legal. Opiates were dispensed by physicians and pharmacists and were readily available in a wide variety of patent medicines. Their use was not viewed as a social problem but as a means of coping with an individual medical problem or as a means of coping with or reducing pain or anxiety. Opiates functioned analogously to modern tranquilizers. A moral crusade was energized by moral entrepreneurs (Becker, 1963), who played upon the international obligations of the United States and the power aspirations of the United States in the Far East to sponsor and successfully pass a series of treaties and laws that were subsequently supported by court decisions. Musto (1973) claims on the basis of his impressive and convincing historical research that the original intent of these laws was the suppression of use as well as the virtual eradication of the trade in and distribution of opiates. This originally moral intent, once legally established, became the legitimate rationale or mandate for a structure of enforcement. The original model for this prohibition model of control (Lemert, 1972:112–121) was predicated upon the modes of pharmacological action, potential for addiction, and the threat of spread thought to be associated with opiates. Soon many other pharmacologically diverse drugs were also made illegal. They were defined and controlled as if they were opiates. The prohibition model was generalized in an attempt to control a striking variety of drugs with highly different actions, addictive potential, and life-threatening consequences. A series of unanticipated effects unfolded:

Use and trade in these kinds of drugs was increasingly redefined from a taxable economic transaction into an intrinsically evil matter to be eradicted.

The social character of the population of users changed; their sources of drugs and life-styles were altered, and trafficking in and use of narcotics was driven into a demimonde.

The image of the user became diabolic.

A black market was created and maintained.

An enforcement system was established and grew periodically until it became a 786-million-dollar federal business in 1976 (Cline and Goldberg, 1976).[1]

These unanticipated changes can be seen as the most significant social effects of employing the prohibition model. This book is primarily directed toward the control structure, in particular the local police enforcement organization. Their legal mandate is shaped chiefly by a series of federal laws, however, the most important of which is the law designating and classifying certain substances as having potential for abuse and requiring control.

The Legal Mandate

Since the early twenties, federal, state, and local police forces have been mandated by a sequence of ever-more-punitive laws covering larger and larger numbers and kinds of drugs to eradicate traffic and the trafficker in these illegal commodities. These laws are the ostensive rationale for local policing drug units. The present basic statute is the Controlled Substances Act of 1970 (Public Law 91-513, 91st Congress, H.R. 18583, October 27, 1970), which consolidated about fifty-five statutes that had previously governed the trade in dangerous drugs. The controls established by the act are listed in table 1.1 and include registration of handlers, recordkeeping, manufacturing quotas, distribution restrictions, dispensing limits, import and export limitations, security (stipulated conditions of storage), required reports of transactions to the government, and criminal penalties for illegal trafficking. The first two conditions apply to all drugs while the others are variously controlled, depending on the schedule (I–V) in which they are placed. The drugs controlled are placed in one of the five categories depending on their potential for abuse, physical and psychological dependence liability, and presently accepted medical use. Schedule I drugs, such as marijuana, heroin, and LSD, are considered to have "high abuse potential" and no recognized medical usage. (This is currently being debated in the courts and among medical researchers.) These are the drugs of most concern to law enforcement agencies and provide the model for regulating others. They are permitted in the country legally only for stipulated research purposes (the University of Mississippi grows marijuana for governmental research at Oxford, Mississippi). Schedule II drugs are considered to have a high abuse potential, but also have a currently acceptable medical use. They also are considered to have a high potential for physical or psychological dependence. Examples of Schedule II drugs are morphine, methadone, and the methamphetamines. Schedule III, IV, and V drugs are controlled by much the same means, as table 1.1 shows, but are differentiated on the basis of their potential for abuse. These drugs have currently accepted medical use. They range from being considered as having a moderate to low potential for dependence of either a physical or psychological kind. Schedule III drugs (for example, amphetamines and barbiturates) may have potential for high psychological dependence. Schedule IV drugs include many familiar household drugs, such as valium, quaaludes, librium, and other tranquilizers. Schedule V drugs are exemplified by those containing small amounts of codeine or opium, such as cough syrups and the like. In general the criminal penalties make trafficking a felony, while possession and use carry lesser penalties. Since the law is federal, it can be used by local officers and federal agents, and cases can be prosecuted in any of several federal or local courts.

Although this chart has the semblance of a scientific classification, it is in fact based loosely on medical opinion, about which there is continued controversy, social value judgments made by politicians and policy makers, and unexamined conventional wisdom. It is at best an ordinal scheme of commonsense knowledge held by policy makers at various times. As many recent events show, drugs are added to the list as public concern rises about their use, and drugs have recently been reclassified by the actions of legislators in several states who passed laws making the drug intended for cancer treatment, laetrile, legally available. Although laetrile is not a controlled substance, the same political dynamics occurred or are occurring with regard to the addition of LSD to the list in the mid-sixties, and the attempt in late 1978 to add the animal tranquilizer, PCP, to the list. This list is not an exclusive or inflexible one. Nor is is free of social value judgments, such as those referring to psychological dependence, a matter of some continued debate among psychologists and physicians. Medical use itself is further a matter as much of politics as it is of science. Public opinion works to change the medical definition of utility as it did after the Linder case when federal harrassment of physicians led to their refusal to prescribe heroin and morphine to individual patients (Musto, 1973). The Supreme Court decision supporting the utility of marijuana smoking in the treatment of glaucoma likewise illustrates the interaction of politics, the

Table 1.1 Control mechanisms of the Controlled Substance Act by schedule

Schedule	Registration	Recordkeeping	Manufacturing Quotas	Distribution Restrictions
I	Required	Separate	Yes	Order forms
II	Required	Separate	Yes	Order forms
III	Required	Readily retrievable	No (but some drugs limited by Schedule II quotas)	DEA regis. number
IV	Required	Readily retrievable	No (but some drugs limited by Schedule II quotas)	DEA regis. number
V	Required	Readily retrievable	No (but some drugs limited by Schedule II quotas)	DEA regis. number

Note: This table is the work of William Vodra, staff attorney formerly with DEA and now with FDA.

From M. Falco and C. Akins, *Federal Drug Abuse Law Enforcement Regulation and Control.* Washington, D.C.: Drug Abuse Council, Inc., 1976.

Dispensing Limits	Import/ Export Narc.- Non-narc.	Security	Mfr.-Dist. Reports To DEA	Criminal Penalties for Trafficking (First offenses) Narc. Non-narc.	
Research use only	Permit	Vault-type	Yes	15 yrs/ $25,000	5 yrs/ $15,000
Rx-written; no refills	Permit	Vault-type	Yes	15 yrs/ $25,000	5 yrs/ $15,000
Rx-written or oral; refills up to 5 times in 6 months (w/ M.D. auth.)	Permit	Surveillance	Narc. Yes Non-narc. No	5 yrs/$15,000	
Rx-written or oral; refills up to 5 times in 6 months (w/M.D. auth.)	Permit	Surveillance	Narc. No Non-narc. No	3 yrs/$10,000	
OTC (Rx drugs limited to M.D.'s order)	Permit to import	Surveillance	Narc. Mfr. only	1 yr/$5,000	
	Notice to export		Non-narc. No		

law, and medicine. Law makers, regulators at the federal level, and politicians have periodically supported new and more harsh legislation (Boggs, Harrison, et al.). This fact is often overlooked in mass media treatment of drugs and their effects, and the classification scheme is accepted almost without question among drug enforcement officers at every level whether or not they personally use any of the listed drugs. It is often an invisible credo, isolated and unsupported by unequivocal research findings, assumed to be scientific, and publicized widely as a statement of the essential features of the listed substances.

It is clear that the creation of the law substantiated the already formed market in these commodities and that the market has continued to shape the regulation as well as the regulators (see Manning and Redlinger, 1977 and 1978). Even the growing public disagreement (see Rossi, et al., 1974; and Gusfield, 1975) and fragmented public opinion on the use of drugs covered in the act, especially marijuana, has little altered the practices of the agents and agencies of control over the last fifteen years. Over 450,000 young people were arrested on marijuana charges in 1976, and the upward trend continues. There is growing evidence that, in spite of some impressive statistics on arrests and seizures, the effort is not always as effective as was intended. Law enforcement regulation organizations are under congressional scrutiny (see Senate Hearings, Committee on Government Operations, 1975–1976 on the federal drug enforcement effort, and the Hearings and Interim Reports of the House Select Committee on Narcotics Abuse and Control, 1976–1978), as well as attack in the popular press (Berlet, 1976; Browning, 1976) and by investigative reporters (Epstein, 1977).

These criticisms, including a recent work by a social scientist closely associated with policy making in the Department of Justice (including the Drug Enforcement Administration itself), James Q. Wilson (1978), suggests that in an odd way the transformation of the drug problem from a moral to a legal and organizational problem may be the basis for additional close, critical analyses of enforcement practices. It is in that spirit that this book is intended, for more and more the problems of order and control, and conversely those of individual freedom, are caught up in organizational process. More and larger organizations have been proposed and created as solutions to drug problems, so we must see drug control in this society as being an organizational problem to a significant extent.

The problems of our society are increasingly handled by organizations, even though the organizational approach has repeatedly failed in the past. More and more the problem of drug use has been viewed as a legalistic matter (defining the problem as a medical one provides a counter-but-still-organizational theme), and it has been allocated or arrogated by large organizations that try to prevent drug use, to educate users or potential users, or to lock up those who persist in using the stipulated illicit substances.

The tendency toward creating larger and better funded agencies to control drugs has gone almost undetected. These agencies have grown in number and size at every level of government, especially in the last ten to fifteen years. They enforce the more than 900 federal laws with criminal penalties relevant to drug use, possession, or trafficking. There are more than thirteen federal agencies that obligate at least a portion of their budget to drug control either in the form of punishment, education, or treatment (Cline and Goldberg, 1976). Several departments with enforcement agencies are involved in the suppression effort: Justice (the Drug Enforcement Administration (DEA), Law Enforcement Assistance Administration (LEAA), and FBI), Treasury (Customs and the Internal Revenue Service); and State. Others have quasi-enforcement or regulatory functions and/or international obligations in the control of drugs: the Departments of State; Defense; Health, Education, and Welfare; and the Central Intelligence Agency (see Interim Report, Committee of Government Operations, Senate, 94th Congress, 2nd Session, 1976:23–25). The costs of these operations in the 1976 federal budget was estimated to be $489. / million for prevention and $296.2 million for law enforcement. In addition there are some 115–150 federally supported "metro drug squads" in the country composed of combined city, county, or state officers (Garza, 1976). It is estimated that there are about 17,000 police units, and that approximately 700,000 officers are now employed in law enforcement (Farmer, 1978). Every state has a drug enforcement capacity in its state patrol, or the equivalent, as does every county, city, and other incorporated area. In addition the private security forces now outnumber police employees in law enforcement and often are involved directly and indirectly in drug investigations and arrests (Spitzer and Scull, 1977). This drug enforcement capacity varies from year to year and is exercised with varying levels of skill, personnel, and resources.

Although it is impossible to provide a secure and accurate estimate of the number of drug enforcement officers in the United States or abroad, figures for DEA and customs are sensitive indicators since all of DEA's activities are drug related, and a large portion of customs agents' activities are drug related. The personnel figures for the CIA, the State Department, the Internal Revenue Service (Treasury), and the Defense and Justice Department (outside of DEA itself) are not sensitive because many of these agents only occasionally work on drug cases. The Drug Enforcement Administration had 2,100 slots in 1976, with some 300 agents working abroad in regional offices in Bangkok, Mexico City, Paris, Buenos Aires, Manila, and Ankara. More than $135 million was budgeted for DEA in 1975–1976. In 1976 DEA had a budget for buying information and drugs of $9.9 million, while in 1974–1975 it was over $10 million. This latter figure, only about 5 percent of which was recovered (for example, through "buy-busts" where the money and the drugs are confiscated), provides each agent with a working capital of about $4,300 a year.[2] The Customs Bureau, under the Department of Treasury, was adversely affected by the Nixon reorganization plan, their numbers reduced, and their mandate abbreviated (Epstein, 1977, especially chapter 12). The past few years have seen a steady decrease in their complement of employees (not all of whom are agents) from a recent high in 1975 of 15,725 (Report of the Secretary of the Treasury, 1976, table 114:414) to a projected or budgetary obligation for fiscal 1979 of 14,332 (United States Budget, 1979).

Studies of the Control of Drug Use

The assumption under which these organizations have been created and expanded, sometimes in balloon fashion as under Nixon in the early seventies, is a corrective-control model in which increased organizational resources, effort, and personnel are expected to produce a sharply reduced drug-use level and diminished associated problems (such as crime, which had been the public rationalization for the massive federal expenditure allocated to the attempt to reduce heroin use). Sociologists on the whole have been little concerned with the impact of organizations on the drug problem. With some notable exceptions, they have accepted the corrective-control model, while looking at the negative effects of the subcultures surrounding use of some drugs[3] or the personalities of drug users[4] either in treatment or, rarely, in situ. Epidemiological studies use the disease metaphor, seeing the use of drugs not as a choice based on values, preferences, and lifestyles but as a contagious viral entity that surrounds, enters, and overwhelms the user much as bubonic plague, Legionaires' disease, or smallpox might.[5] Even a more structural approach to the drug problem, found in work trying to explicate the sources, political interests, and moral meanings lying behind the development of the characteristic American legalistic-moralistic preoccupation with prohibition and denial, rarely roots these analyses in organizational paradigms or theories.[6] In recent years the view that the law is a regulative force, in this case used to regulate or to tax in a generic sense, or place a risk cost on the drug trade, has grown in support, especially among a select group of lawyers and economists.[7] These attempts to model the system of control and the differential costs it imposes represent studies of the "control side" of the analysis of the drug system as an economic/oligopistic market.[8]

Police Studies as Organizational Studies

Although the sociological study of the police has grown significantly in Anglo-American societies since Westley's research was submitted as a dissertation at the University of Chicago in 1951, it has focused primarily on police role, especially role-consensus and perceptions, police-public interactions, police strategies and tactics, and to a lesser degree police history.[9] Among the works that treat the police specifically as an organization, the works of Bordua and Reiss (Bordua, 1967; Bordua and Reiss, 1967; Reiss and Bordua, 1967; Reiss, 1971), Wilson

(1968) and Gardiner (1969) are outstanding, but do not focus on police control of drugs as a specific organizational assignment or strategic concern.

Studies of police drug control in the United States are recent,[10] and of these studies three are significant background for my analysis: McDonald, DeFleur, and Johnson and Bogomolny. Each attempts to describe the ways in which organizational actors perceive, define, and articulate the organization's goals in reference to an environment; each assembles data on the means by which these goals are said to be pursued (they describe the strategies of drug enforcement); they outline organizational structure and describe its dynamics (to varying extent from the detail of Skolnick and McDonald to the inferential material presented by DeFleur, and Johnson and Bogomolny), and the articles contain data on the outcomes of enforcement practices (arrests and charges).

Two other studies are useful reading: Jerome Skolnick's *Justice Without Trial* (1966, 1975; the second edition contains an epilogue discussing changes in drug use and policing since the early sixties when Skolnick did the original study), and Wilson's *The Investigators* (1978). These books deserve detailed attention due to the similarity in their focus to that of this work and because of the quality and perceptiveness of the studies themselves. *Justice Without Trial*'s main theme is that police discretion, some of it inherent in the enforcement of certain laws (especially those designed to control vice) and some of it created on the streets, in effect allows the police to establish the guilt or innocence of individuals by their enforcement practices. *Justice Without Trial* is both an ironic and literal title. Skolnick feels there is little justice dispensed by policemen and that decisions legally reserved for the courts are made by the police who have arrogated judicial functions to themselves. Skolnick suggest that the enforcement dynamic is both moral and practical: police officers view vice practitioners as evil and as symbolic assailants, while seeking to maintain control and definition of the work tasks they undertake. Narcotics police respond to the exigencies of the job and to the immediate evaluation context (see pp. 148 ff, 179–180 ff). However, we do not know from this study whether

Skolnick offers a description of a particular organization or of the generic pattern of narcotics enforcement.

It would appear that several aspects of Skolnick's study deserve further analysis. These considerations suggest the need for contemporary organizationally focused studies of police drug law enforcement. We lack research that attempts to elucidate and link the structural characteristics of policing as they bear on decisions to enforce particular laws or to intervene in certain kinds of allegedly illegal transactions. Since the book was written almost fifteen years ago, the procedural law governing narcotics enforcement has changed (see Skolnick 1975, epilogue). A number of changes have occurred in drug laws at several levels, in the distribution of drugs, the types of drugs used, and the numbers of users. Second, Skolnick studied an organization that, according to his description, employed primarily an informant strategy and did not employ alternative modes of enforcement found in many departments for example, developing conspiracy cases, and "falling on" street dealers. Skolnick's concern was the ways in which the legal context is perceived and modified by the discretionary action of the officers, rather than the way in which organizational policies might have determined or set these options. Finally, there are regional differences in enforcement practices, levels of use, and kinds of drugs favored (Johnson, Peterson, and Wells, 1977) that in turn may affect the strategies employed by various departments.

The study of police enforcement of economic or transactional crimes is critical from the perspective of police studies, for it bears on the informational or systems theory view of policing (see Larson, 1972, and Manning, 1977a). This form of policing, in particular drug policing, provides an opportunity to examine the claim that the greater the level of police capacity to know crime (in turn based on their resources and organizational structure and strategy), the more arrests will be made (or some other independent measure of the impact of the police on the environment). The level of enforcement of vice crimes, it has been asserted by Skolnick (1966) and Bordua and Reiss (1967:40–48), can be decisively controlled by the organization. It is claimed that the organization, through its administrators passing on policy and priorities to enforcement or agent-level personnel, can define and şet targets, seek to attain them through the articulation of strategies and tactics of enforcement, identify desired outcomes, and effectively utilize the information and intelligence available to mobilize agents. In this view, the less organized the crime to be detected, the greater the organizational capacity to monitor (and control) it.

This assumptive theory or proposition has been questioned by James Q. Wilson on the basis of his study of the Drug Enforcement Administration and the Federal Bureau of Investigation (1978). His view is that the environment in which the DEA operates is sufficiently problematic to obviate or diminish the capacity of the organization to regulate it. His principal argument is that the mandate of DEA is insufficiently solid to permit accomplishing the tasks, which are themselves problematic in any case, and that constraints derived from the task and reward structure as well as the political environment are far more significant than resources or even the level of drug use or trade toward which regulatory efforts are said to be directed. Because the informal reward system, the supervisory system, and the traditional view of the agents of their work and its imperatives control the organization's allocation of resources and basic mission, the agents' tasks and their view and perspective of them are determinant of the day-to-day work of the agency. Although this view contrasts with that of the supervisors and executives of DEA (and this is also true at local level organizations), they are unable to assert and maintain control. An organizational tension is created among administrative aims, public front-work and rhetoric (the drama of enforcement), and the agents' aims and operations.

The important works of Wilson and Skolnick suggest that one must look as much at the constraints upon organizational action as upon the characteristics of organizational structure and function. Thus one must elicit and understand the official mandate, legal tools, and aims of the organization as well as the internal and external problem and commitments that make unusual the accomplishment of these stated ends. As was suggested in the preface, and by Skolnick's and Wilson's analysis, the decisions made by the agent in line with his or her own interests substantially set the direction of police drug enforcement. Even when policy is set, articulated, and flows down the line to agents, it rarely actually constrains them, and they continue to act in line with their own perceptions of the practical problems of drug enforcement. The central problem of drug policing, from the agent's perspective, is not moral but distinctively practical. The aim is to define the work in ways that will allow the occupational members involved to manage it, to make reasonable decisions, control it, parcel it out into meaningful, solvable, and understandable units and episodes, and make this accomplishment somewhat satisfying day after day. Administrative aims and rhetoric differ from agents' praxis and perspectives, and an organizationally induced tension results. This makes it clear that a study of the process of narcotics law enforcement requires concepts and insights that can be gathered from a review of the literature on complex organizations.

A Perspective on Formal Organization Theory

Studies of complex, rational, or formal organizations have been guided by the ideas of Max Weber, especially the characteristics that he derived as features of the ideal bureaucracy.[11]

Researchers seize on Weber's emphasis on rational ends-means relationships, formal role and status systems, and the link between plans and actions and rational feedback loops that are self-corrective with respect to the organization's goals. Weberian rationality as an image has dominated organizational analysis in Anglo-American society. Research on bureaucracy is often an elaboration of what analysts have assumed about bureaucracies: that there is a close relationship among plans, intentions, conduct, and outcomes; that this relationship operates as the guiding and perhaps exclusive principle of participants; and that they assess and understand their own actions and others' actions within this rational frame. Rationality within the action system described is assumed to be the normal background knowledge of all participants and thus goes unexamined (Bittner, 1965; Weick, 1976). The extent to which organizations are negotiated orders, predicated on different kinds of assumptions and contexts in which notions of rationality are various and are not shared, has not been studied. Perhaps as a correlate of this students of organizations have overlooked or ignored alternative methodologies for the study of formal organizations, focused largely on single organizations, and reified the process of organizational decision making.[12] These characteristics of organizational studies have limited both the kinds of questions asked and the kinds of analyses undertaken. It would appear that several trends are working to produce a dissatisfaction with these kinds of organizational studies. Alternatives are needed.

Changing Organizations: Static Theories

These characteristics of organizational studies have limited both the kinds of questions asked and the kinds of analyses undertaken (see Benson, 1977a, 1977b), and especially in the context of a rapidly changing society with emergent problems and forms, traditional assumptions are increasingly inadequate. As Wilson has pointed out, we tend to delegate messy problems to public bureaucracies and as a result they are expected to attain ". . . vague, complex, controversial, hard-to-produce objectives" (1978:204). Of course, social rationality and certainty of goals are social productions everywhere; in nonprofit public bureaucracies and in profit-making business organizations. Perhaps some of the more interesting studies generated by this new interest in public organizations and organizational theories are those that ask the old questions, such as those of rationality, efficiency, and effectiveness, in new organizational contexts, for example, schools, police departments, and public service organizations (J. Meyer, 1977; Kamens, 1977; Meyer and Rowan, 1977; Greenwood, Chaiken, and Petersilia, 1977; M. Moore, 1977; Wilson, 1978).

Critiques relevant to the study of drug control bureaucracies have also been published. No single perspective unifies these critiques (see Crozier, 1964, 1971; Jehenson, 1973; Silverman, 1971; Blankenship, 1977; Benson, 1975, 1977a, 1977b; Weick, 1976; March and Olsen, 1976; Day and Day, 1977). These authors more clearly articulate what they are not concerned with explaining than what they believe should be explained; they are long on commentary and short on data; they tend on the whole to issue from the "soft methodologies" and to be linked to the symbolic interactionist, phenomenological, and Marxist perspectives; and they have raised more queries than they have answered. However, in order to examine the relevance of this perspective for the study of organizations, it is useful to overview its most salient themes and concepts.

A Perspective on Organizations

The emerging perspective on organizations and organizational analysis is indebted to symbolic interactionism for its root metaphors.[13] Analysts in this tradition have maintained a sensitivity to the notions of process, change, and flux, have reserved great domains of autonomy and choice for the individual actor, and have avoided the reification of social structures. They have provided close description of the meaningful context of work, especially as it appears to the lower participants, the assumptions that underlie organizational order and negotiation as well as explication of the kinds and circumstances of negotiations. In these negotiated situations, the organization is said to come alive or to act in the sense that it displays the actor's loyalties and commitments to the organization and occupation, gives rise to routinely utilized strategies and tactics, and outlines the salient identities and selves of the participants. From this perspective also, the developmental and historical aspects of the task specialization, division of labor, and authority base can be analyzed. The static or snapshot-like analyses of structural functional studies is eschewed, and a negotiated or problematic element is made foremost in the study of organizational work.[14]

The perspective adopted here develops from an interactionist approach. It includes an imagery of social structure as changing, fluid, contradictory, and partial rather than absolute in its hold on conduct; contains a view of persons as creative, active, and choosing, actors who assess meanings within specific contexts of symbols and relationships; advances an appreciation of the enduring nature of conflict, contradiction, and change in any social pattern, and the relevance of power and authority to such changes. Further, it permits the understanding of inter- and intra-organizational relationships within the same paradigmatic discourse. It gives salience not only to the obdurate material and technological constraints on action but to the symbolic manifolds of actors within organizations and of organizations themselves as multilayered, multi-meaning structures of relevance. The organization is seen less as a whole and more as a set of symbols or fronts attributed to the collective conduct by various audiences, other organizations, and different segments within the organization itself (Manning, 1977a, especially chapters 4–8). This imprecision characterizes actors' conduct and collective actions found in any segment of the organization. The organizations studied here, and by others, are integrated internally by "loose coupling" (Weick, 1976; March and Olsen, 1976; Meyer and Rowan, 1977). The overriding metaphor "loose coupling" indicates the often inexact nature of the relationships between intentions, actions, and outcomes. The loose coupling of the organization internally and with the environment creates important problems with regard to control and evaluation (Meyer and Rowan, 1977).

As we show in the later chapters of this book, traditional approaches to evaluation and efficiency are of questionable value in loosely coupled organizations like the police. Multiple methods and approaches are needed to capture flux and flow, integrate several levels in the organization, and capture the tensions between segments and between individual members and the organizational mandate.[15] This view implies, in turn, that one should look at both how the organization defines its project or intentions in the world and how individual actors go about constructing that vision of the world and act in line with it. As Schutz (1967), Weick (1969), and others remind us, a set of issues is created by looking at the phenomenology of organizations, including analyzing the inter-subjective meanings that cohere to form organizational structures, the intentionalities of actors who create and maintain organizations as structures of relevance, and the grounding of these meanings and intentions in a commonsense world of assumptions and taken-for-granted understandings.[16] Goffman (1959) and Collins (1975), combining both micro- and macro-level analysis, make convincing arguments to the effect that in playing out their roles internally toward each other and externally toward organizational audiences, actors idealize and in effect reify their own positions (Collins, 1975:301). In attempting to maintain power and authority, they act as if the organization and their positions within it are concrete.Thus we are often lead into thinking that organizations are more than labels for repeated behavioral patterns within somewhat bounded ecological systems or territories. Transactions between individuals within organizations, such as patterns of deference and demeanor, and between organizations may be constraining, but they are constraining precisely because they are made real day after day by the actions that actors direct toward them. Actors create and recreate social worlds, but they also objectivate and communicate the reality of these socially defined constraints to each other. The ways in which organizations, in turn, are known to participants and others, the shape and changing nature of the mandate of an organization, are socially constructed and historically rooted.[17]

Thus, rather than isolate and reify certain structures in the world, such as technology or organizational structure, which are dynamic and multivalent symbols, this approach will seek to understand their perceived uses, meanings, and consequences. Static depictions of organizations as congeries of measures such as size, levels of hierarchy, or differentiation, or objective measures of the degree of change or complexity in the environment, are less valuable in this context than an analysis of the substantive relations between segments and units and associated modes of sense making, rules of thumb, or tacit decision-rules. These depictions of organizational structures contain an image of human interaction and decision-making that is not consistent with other general conceptions of the ways in which human interaction builds up structures based on decision- and choice-making (see, for example, Garfinkel, 1967; Gluckman, 1971; Cicourel, 1973). It has been found that at the higher levels of most organizations, substantial rationality obtains (Mannheim 1949:53): decisions are made that show a degree of insight into the immediate context and are based upon understanding and readings of the present circumstances (Kanter, 1977; Carter, 1974; Wildavsky, 1974). Even when rationality is the formal norm of decision, patterned conflicts and ambiguities produce characteristic modes of adjustment. When the values of individual actors are in conflict, where short- and long-run rationality collide or are mutually exclusive, when formal and substantive rationality are in opposition (Weber, 1967:224–265), or where the formal stipulated procedures are eroded or otherwise neutralized by the traditional deference in the work group to working rules (Dalton, 1959; Roy, 1953; Horning, 1970;

Sykes, 1958; Manning and Redlinger, 1978), then knowledge of the selective, sorting, and sense making of individual actors is more revealing of organizational process than structural correlates of outcome measures. The degree to which individual discretion is permitted is organizationally rooted and controlled, although in neither unit is this reserved power exercised sufficiently to control the vast majority of choices made by the investigators.

This perspective, with its emphasis on explicating the contexts of decision making and organizational constraints, as well as the decision making accomplished by individual investigators, will guide the analysis in the remaining chapters. It is useful, after the methods chapter, to review the enacted environment of policing and then the enacted environment of drug enforcement units within police organizations. For from this frame of reference used by officers comes their primary sense of organizational purpose, structure, and function. When they act in the name of the organization, they act to recreate again and again the reality of this conception of the environment. They act out their reality and so live within it.

This chapter describes the political and social aspects of the area in which the two departments studied are located, the two departments with respect to their personnel, resources, and organizational structure, and some aspects of the methods employed in the study. These data are provided to give the reader a feel for the area, the organizations, and my approach to the research.

The data on the environment and the organizations are descriptive. I do not claim that the material aspects of the scenes of observation can be affirmed or denied, only that the way in which content comes to the attention and is recognized as significant is enacted, not given in the world. Choices made in respect to enforcement are not based on physical features of the environment, the level of resources, or on a close reading of the political or social environment but on the basis of a sense of what the community expects and the practical interests of the officer and his squad.

It is my contention that narcotics enforcement is constrained more by social, cultural, and social-psychological matters of belief and practice than by the presence or absence of technical, technological, legal, or other sorts of resources. The assumptions made about the environment and what can and ought to be done have already set the options for officers before any question is raised about how to enforce the law in the specific case at hand. The practice of enforcement, based on the knowledge officers have and the way they "see" and make sense of the environment, is only marginally patterned by their skills and what is available in a technological or resource sense. Numerous other powerful antecedent constraints operate. To seize on a few objectively identifiable features of the site and setting is to overlook the proximal and immediate controls upon actors' choices that have little or no connection to the local social structure. These choices are patterned by the "narcs' game."

The Site

The research was undertaken in two police departments in a large metropolitan center of some one-half million in the Southeastern United States. The area combined a number of sociological, ecological, and political characteristics that made it a worthwhile location for the study. The area was large enough to support a number of professionalized police departments with specialized drug enforcement units. It had a history of public concern about drug use and effective enforcement and was not dominated by federal drug enforcement presence (as are border cities and large ports such as Miami) so that local decisions, strategies, and operations could be observed. There were practical limits as well in my choice of settings. The units had to be within driving distance of my home, be large enough to have a functioning drug unit but not so large that I could not interview a substantial number of the officers involved and allow me freedom to interview, ask questions and observe, and examine their records. Fortunately, the first two organizations I approached graciously granted me access and were cooperative throughout the study.

The two units chosen for study were called, prosaically, "Metro" and "Suburban." Their salient characteristics are that the Metro City Department employs over 4,600 persons, approximately 13 percent of whom are civilian. The Suburban Police Department, located in a large city, employs slightly over 800 officers. The political boundaries of the county in which Suburban Department is located are coterminous on the south with the northern boundaries of Metro City. This juxtaposition leads to some cooperative work, administrative coordination on some occasions, and potential cooperative arrangements formalized into a metropolitan area council of governments agreement stipulating manpower exchange arrangements.

I had intended initially to try to trace how community structure influences or produces certain patterns of cases and case outcomes, but I soon found that the records were not kept in a way that would make the study possible. Many of the cases are never officially opened or closed, and the ones closed officially are a sample of an unknown population of cases worked. There were also more commonalities among the problems both organizations faced than there were differences attributable to the political, social, or economic environment of the two units. Although the aim of the study was comparison, it was clear as the work commenced that the problems of drug enforcement, especially those of establishing targets and priorities (clearly, the central

administrative issue in drug law enforcement), were more alike than `
different in the two departments. The themes of this book reflect my
sense of this similarity. This claim is not meant as a denial of a range of
other variations within each site that either were not studied or were not
revealed by my method or approach.

The Social Characteristics of the Region

The political and social characteristics of the two jurisdictions most relevant to the research can be summarized. Both are large, dense,
highly urbanized areas; although Suburban contains large rural areas,
it is nearly 90 percent urban, and most of the population is clustered in
four cities. The rate of growth for the Suburban County is very high,
while Metro City grew only 1 percent between 1960 and 1970. Slightly
over half of the population in both areas is under thirty years old. The
percentage of the population in the high drug-use category (in terms of
national self-report figures on distribution of drug use), ages fifteen to
twenty-four is slightly higher in Metro City. Both have a small percentage of blue-collar workers in their labor force, and show high average
educational and income levels. The median income figures for the two
areas show Suburban County to have almost twice as high a median
income as Metro City. Suburban County is a residential, white-collar
suburb with a median income that is among the highest in the nation. It
should be noted that although the median income figures for blacks
and whites are similar (blacks are lower in both jurisdictions), an examination of extremes of the distribution reveals that in Metro City nearly
34 percent earn below $7,000 and 47.7 percent above $10,000; while
in Suburban County, it is apparent that the majority of the higher income groups are white.

A number of political-organizational differences exist. In Suburban
County, the council-city manager form of government provides for the
appointment of the chief of police, and the chief is accountable to the
County Executive and County Board of Supervisors. The county is a
Republican stronghold, and most of the local office holders are Republican. The high income of Suburban County would suggest this pattern
of allegiance. In Metro City there is a mayor-city council form of government. Each council member is either elected to represent a pre-

cinct in the city or at large. The mayor runs independently on a nonpartisan ballot, but the city is virtually a Democratic monopoly. The chief of police in Metro City is an important political position not only because of the size and national reputation of the department he administers but because his policies ramify throughout the region and affect all adjoining jurisdictions.

The treatment, rehabilitation, enforcement, and judicial systems of Metro city, along with the other large urban centers of the country, sustained a massive infusion of federal support in the first Nixon administration, one feature of what Caplan (1973) perceptively calls the "nationalization of crime," the attempt to make the federal government responsible for crime prevention, enforcement, and "cure."

Organization Milieu
Suburban County operates its police force in conjunction with the local police agencies of each of the four major cities in the county and the state police, and it cooperates with the Federal Drug Enforcement Administration (DEA) in drug cases. The DEA has a nearby regional office that covers a region including four states. The DEA aims to control "major violators": dealers in an ounce or more—multi-ounce, fractional kilo, kilo, and multi-kilo—of heroin and cocaine. (In 1974–1975, these were considered high priority drugs by the DEA.) The DEA asserts that their mission is not to deal with street users, small time "jugglers," or street peddlers,[1] nor even middle-level wholesalers (Senate Hearings, 1975:55). They have agents in this area and ostensively aim to cooperate with local departments in the following ways: the supply of money, expertise (electronics skills, for example), and personnel and information to local departments. Usually the DEA establishes its own priority or claim for credit for arrests, any seized evidence (vehicles, drugs, money, or stolen goods), and the prosecution of any defendents. The bargain with DEA for help is often perceived as an expensive one by local departments and may be rejected or contact never made with DEA. On the other hand, if an investigation exceeds the political boundaries of the county, cooperation either with other county forces, state police, or DEA becomes almost imperative. There are a number of devices for avoiding or circumventing cooperation,

but the desire to facilitate prosecution tends to constrain units to minimal cooperation.

The state police of the state in which Suburban Department is located have a drug squad that also cooperates in theory in investigations with Suburban. Nearby county agencies also compete with Suburban, and many cases involve crossing county boundaries for raids, buys, and arrests. Virtually all opiates flow from Metro City into the suburbs so that many "larger cases" result in investigation in the city by county police officers and vice versa. The relationships between agencies within the control domain with special interests in drugs are conflictful in general because of the competition for arrests, seizures of drugs, property and money, convictions, and the public praise and publicity that results from a "big bust."

In Metro City there are as many as eleven agencies involved in the enforcement of drug laws, with the two principal ones being DEA and the Metro Department. These forces have a sworn capacity for some 10,000 officers. Customs, the Post Office and DEA special task forces (CENTAC), operating from headquarters in Washington, D.C., were involved from time to time during this period in enforcement activities within Metro City. Thus at any given time, any illicit drug operation can be under investigation simultaneously by representatives of many competing units. It may be investigated by agents within Metro Police Department: the central narcotics unit, the district vice units, patrol and/or Internal Affairs (if there is an allegation of corruption of police officers themselves); the DEA (either the local unit, the regional unit, or the CENTAC force); Customs, the Post Office, the Department of Defense (or any of nine other federal agencies involved in drug law enforcement in the area); the county police from any of the four contiguous counties, or the state police of several adjoining states. Cooperation under these conditions is a continuing problem.

Settings

The two organizations have experienced a different pattern of growth, differ in size and structure and are funded at different levels. It is important to recall that the years prior to the study, the first few years of the Nixon administration, were the years of the war on crime and the associated public concern, political action, and control efforts. The subsequent reduction in public concern and funding was just being felt as the study began in late 1974 (a few months after President Nixon had resigned and approximately a year after the drug war was abandoned as an administration priority). Although no data were gathered to this effect, there was a sense in these two units that although drug use was again on the upswing, the major enforcement push, symbolized by federal dollars, mass media publicity, and public concern, was moribund. The irony of this was not lost on the officers, in my opinion. Although the correlation of the level of use, types of drugs used, and number of users is by no means an established one, the sense of the officers that the problem was growing while public concern was diminishing added to their cynicism about the commitment of the general public and the government to their work.

Organization and Personnel in Metro and Suburban
Both Metro and Suburban have a specialized unit for the enforcement of the drug laws, and the officers there are assigned work on a variety of kinds of cases using several different kinds of strategies. Suburban Department relies on undercover work, with all agents dressed in street clothes and working the streets or informants; there is no pharmacy unit to deal with drugs diverted from the licit market to the illicit market, and indeed no specialized squads of any kind. Metro Department has several specialized squads in the central narcotics unit, and officers not assigned to specialized squads are free to work in whatever manner they choose—in street clothes, through informants, on conspiracy cases. In addition to the fifty-seven officers included in the complement at headquarters of Metro, there are detectives who work general vice (including prostitution, pornography, obscenity, gambling, and drugs) in each of the seven districts of the city. From time to time young officers are recruited directly from the police academy to work undercover in central narcotics; I did not find evidence that there were such undercover officers at the time of the study although no one would discuss this with me. In both units, it should be emphasized, the patrol units make the majority of all drug-related arrests and charges;

even in a department with a specialized unit most drug enforcement is done by patrol officers.

In both units the "typical" narcotics officer was a young male under thirty, married, white, with a high school education. Most of them work narcotics, according to their own description, because it gives them freedom from supervision, they can set their own hours (within limits), they have great discretion in whether, to what degree, and how they pursue their cases, and they feel it is a good experience for a person who wants to move up in the department. Some expressed moral reasons such as, "I want to keep my kids and your kids from being destroyed by dope," but most generally liked the hours, the freedom, and the discretion built into the job. Further, they were given a clothing allowance in both units and shared the miscellaneous perks of the office such as the freedom to drink on the job and have their expenses paid when they used their own cars on the job. (In Suburban, each officer was given a new car to drive home and care for as a personal vehicle. All maintenance, gas, and repair costs were covered by the department.)

In both units overtime pay was an important source of job satisfaction. In Suburban, overtime was rather easy to acquire if an officer applied for it in advance in connection with his work or for court appearances. In Metro, although there was a complicated system of allocation of overtime, it was an important attraction to those who were motivated to acquire it. Each arrest and charge increased the probability that the officer would appear in court, and each court appearance produced overtime pay. Thus, for a number of reasons, the assignment to narcotics was sought by a segment of the department, and because it was voluntary, officers who served there were motivated to do the job. (They were often described ideally as "self-starters" and "go-getters" and served essentially at the pleasure of the lieutenant, captain and inspector, or lieutenant and captain in Suburban.) Unlike virtually any other assignment in the police department, working in vice-narcotics or organized crime as it was called in Suburban was voluntary, sought-after, and officers were subject to rather arbitrary dismissal. Unlike detective work, there was no necessary implication that serving there meant upward mobility on the "investigative side" and was viewed by patrol officers as a kind of unusual, attractive but mysterious sort of work. Drug law enforcement officers were generally viewed by uniformed officers with respect and considerable ambivalence.

It is not easy to extrapolate from structural characteristics of the region to personnel levels or from these to some sense of the level of drug problem in the area. This is true because there are no reliable figures on the level of use or trade in either area, and narcotics units, although they generally constitute about one and one-half of a percent of the total personnel of a department, are more sensitive to local demands and political pressures than are other units in the department (see Manning, 1977d; and Williams, Redlinger, and Manning, 1978). A high priority item in the "war on drugs" was increased police personnel. Increases occurred in Metro both in the central or headquarters units and in the seven districts that also employ vice-narcotics officers. The total number of officers in the Metro Department increased from 2,958 in mid-1968 to a high of 5,100 in September 1970. By late (October) 1971, it had dropped to 4,900 and has slowly declined to the present 4,613. Metro (Central) drug unit in 1975 (57) was 1.23 percent of the total personnel in the Metro Department (4,613) while Suburban's (13) was 1.61 percent of the 809 officers in that department.[2]

There are at least two ways of calculating the number of narcotics enforcement officers available per capita in Metro city. If Central Narcotics officers only are counted (57) with four undercover officers (as a guess), there are 0.844 narcotics officers per 10,000 population. If, on the other hand, one adds to these 61 the 49 district vice officers, a total of 110, then the ratio per 10,000 is 1.52. In any case, the Suburban district maintains a far lower ratio of narcotics officers to the population: 0.23 per 10,000. Roughly 3.7 times as many narcotics officers (or 6.66 using the total figure of 110) were employed in the Metro Department than in the Suburban Department in 1975.

Estimates of the number of dependent users of opiates in a given area are always subject to debate and criticism and are matters of conjecture. In the summer of 1975, the police estimated that there was a population of nine to ten thousand opiate users in Metro City. Metro

City, according to other experts, contains one of the largest addict/
user populations in the country. Suburban County, on the other hand,
maintains no official estimates of size of the opiate user population. Police informants felt that it was probably relatively small. However, it was
thought by Suburban County police that substantial numbers of persons in the county under thirty years old smoke marijuana and use hallucinogens of various kinds.[3] They assert that large dealers in cocaine,
hallucinogens, and amphetamines live in the area but deal primarily
through trusted associates in the central areas of Metro City. The
county has been the site of several large labs and production centers.
These labs, which produce primarily hallucinogens (LSD and PCP),
were under observation at the time of the study, and in 1973 to 1974
several had been closed in dramatic raids organized by Suburban
County and DEA. These raids resulted in seizures and publicity and
were counted among the most significant operations of the Suburban
unit.

The budget for Metro City Department for 1972–1973 totaled $94
million, with some $3 million for narcotics control. Suburban supports
its force at slightly more than $14 million. In 1972–1973, the Metro De-
partment had a $25,000 replenished enforcement fund provided by
LEAA, which was recycled three times (that is, nearly $75,000 was ex-
pended). The same type of grant was made by LEAA to Suburban
County Police Department for 1974–1976. In addition to these grant
funds, both forces maintain an enforcement fund for covering miscellaneous expenses associated with a drug investigation, paying informants, rewards for seizures, and making drug buys. The narcotics enforcement fund in Metro was $120,000 for 1975–1976. This amount
was divided between the seven districts and the central unit in Metro.

Organizational Structure

The two departments differ in organizational structure. Neither had a
specific written policy defining the scope, objectives, and means of
controlling the narcotics problem within their respective jurisdictions.
The choice of organizations was made on the basis of the above similarities in an attempt to discover what influences existed in the setting

of policies in large professional police departments in the narcotics domain, and how, given a policy, certain identifiable outcomes were produced.

Figures 2.1 and 2.2 show the outlines of the formal authority system in the two departments. Metro City Department, which underwent a major reorganization in 1970 on the advice of the International Association of Chiefs of Police after a new chief was appointed, places the Morals Division, in which responsibility for drug law enforcement is primarily vested, under the commander of the Inspectional Services Bureau. It is defined as a staff function, as are internal affairs, field inspections, and intelligence, and is thus organizationally seen as functioning

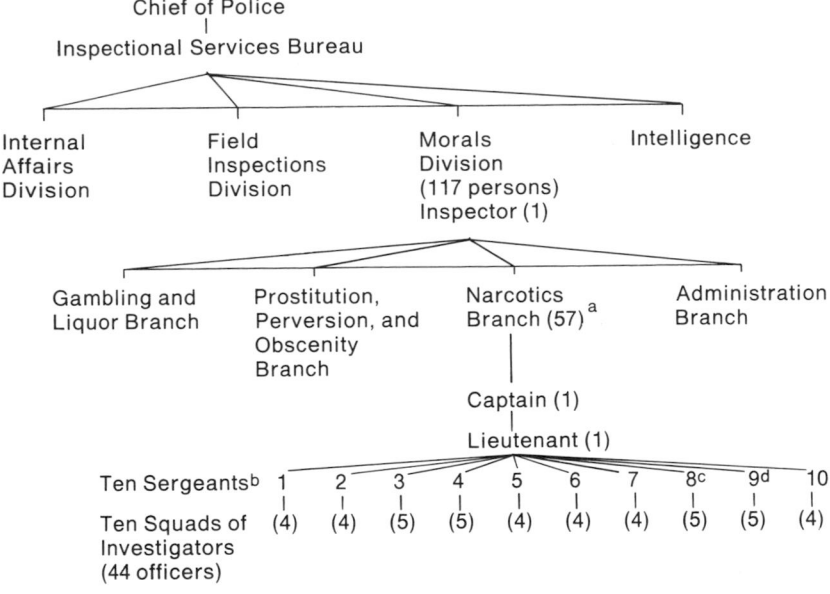

a. Omits a variable (1–5) number of officers on undercover assignment.

b. An additional sergeant is assigned to maintain and operate electronic equipment as required by investigations. Although he is listed on the strength of the branch, he is not an operational sergeant. Sergeant 10 is an administrator in charge of the Branch Office. His squad is assigned exclusively to clerical duties.

c. Supervises compliance squad.

d. Supervises schools and pharmacy squads.

Figure 2.1 Partial organization chart of Metro Police Department showing detail of narcotics branch (August, 1975)

in a fashion analogous to these divisions. In many ways, as will be explained, this type of proactive or initiatory policing stands in the same relationship to citizens' demands and claims on police time and energy as do these other functions. From an organizational point of view, this position on the ladder of authority symbolizes the general view that such investigative functions require a different quality of supervision. The requirements for supervision are believed to grow from the great discretion granted to officers dealing in transactional crimes, the risks of corruption and bribery, and the need for close guidance in the expenditures of enforcement funds. The supervisory ratio (sergeants to officers) in patrol divisions generally runs around seven to one, while it is usually lower in detective work and in staff level functions (such as those grouped under the Inspectional Services Bureau in Metro). In Metro, the supervisory ratio in the narcotics branch was slightly higher than four to one (4.4), while in Suburban, it was slightly above five in the narcotics unit. Since two sergeants worked alone in vice enforcement in Suburban, any ratio for the entire Vice Intelligence Division would be misleading (overall, there are five sergeants and thirteen officers). However, as has been shown by Tifft (1975), Wilson (1978), and by research in narcotics units (Williams, Redlinger, and Manning, 1978), this organizational symbolization of close supervision does not

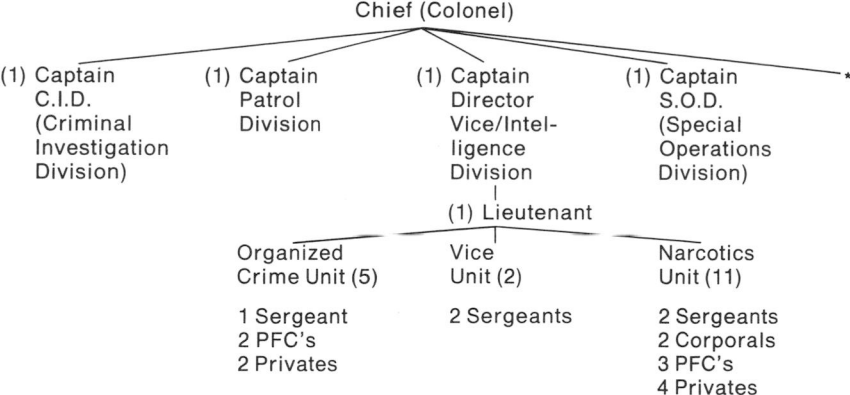

*Additional staff functions supervised by headquarters-based captains.

Figure 2.2 Partial organization chart of Suburban Department showing detail of Vice-Intelligence Division (August, 1975)

occur in practice for a number of reasons, which are closely examined in later chapters. The organization creates a structure that symbolizes one thing, although individual level tasks and role definitions are contradictory. The belief that officers must be "self-starters," self-motivated, and allowed to creatively and flexibly adapt to the highly uncertain nature of drug crime rationalizes the wide freedom granted and permits the investigators to control the resulting level and kind of enforcement.

It should be noted that within the Metro Narcotics Branch there are specialized squads for investigating schools, pharmacies, and physicians (to verify compliance with the requirements of the Controlled Substances Act of 1970). Figure 2.1 displays only the central narcotics unit; district vice units, one in each of the seven districts in the city, also enforce drug laws. Four categories of officers in the department enforce drug laws: central narcotics officers where authority flows to the forty-four investigators through the ten sergeants; district vice officers (who control gambling, prostitution, and pornography, as well as narcotics); district casual clothes officers (often used in saturation patrol in high crime areas); and patrol officers. If one examines the breakdown by charge (table 9.1) it is clear that patrol officers typically make charges involving marijuana, and that opiate charges are made almost entirely by central and district investigators.

Suburban Department is a more decentralized operation. This is, in part, a result of the large area covered by the department (it has county-wide responsibilities in a county of over five hundred square miles) and in part a function of a lack of a single headquarters building housing command and control functions. At the time of the study there were five main sub-buildings in the Suburban Department. One building contains the headquarters staff, robbery-burglary, and narcotics. Another houses the juvenile division and a patrol unit. Three buildings serve as centers for patrol units only. This decentralized organization has several consequences for the enforcement process: four separate radio channels must be maintained, one for each of the four areas. Narcotics officers must switch radio channels and report on which of the four they can be reached as they move from section to section. In 1975, the narcotics unit was housed in the headquarters unit, located at that time in the basement of a large shopping center. This created some problems when a raid or other semisecret operation was mounted, since the investigators had to enter and leave in public view through the only exit and entrance to the unit's office in headquarters. They had to drive in and out through the shopping center's parking lot.

Methods

This research was designed to draw upon the strengths of three kinds of data: interview, observational, and official records.

Interviews of one to three hours duration were gathered in both departments with the command personnel who have direct responsibility for setting policy in the narcotics enforcement area. Included in this category were the chief, a captain, a lieutenant, and two sergeants in the Suburban Department. Six investigators were also interviewed. Prior to interviews in the Metro Department, the ex-chief of police of the department was interviewed at length (three plus hours) concerning his policy and its implementation over the period of maximal growth of narcotics use in the city (1968–1972) and the parallel growth in the Narcotics Branch. The immediate past director of the Morals Division, which includes the Narcotics Branch, was also interviewed. (His introduction to the present director represented the formal initiation of the research.) In the Metro Department, the director of the Morals Division, the former head of the Narcotics Branch, the present captain in charge of the Narcotics Branch, the lieutenant, and ten sergeants were interviewed. In addition, semistructured interviews were repeated with five principal informants and with twelve other officers in Metro Department. All investigators in both departments were observed or interviewed, and at least one and often two members of each of the eleven squads in the Metro Department and the two in the Suburban Department were interviewed. (Data on interviews shown in table 2.1.)

Systematic observation was also carried out in both departments (see table 2.2). The table shows that observations were concentrated in the day-work time (8:00 A.M.–4:00 P.M.) period, secondarily in the afternoons (4:00 P.M.–12:00 P.M.) and lastly on midnights. (Only one or two persons worked midnights in Metro, and they picked up drug evi-

Table 2.1 Interviews obtained in Metro and Suburban by rank, 1975

Rank of Interviewee	Metro Number	Percent	Suburban Number	Percent
Officers	17/44	39	6/13	46
Sergeants	10/10	100	2/2	100
Command personnel				
Inspector Captain Lieutenant	2/3	66	3/3	100
Others Former chief of Metro	1			
Two former directors of the Metro Narcotics Unit	2			
Sergeant (electronics expert)	1			

Table 2.2 Distributions of hours spent in observation in Metro and Suburban Departments, May–August, 1975, by shift

	Mornings/Days 8:00 A.M.– 4:00 P.M.	Afternoons 4:00 P.M.– 12:00 A.M.	Midnight 12:00 A.M.– 8:00 A.M.	Total
Metro	91	28½	14	133½
Suburban	46¼	28¾	1	76

Number of days in which observation was made by shift

	Base of days in which any obser- vation was made	Days	Afternoons	Midnights
Metro	(27)	25	15	2
Suburban	(10)	10	8	1

dence during these hours. Suburban did not technically work midnights, although some surveillances and raids did occur during those hours.) Squads of four to six men with a sergeant rotated from mornings (7:30–4:30) to afternoons (4:00–12:00) on two-week segments in the following pattern: day/4–12/day/4–12/day/midnight/4–12. The times at which I worked were distributed across turns, although the work load tends to be equal on day and 4–12 turns. The purpose of the research was not related to the times at which activities occurred, but was designed to gather observations of the greatest number of officers. This was accomplished, to lesser or greater degrees, in both departments. The squads with whom I participated in raids and surveillances were perhaps more trusting of my presence than others simply because I persuaded them to be allowed to observe.

Of particular concern were observations made of key episodes: the interrogation of suspects, informants, and arrested persons; serving of arrest and search warrants (raids); "cruising" dealing and/or using areas to observe activity; squad meetings and planning sessions; and informal and off-duty interviews. A set of field notes covering these key episodes as well as data on career lines, age, conceptions of the job, dealers and users of narcotics, strategies of enforcement—personal and departmental—were gathered from observation and interviews and dictated nightly. They were subsequently transcribed into some 561 pages of qualitative data which were coded by topic and used to inform the following analysis.

Official records of investigative reports, arrests, buy expenditures, seizures, search warrants served and annual and semiannual reports for 1974 and 1975 (through July) were also obtained.

The general approach utilized was overt participant observation. Although I was involved in several aspects of the work, I was only a marginal member of the ongoing organization. I used my personal contacts with various officers, which resulted from an introduction by the inspector to the administrative sergeant and by the administrative sergeant to a few officers who were frequently hanging around the office, to chat informally with them. After meeting a few officers in this fashion, I attempted more formal, semifocused interviewing. After a few weeks on the site, I found that I depended on a few key informants. It was

through them that I checked facts for validity and reliability, raised new
ideas and hunches, and derived, I think, a fairly subtle sense of what
the work was about. The details of this approach, and how I moved
from concept to data and to new conceptual linkages is found elsewhere (Manning, forthcoming a).

Summary

The ecological system in which the enforcement action described here
is found is rather arbitrarily divided into political jurisdictions from the
perspective of drug law violations. As a result, many problems of organizational coordination and exchange arise. However, the study does
not intend to describe or analyze all the enforcement practices in the
site. This is a limited study of two organizations that yields a perspective on enforcement in the region. Nor do I argue that in an important
way the problems of the two organizations are different; I focus on similarities and on the primary identifiable constraints on the enforcement
of laws against transactional crimes. These are to some extent a function of the organizational structure (personnel, funding, degree of supervision and administrative structure) but more importantly are a
function of the ways in which the problem is defined and acted upon,
especially as investigators "see it." I have tried to suggest in this chapter that because there are no accurate figures kept on the drug problem in the area, an evaluation of an enforcement strategy, its impact,
and general purpose or focus cannot be based on valid and reliable
informational feedback.

My approach to the constraints on enforcement involves interweav-
ing the basic methods and theoretic perspective. The characteristics
of the sites, settings, and the particular organization of enforcement
are seen as the context in which the organizational control of drugs is
studied, but they are neither the primary determinants of success or
failure nor the primary constraints upon the enforcement process. The
primary constraints are those that the agents or operators construct,
objectivate, and enact in the course of their duties. It is the enacted
environment that makes the problems real and is the context of the
narcs' game.

II

Foreground

This chapter presents a conception of organization as a creation of acting, defining, and working persons dealing with ongoing practical tasks and problems. The enacted environment of policing and drug policing is given a structural form so that the reader might better understand how the formal rules and regulations of the two organizations bear on the practice of enforcement. They constrain it very little, as chapter 4 makes dramatically clear. In chapter 4 the centrality of the perspective of the agent in determining the outlines, objectives, and kinds of drug enforcement is shown. This consequence is but one of the enacted environment described here and is possible because the informational base for rational deployment of organizational resources is limited, especially with respect to the drug markets and the users. This informational base is subject to enormous error and is of limited utility even when available. The system is closed and self-confirmatory and thus easily lends itself to generating symbolizations that are ritualistic affirmation. The information available is limited, and the most credible information from their perspective, as well as that most readily available, is official police information. This information is interpreted using the implicit propositions or assumptions about the environment that led those statistics to be gathered initially. Results are seen as bearing on the problem as it was initially defined. Since alternative sources of information are neither sought, used, nor wanted, they are not bases for an examination of patterns of routine action. Each action of officers is seen within the context of what is assumed about why this action is undertaken and what results are expected. This can take place because the conception of the enacted environment is durable, flexible, and controls the meanings of actions that take place under the rubric of enforcement. Complementing this conception of the environment is a particular kind of organizational structure that seems to mirror the world of drug use and dealing, thus facilitating interchange based on symbolic and structural compatibility. Insofar as the organization and its members adapt to the character of the criminal world they are regulating, they share the symbolic, linguistic, cultural, and social world of those they regulate. This should in theory improve the organization's capacity to eradicate the market, but it brings with it increasing organizational (unit) autonomy from the controls of the police department and from the public at large to whom they are accountable. The individual officer faces this problem in an acute form. This produces a contradiction or constraint upon action that grows directly from the shaping of the organization by members' actions.

The Enacted Environment of Policing

The police see themselves, individually and collectively, as working in an environment that they cannot fully control. They see parts of it at least as being uncertain. Organizational analysts, although they have defined the term in slightly different ways, have argued that there is a set of correlates of uncertainty in the environment and in the structure and functioning of the police and other similar organizations.[1] This position is a logical extension of a quasi-evolutionary theory that sees organizations as if they were rational, adaptive systems that adjust to their environments as do slugs, hyenas, and bramble bushes (March and Simon, 1958; Terreberry, 1968; Simon, 1957). Given its multiple usage and general application, it may be that the concept of uncertainty is a metaphor that points to certain characteristic problems rather than to an empirically useful measurable concept.[2] It would appear to be a commonsense construct that directs the attention of researchers to certain features of organizations. Perhaps the most difficult problem in research, which links organizational features to the environment and associates some features with uncertainty, is that these correlates do not in themselves allow one to establish a causal or directional statement concerning the flow of influence. Are the features of policing, such as high discretion and a complex task structure, produced by the influences or pressures of the environment upon an emerging organizational form, or does the environment, through decision making, managerial allocation of resources and planning, take on a certain shape? In less abstract terms, do the police have specialized drug units because the environment creates a press for them, or do police departments create drug units in order to create a sense of efficacy and establish or mark aspects of the environment they perceive as problematic and which they claim to control? Collective and semi-shared orientations to an environment may well give rise to belief systems which in turn sustain a pattern of organizing and acting toward that perceived environment (see Child, 1972; Aldrich and Pfeffer, 1976; Meyer and Rowan, 1977).

Weick (1969:63–64), following these implications, argues persuasively that the evolutionary conception of organizational adaptation is imprecise, lacks clarity, and contains a gross portrait of the environment. Instead of assuming that an external environment exists independently of human processing of information, the organizing and sense making of human interaction, human memory, and socially constructed constraints on subsequent actions, an alternative conception of the environment is required. This conception, called by Weick "the enacted environment," is adopted here as a basic metaphor for articulating organization-environment relations:

Instead of discussing the "external environment," we will discuss the "enacted environment." The phrase the enacted environment preserves the crucial distinctions that we wish to make, the most important being that the human *creates* the environment to which the system then adapts. The human act does not *react* to any environment, he *en*acts to it. It is this enacted environment, and nothing else, that is worked upon by the process of organizing. (Weick, 1969:63–64)

Weick further argues that an important aspect of the enacted environment is time. We act in line with intentions, but these are known reflectively or after the action. "All knowing and meaning arise from reflection, from a backward glance" (Weick, 1969:64). The future, on the other hand, is envisioned as a plan or project, and it is only through the envisioning of the whole project that component parts can be isolated. Even when one tries to anticipate the future, it is anticipated in terms of what might have been the consequence of some already completed act. Meanings themselves arise from selective attention to the present by the actor; the selection is guided by pragmatic or practical concerns in the here and now, as well as by past selections from among variations in information with which he is presented. "Whatever items are singled out of the flow of experience for closer attention will take on whatever meaning is implicit in the pragmatic reflective glance" (Weick, 1969:67). The pragmatic attitude means that whatever meanings are attributed to events are patterned by the present and that, conversely, some aspects of any situation will be overlooked, ignored, and only partially represented in a decision-making context. Any explanation for a decision will be partial because it will not include aspects of the events that cannot be expressed verbally, recalled, or coded in ways not relevant to that event. Pragmatic considerations in an organizational context are linked to tasks and location within the organizational structure (especially in segmentalized organizations). Individual actors, in their actions of reacting to, creating, and maintaining an environment, take an active part in constructing the central meaningful components of organizations and their environments.

If the ways in which participants perceive, define, and act upon the environment and the ways in which they chunk and decode memories of experience are socially rooted and to some extent patterned by the segments in the organization in which they experience organizational activities, then the environment cannot usefully be seen as a single object but as an entity that variably and phenomenologically links the organization and external events. The potential for loose coupling is maintained. The enacted aspects of the environment cannot easily be seen as flowing from long-term rationality and planning, since the central implication of the loose-coupling concept is the gap between plans, intentions, and outcomes.

The capacity, then, of the organization to produce its own coding system by which received messages are encoded and then decoded is greater under these conditions, and as a result the organization has important independent symbolic and symbolizing capacities. The organization is a system of signs by which other signs are encoded and stored, hence to be decoded. It is, in effect, a crude semiological system. Thus, the term enacted environment is a reflexive concept: it refers not only to what is "seen" in the external world but also to the structure by which such seeing is made possible. In a sense, seeing and the seen are two sides of the same system of thought, action, and praxis. To separate them is to do a logical injustice (see Dewey and Bentley, 1949). It is a differentiated semiotic system based on information and encoding processes. If we look at the differentiation of drug work from other police work, we can subsequently scrutinize the enacted environment of drug law enforcement.

The Differentiation of Police Work

Police work is differentiated along at least two dimensions, one a task and informational dimension and the other a symbolic or expressive dimension. The patrol officer and the drug officer represent, as ideal typical examples, very distinctive informational and symbolic characteristics. The informational problems facing the patrol officer and the drug officer are presented in table 3.1. The expressive or symbolic dimensions of police work also differentiate the patrol officer from the drug officer because the roles and the positions that they occupy, respectively, in segments of the organization, have different meanings for the selves of officers. This section discusses not only what officers do, but what these doings have to do with beings or self-symbolizations. The distinctions drawn here are generalizations rather than empirically based descriptions of particular activities found in either of the two units. The instances and examples are drawn from field notes, but the general organizational pattern is found in all police departments and is based on review and synthesis of the relevant materials on these two types of policing.

The sources of information available and utilized by the two types differ (see table 3.2). Whereas the patrol officer responds to citizen complaints, requests, and demands for service either on view or from dispatch, the investigator rarely works with citizen complaints and must assemble information from informants, previous arrestees, other officers, or intelligence units. The legal basis for action differs (that is, the degree of control over the use of law). Although a citizen complaint in patrol is virtually legal grounds for action, citizen complaints rarely constitute a basis of legally based action in the vice area, and if the officer is not an eyewitness to the transaction, additional evidence of possession, sale, or intent to sell is required for an acceptable or prosecutable case to be assembled and presented. The time at which intervention occurs in the crime sequence varies. The initial information base is different. Vice officers must in a sense "make crime happen" or construct circumstances in which evidence can be obtained, and a variety of consequences flow from the fact that the officer, not a citizen, is the complainant in the typical vice case. A number of techniques are used to facilitate the appearance of crime under controlled circum-

Table 3.1 Crime-relevant features of police work in patrol and drug units

Features	Drug Unit [a]	Patrol Unit
Sources of information	Informants, citizen's calls, previous arrestees, intelligence units, and other officers.	Citizen phone calls; on-view police intervention; citizen encounters with police (face-to-face call for help, appearance at station, etc.)
Legal bases for action	Office typically brings complaint	Citizen or citizen and officer file complaint
Time of intervention	Prior to, simultaneously with, or after a crime has been committed; tends to be "proactive" (Black, 1968)	Variable, but most typically after the fact or "reactive" intervention
Aim	Use techniques to observe, recreate, or "create" the crime; evidence of crime must be made court-relevant	Crime must be founded; facts established and perpetrator arrested if required
Targets	Selection of targets (groups, persons, locales) is individually patterned and discretionary	Some targets based on discretion; vast majority are assigned to an officer or officer-pairs who then are accountable for handling
Measures of efficiency	Clearance rate cannot be used; base number of cases is unknown	Rate of cleared assignments can be calculated from those assigned or reported (either on view or dispatch)

a. Many of these apply to vice enforcement and the enforcement of other economic/regulatory violations.

stances, all limited to use by vice officers: direct hand-to-hand buys from dealer to agent; "buy and bust" situations when arrests are made at the time of the sale, or by establishing a pattern of conspiracy to sell drugs by assembling wire-intercept evidence, surveillance, photographs, videotapes, films, or the testimony of informants. The agent relies on informants to make buys, provide information on dealing/using activities, make introductions (to "duke in" or "cut in" an undercover agent to make buys), and occasionally to testify. Informants sometimes come forward voluntarily but for the most part are previously arrested persons (charged with drug or other offenses) who agree to "work off the beef" (act as an informant in hopes of having charges dropped or reduced, having bail reduced, or obtaining altered conditions of probation). Narcotics work is nearly impossible without informants.[3] Thus the recruitment, interrogation, working, and protection of informants is a focal or key activity in narcotics work. The facts of an alleged crime are either "on view" or "presented" to a patrol officer. Narcotics agents must "work forward" from information on a potential or known violator rather than "backward" from the alleged or established facts of crime (for example, in murder, a body must exist; a crime must be established or "founded" prior to investigation). The selection of targets is highly discretionary, and the scope of a case is infinitely expandable (every buyer has a seller, etc., on up or down the dealing hierarchy). Uncertainty obtains between the effort and time expended and the "pay-off" it might yield.

The contrasts of the aim and targets involved in these two kinds of police work, as table 3.1 shows, are striking. A "clearance rate" is problematic since cases are typically not assigned to officers in narcotics but built by them with their partners or on their own from information. Even when assignments are made, calls are not recorded, making it impossible to independently verify the clues officers receive. Much activity is not reported if it does not lead to an arrest, buy, or long-term surveillance, and in general sergeants are ignorant of the precise number of cases (potential or otherwise), informants, and "clues" (leads to potential cases) being worked by investigators under their supervision.

In both patrol and narcotics, to varying degrees depending on the supervision attempted, there are pressures to "produce" in terms of established criteria. In patrol, it may be number of "stops," traffic tickets, or field interviews obtained in a given period of time, or production may be defined in terms of the handling of dispatched calls.[4] Since the number of stops, tickets, or field interviews generated by an officer is in a sense "proactive work" similar to that of narcotics, the principal difference lies in the fact that the patrol division has records of accepted and handled routine calls and whether they eventuate in arrest or other forms of official paper, while the narcotics unit virtually never has a record of clues, cases, tips, names, and alleged events that officers did not undertake to investigate (and moreover there is no record of most that were investigated). The essential point is that pressure to produce can be anticipated by the patrol officer to be based on his showing on standardized measures of performance, assigned work, and limited time and space obligations (while on shift, in his district, while on duty). The narcotics officer cannot do so; he may seek to produce but is rarely assigned work and is given wide latitude in the time given to and the places in which an investigation is conducted. The investigator, in the absence of prospective guidance, must personally socially construct the meanings and prospects associated with a given set of clues. The reasons that this tends to be individualistic in the two departments studied (exceptions are noted below) brings us to the symbolic aspects of the drug officer's role.

The role of the drug investigator is patterned as much by the stylistic and expressive aspects of the role as by the structural features that are based upon the level and kind of information he or she processes. The role of the narcotics or drug investigator, as shown in the previous discussion, contrasts greatly with the patrol officer's role. In fact, the distinctiveness of the drug investigator's role in contrast to the patrol officer's role is one of the reasons many people seek out a position in the drug investigative unit. For many, the freedom associated with that role is a salient factor in their staying in police work.

In a sense, then, the role of the drug investigator cannot be understood unless one compares it with the role of the patrol officer. One must appreciate the dominant position of the patrol division and patrol officers in any department in order to appreciate how it is the base for contrasts. Patrol officers represent the numerical majority in the department (somewhere around 90 percent of most departments are uniformed or patrol officers). They represent the traditional mode of policing in this country and are associated with the most important and salient social symbols of policing: the patrol car, the uniform, the weaponery, the badge, and other visible symbols of authority carried by the officer or seen on the vehicle. All officers share a sense of the importance of police work on the streets. It is the baseline function and the central locus for comparisons in police departments.

A second feature of this comparison is the relevance of the content of information rather than the absolute level of it. Narcotics officers must work with secondhand information since they often cannot personally observe the crime taking place but must rely on informants. They must rely not so much on the level of information or the absolute amount they possess as upon the degree of credibility attributable to the information received.

Evaluation in narcotics work becomes a game based on how well a supervisor interprets an officer's reading of informants. The supervisor, because he lacks firsthand information in almost every case, is on the edge of an interpersonal perception game that staggers the imagination. However, decisions, rather than being based on the classic information-assessment paradigm, are based on those features of the situation the officer deems as credible for the purposes of the investigation. Messages do not function so much as matters of information but more as signs of the credibility of the source of the information. The assessment of credibility is prior to the operational question of ascertaining the amount, content, social location, and actionable consequences of the receipt of such information.

Work-related situations for officers in patrol and in narcotics/vice produce levels of information received and acted upon and expressive features of social interaction by which the situations are defined and made actionable. The content as well as the form of the communication is critical to the decisions made, the outcomes generated, and resultant organizational consequences. The problematic nature of the relationship of the officer to the informational bases of the work and the content differences in social processing of information have correlates in the "expressive features" of the role. Goffman (1969) has defined these as the messages that are "given off" rather than given in the course of a performance. The "idiosyncratic particulars" of the person's performance, those signs that indicate the extent to which the person is linked to the socially defined role compose the expressive dimension of role behavior. It can be seen that although the structure of information may pattern the variability in the tasks performed (the targeting modes), the ways in which the tasks are performed are socially constructed. The expressive or stylistic aspects of the role must be negotiated within the limits of information control provided by targeting modalities.

One of the most important sources of identity for the police officer is his uniform. Conversely, the absence of a uniform is a very salient source of negative identity to drug investigators. One of the major dimensions of the role derives from the absence of a uniform. They are not "harness bulls" or "uniformed men." The police uniform is at once a statement of the wearer's identity, a degree of organizational attachment, a visible sign of commitment to a consistent line of action, and a source of uniformity of behavior on which an audience can rely (see Stone, in Rose, ed., 1963). Uniformed officers wear a uniform at all times while on duty, and most wear it to and from duty. The symbols of authority (gun, badge, truncheon, radio, handcuffs, patch of the city, the uniform itself) produce an overt statement of identity, increase the attachment of the officer to the role, and offer a program for others to follow in affirming or denying the role. Agents do not wear uniforms, with a single exception: when in the course of an investigation they are "playing at" being a mailman, utility repairman, a city inspector, or a uniformed officer. Usually playing at occurs when duplicity is needed to enter a house without violence, for surveillance, or to serve an arrest warrant on an unsuspecting person. Thus these uniforms become an affirmation of what officers are not rather than what they are. Conversely, drug investigators are encouraged to wear whatever is acceptable on the street when they work undercover: T-shirts, jeans, sandals. These clothes are paid for by the uniform allowance (insofar as it cannot be used for a uniform). In Suburban, cleaning costs for clothes required for court appearances were also paid by the department.

This flexibility in dress is complemented by freedom of action while on duty. The key device of undercover officers is dissimulation of the criminal. Thus when going on a surveillance, they might rendezvous in a supermarket parking lot to drink a half-case of beer; when in a bar, they will drink, shoot pool, and talk about drugs, as well as adopt "street language." Their role requires that they reduce distance between themselves and the criminal, whereas the uniform, the symbols of authority associated with it, and the tasks of the patrolman serve to distance them from the criminal. Patrol officers succeed, in part, by appearing and acting less and less like the persons they confront in conflict situations, whereas narcs succeed by utilizing precisely the opposite interpersonal strategy, front-work, line, and manner. The closer he is to the criminal's style of life, argot, and behavior,—the less he is like a cop,—the more successful he is.

Control over the drug officer's behavior and demeanor is always problematic, not only because of the informational variation noted above, but because the symbolism of the role frees him to redefine the significance of stylistic features of his behavior. He is free and expected to work overtime (in limited paid amounts in Suburban; without pay in Metro except for court), wear a beard or mustache, and negotiate the timing of his reports, time of arrival and leaving work. He does not answer roll calls and can be in odd places at odd hours with strange associates. He can drink on duty (and be paid for it as well) and typically is out of radio communication with the department. Radio messages between drug officers on surveillance are coded in a nonofficial format ("Hey, Bill, are you there?" not "Metro 1 to Metro 2") and are transmitted through a special investigative channel reserved for detective and vice-drug units. On the other hand, when radio messages are transmitted on the departmental frequency, they are partly in code and use official numbers rather than names, thus tying patrol officers to an official identity. Street names used by narcs, such as "Red," "Slim," or "Jerry," are used interchangeably with actual personal names in and out of the department. Street names deny the relevance of the tie between person and organization except through that false or dissimulated identity.

Pay and rewards are differentially distributed between patrol and drug units. Patrol is the entry point for all officers; initial transfers to other units are effectuated from that point. Narcotics officers are chosen or handpicked through informal decision making engaged in by sergeants and lieutenants. Whereas patrol officers are transferred in and out of patrol by official policy, drug officers are assigned at the pleasure of the administrators of the unit. They can be asked to leave or be transferred at any time. They have no job security.

Narcs on duty have all their personal expenses paid. In Suburban, they were supplied with personal cars paid for from the city budget, which they gassed, washed, and repaired outside the city's garages. Narcs are fronted money for miscellaneous personal expenses and keep city money varying from a few dollars to a few thousand in their pockets when going on a buy or an attempt to arrest a person at the time of an expected buy. Patrol officers are paid a salary and a uniform allowance and may earn overtime.

The authority of the investigator is wide, and his discretion is great. He can dispense favors of money, drugs, relief from charges and work, and can either pursue or drop cases and informants at virtually his own discretion.

All officers respect traffic laws to variable degrees; they are permitted to violate them under stipulated conditions (pursuit, crime in progress, officer in trouble). Narcs drive as they please: on sidewalks, at high speeds, and through stop lights and signs; they will make illegal U-turns in mid-block, park illegally while on surveillances, drive on the wrong side of the street, and violate miscellaneous niceties of the road (yields, crosswalks) with impunity. Their lack of uniform, visibility, ultimate protection through the department, and their moral mandate cover such miscellaneous delicts. Conversely, it loosens the commitment of the officer to both the law and the police role.

Agents, like patrol officers, handle illegal materials and substances and persons whom many, including themselves, view as stigmatized, immoral, or polluted: "junkies," "whores," and criminals of many varieties. The agents come in direct contact with drugs (they claim to simulate use if asked to smoke a joint or only smell heroin if asked to taste). The more frequently they have close contact with such "polluting" substances, the more successful they will be in carrying out the role. This freedom also means that opportunities to manipulate the law to create the condition of crime are high. Thus the informational dimensions of the role produce stylistic variations in the opportunities to act in ways contrary to those associated with the role of patrol officers. The special relationships they have with the drug world and the opportunities they have to create the conditions of crime and working informants gives them a special relationship to prosecuting attorneys, which is shared with detectives. They possess the opportunity to alter, change, redefine, drop, or add to the charge(s) against a person. The freedom exercised in this respect also marks them from the patrol officers who may utilize discretion at lower levels of the system (in the arrest and charge situation) but are denied significant influence thereafter.

This analysis and comparison of the stylistic aspects of these two types of police roles implicitly contains an indication of the types of involvements required, permitted, and avoided by these officers. Some features of the occupationally relevant situations determining the extent of involvement in the role itself have been presented. On the one hand, the role of the patrol officer contains a number of scripts for the unfolding of demeanor by the participants in the action, guided by some proximal rules such as maintaining interpersonal control, affective neutrality, and controlling or guiding the probability of certain outcomes of a situation (see Manning, 1977a:265). The officer is expected to be less deferential than the citizen, more deferential to women than men, to adults than to children, to middle- rather than lower-class persons, and to whites more than blacks (see Sykes and Clark, 1974). The investigator cannot rely on such prescribed deterence patterns nor is he locked into a single status indicated by multiple complementary lines, props, and appearances. His identities are shifting; he wears no standard symbols of authority: he must play at being the very thing he attempts to control and to participate in the market he is meant to eradicate. Even when the informational level is high, the aleatory features of playing out a deal (in the case of undercover work) are so salient that all planning, regulation, advisos, and principles can only be applied to situations by individual officers making discrete and invisible decisions. Conversely, the structure in which he works places him in a loose relationship to the role of police officer, thus freeing him to innovate and to play it by ear in the street (narcs who maintain the "patrolman's mentality" are transferred out of the unit).

Although the degree of uncertainty within a police department varies from the patrol to the vice/narcotics unit, members of both units must resolve episodes in which the information level is low. In the case of vice/narcotics units, however, the informational problems involve not only the level of information received but the credibility of the source. Interpersonal trust and credibility are central.

Situational rationality and discretionary judgment are more characteristic of vice/narcotics than of patrol in part because there is greater certainty (more information from more credible sources) in patrol than in narcotics. Segments vary in degree of uncertainty and can produce the processes of differentiation and functional autonomy. The entropy in narcotics units rests on an informational base, producing operational differences in resolution of problematics. Increases in the degree of competence within a narcotics unit will produce greater organizational differentiation, rule specialization, and stylistic variations in supervision. The more narcotics units succeed, the less like police officers they will be in terms of style, appearance, supervisory modes, and procedural guidelines. Subsequently, then, the narcotics officer becomes less and less committed to the organization and more and more committed to himself (herself) and to other normative commitments. Ironically, success pulls officers farther and farther from the organization (hence the limitations usually placed on the length of time any officer will be allowed to work undercover). Conversely, if they "fail," they are drawn back in both literally, since they will be transferred back into patrol, and figuratively, since their commitment will be toward more conventional modes of policing. A tension is produced that paralyzes and divides many units, and sets vice officers apart from other police officers. The different modes of authority (more patrimonial, personalistic, and squad-sergeant related), variable hours, times, and locales of work, degree of involvement with the target groups (criminals, drug dealers, or villians, bad guys, crooks, or bandits as they were variously called), and variations in information and work demand produce role styles that serve to locate the officer's sense of himself in relationships with participants in the drug markets.

The differentiation of police work, based on information and role expressiveness, structures the work on a day-to-day basis. Thus far, the features of drug law enforcement have been described as if they were a function only of factual or objective matters that can be located in some consensually defined "real world." There are constraints and patterning influences in the present role and task structure of police work. However, these do not provide the determinant features of the strategies of enforcement. There are other more important determinants that arise from perceptions and understandings of what the mandate and aims of drug law enforcement are, the intended effects, and the legitimate techniques and strategies that are associated with "good police work." Importantly, the environment in which the officers act is one they largely project, act in accord with, and thus reify. The role and structure of the police department has developed over time, and the relative contribution to that structuring by elements of the objectively measurable environment and the perceived or enacted environment cannot be established. The enacted environment of the police in the two organizations studied was consistent with the structuring of the drug markets they intend to regulate.

The Enacted Environment of Drug Enforcement

It has been argued (Thompson, 1967) that administrative certainty results when the organization can specify in detail a notion of cause and effect with regard to its actions and outputs and when a clear or crystallized set of standards of desirability can be set and adhered to by participants. In this perspective, organizations can be arrayed by the extent to which the standards of desirability are either ambiguous or crystallized and the degree to which their knowledge of cause and effect relationships in the environment is either complete or incomplete. The classic example of crystallized standards is found in an auto plant where levels of production are set and performance is judged against profits. With a given number of workers, working a given number of hours with the required equipment and materials, a predictable output can be expected. Knowledge of cause and effect is relatively complete, and minute adjustments in input are revealed in altered output figures. It would appear that more ambiguous standards exist in people-processing organizations (Wilson, 1968; Goffman, 1961; Hasenfeld and English, ed., 1974).

The two narcotics law enforcement units studied do not operate with unequivocal standards of desirability. In both, officers must interpret a number of facts and make them relevant to their practice. Neither unit has clearly stated standards of a desirable environment. Differences exist in the perception of the danger to society involved in victimless crimes; drugs are perceived as having different effects, meanings, danger-criminogenic potential, and as being of different concern to their significant public audiences (compare marijuana and heroin). It is not clear whether dealers, users, or both should be the target of enforcement, given the belief that users may be dissuaded from further use if deterred early (Green and DuPont, 1974; Hughes, et al., 1972), and some dealers supply large numbers of users; public awareness and levels of concern about the drug problem shift temporally and volatilely (DeFleur, 1975); and costs and time constraints must be weighed against the ethics of absolutism surrounding drug use (Gusfield, 1975). Internally, indices of success, competent work, and failure vary (compare Skolnick, 1966; and chapter 4).

Cause and effect notions here resemble those in other control agencies that maintain incomplete, contradictory, or unarticulated notions of cause and effect (compare Lemert, 1972; Stoll, 1968; Strauss, et al., 1964). Does arresting persons deter them from recidivism or should arrests be used as harrassment? (Heller, 1973b). Can information received from informants on dealing-using activities be trusted; is it legally actionable (that is, can a case be made worthy of arrest)? To what extent can arrests, seizures and cases brought to court be taken as valid measures of police impact on the dealing-using system? (see Senate Testimony, 1975; Mandel, 1969; Lindesmith, 1965). In part because the use, possession, and distribution of a number of kinds of drugs has been made illegal, there are no accurate national or local figures on the number of users, their location, patterns of consumption, preferences, and on the market system of use (for a rare exception, see Redlinger, 1975a). Also partly as a result of the illegality, the systematic relations between the actions of enforcement (and treatment) and the dynamics of the using-dealing system are not well understood and empirical data are scanty or absent.

Let us pose a hypothetical situation at this point, bearing on the scheme or organizational analysis that has been presented by theorists such as Thompson, Lorsch, and Lawrence and other open-systems theorists. If cause and effect notions and standards of desirability were governing concerns of narcotics law enforcement organizations, then one would expect that the information bearing on police impact on the use-dealing-market system and on the judgment of the performance of individual officers and units would be sought and refined. It is not. As long as organizations seek to monitor the environment, they will have to test various sources, kinds, and qualities of data. If, on the other hand, they resort to the internal management of organizational processes, then more refined data on the evaluation of individual performances, recruitment standards, and the link between individual performance and organizational success will have to be acquired. The choice between these two strategies is not really a choice at all but a slow accretion of inertia in one or the other direction. Illustrative of this accretion are the two very different tendencies of the DEA, which has adopted the external monitoring position to a greater extent, and the FBI (Wilson, 1978).

Local police do not gather data on the drug problem in any serious fashion: their files are out of date and frequently only partially accurate, they are not cross-referenced so that one can use one bit of data on a person to check another, officers are not encouraged to gather and systematize data, and clerks are often left to maintain the files. Case records are not systematically kept during the course of an investigation or afterwards (compare the similar behavior of detectives, discovered by Greenwood, Chaiken, and Petersilia, 1977). Drug agents do not keep systematic information on paper on any critical aspect of their work. Why this is so is developed further later. The point to be emphasized here is the absence of this information, the absence of systematic attempts to attain it, and the tendency that organizational theorists, media, and the public have to assume that such data are available and that it guides enforcement. It is not available and therefore clearly does not guide enforcement. What are the limits on acquiring it then?

The limits on acquiring this critical information are many, and they have been often mentioned by critics of drug enforcement—the secrecy of the market, the illicit nature of the profits and the business relationships established, the sporadic and uncertain nature of the work and the variable level of profit, the tendency to oligopolistic markets with polycentric street-level dealing—all of which make regulatory monitoring very difficult. These factors are indeed critical constraints of an informational sort upon drug law enforcement. They are critical but frequently recognized. What is not frequently recognized is that the police have no interest in and make no effort to acquire this information.

Much of the debate about the effect of drug law enforcement is, strictly speaking, academic. This information is not sought. The information that is available is not used and is seriously flawed from an informational perspective—it has low validity as a measure of use. Police act anyway on the basis of what they assume to be the case; information of this kind is neither wanted nor needed.

Data on Opiate Users: Errors and Ignorance
The most obvious data, on which police might base their allocation of resources or their enacted strategies, would be figures on the actual number of users in their political jurisdiction. Prior to discussing in more detail the police notion of an enacted environment on which they do predicate their actions, the problem of estimating the number of users of opiates in an area is reviewed, for it is here that perception and politics merge with statistics and policies.

Police compilation of arrests on drug charges and the file once kept by the Bureau of Narcotics and Dangerous Drugs (BNDD) long served as the basis for estimating the heroin addict population. The BNDD file was a previously maintained federal listing of addicts based on the records kept by local police officers of the persons arrested on drug charges. Local police were instructed to fill out a card on every person who they believed to be an addict on the basis of an interview or their own information. In a sense this listing was tautological since all persons arrested on drug charges were labeled as addicts or users. Other users or addicts were not listed because, in practice, cards were only filled out as required when someone was arrested. This suspicion was in fact the necessary condition for their being arrested on such a charge. When BNDD was disbanded, the system was abandoned.

At the present time there are four other commonly used ways of estimating the population of addicts in an area. The first type is from sampling formulas based on BNDD or police files. The second type is based on an extrapolation of overdose deaths due to opiates. The "Baden formula," developed in New York, is the most popular of these, and assumes that one out of every 200 heroin addicts dies of an overdose reaction each year. For example, if the number of overdose deaths in a city for a year was 20, the best estimate of the number of heroin addicts in that city would be 20 × 200, or 4,000. This formula has been used by DuPont in his research (1971, 1972, and 1973). A third type of formula combines an extrapolation based on the number and size of the dealing areas in a city, an estimate of the number of major dealers, and police estimates of the drug-using population (Redlinger, 1975b). A fourth means of estimation, the self-report, has been used by Chambers and associates, and O'Donnell et al. (1976). If we take a set of estimates for Washington, D.C., and see how they were modified over a period of years, we can identify some of the sources of error that can operate in such figures. (See table 3.2 for an example of differing estimates of addicts in treatment, at large, and arrested, based on Washington, D.C., data gathered by DuPont and others.) This data suggests that estimating the number of addicts is not simply a matter of data gathering and analysis but is basically a political process.

Estimating the number of opiate users   There are a number of ways that one can define an opiate user: a person who has ever used; who uses infrequently; who uses daily and who is technically addicted; who uses daily at a certain level (usually estimated by the dollar value of the drugs bought per day; the size of the habit); or anyone who admits to use. All of these definitions have been used in research and in government-sponsored programs. The definitions used are not based on a theory of addiction, such as Lindesmith's (1947), and no attempt has been made to create a standardized and acceptable meaning for the

Table 3.2 Estimated number of users, number of users in treatment, and number of police opiate charges, Washington, D.C., 1965–1975.

Year	Estimated Number of Opiate Users	Number of Users in Treatment	Number of Opiate Charges[k]	
1965	1,116[a]			
1966	1,164[a]			
1967	1,106[a]			
1968	1,162[a]	4,200[d]		408[b]
1969	1,636[a]	4,200[d]	1,046[g]	958[b]
1970	1,743[a], 5,000[c], 10,400[d]		2,920[g]	1,588[b]
	12,400[j]	150[c]		
1971	16,400[j], 16,800[c], 20,000[d] 3,133[d], 20,000[d].			
	17,000[d]	2,700[e]	3,574[g]	3,144[b]
1972	14,200[j]	4,200[c]	2,525[g]	2,108[b]
1973	3,800[j], 18,000[c] 2,000[h]		1,453[g]	958[f]
1974	3,100[i]		1,327[g]	900[f]
1975	3,100[c]	1,600[g]	1,300[g]	

a. Bureau of Narcotics and Dangerous Drugs File of Addicts; cited in DuPont, 1971:323.
b. DuPont and Greene, 1973: 719, see k
c. DuPont, 1973
d. DuPont, 1971
e. DuPont, 1972
f. Greene, 1975
g. Data supplied to the author by the Washington, D.C. department, see k
h. McDonald, 1973 a
i. Chambers, 1975
j. Greene and DuPont, 1974
k. The discrepancy between arrests and charges is considerable, charges varying from somewhere around 44 to 55 percent of those arrested for the years covered. The discrepancy between the two columns under opiate charges probably comes from decisions made about what to count as an "opiate charge." This is not a simple matter because the law changed (the controlled substance act took effect in May 1971), changing the bases for the charges and the older act, the Harrison Act, was no longer used. Further, decisions have to be made concerning whether such charges as "possession of implements of crime" (needles, syringes, burned spoons used for "cooking" heroin, bloody cotton), "present in an illegal establishment," or "uttering forged narcotic prescriptions" will be counted as equivalent to "conspiracy to violate

term "opiate user" or "addict." The absence of any such shared definition has permitted government officials, politicians, public health officers, the police, and epidemiologists to use the term in whatever fashion best suits their own purposes. Changes in the definition of "addict"
alter the base figures for the number of users, for example, and obviously create shifting error terms in any equation. Estimates of
changes in the level of use or number of users are both invalid and
unreliable. The figures are misleading to the public and scholars because they are incomparable over time.

The first source of error derives from the changing definitions of
the term "overdose." (See DuPont, 1971; DuPont and Greene, 1973;
Greene and DuPont, 1974.) A second source of error in estimates is
the small number of cases on which overdose extrapolations are
based.[5] A third source of error comes in the use of various definitions
of addict.[6] A fourth source of error comes in the extrapolation of addiction populations from samples of new users who are most likely to overdose and are therefore not representative of the entire using population.[7] A fifth source of error comes from comparison across methods.[8]

These sources of error hold also for the discussion of treatment and
treatment populations.[9] One can see by examining the figures on the
treatment population at various intervals according to DuPont that substantial changes occur from year to year according to published reports (see table 3.2).[10]

The centrality of these ideas resides in the fact that they are the conventional wisdom in many police departments. It is assumed that reducing the opiate-using population directly reduces the property crime
rate. These notions are rooted in the assumptive world of the police
and have become a part of the enacted environment of police departments, including the two studied. To reveal the fallacious logic of the

federal drug laws," "intent to distribute narcotics," and "possession of narcotic
drugs." From the point of view of the "crime problem" a more restrictive
definition might be used, while if one wanted a sensitive indicator of police
activities, the broader definition might be used. I do not know what DuPont and
Greene (1973) and Greene (1975) used as a definition of an opiate charge and
they do not indicate this in their articles.

argument is not to engage in discrediting the police belief. The episte-
mological status of police beliefs is equivalent to a myth that supports
a set of self-serving rituals (Manning, 1977a). It should be recalled that
the police do not gather these data. The data referred to by the police
are based not on hard data, but on estimates, commonsense wisdom,
rumors, and generalizations. The police respond to what they hear
from others: newspaper reporters, other media people, and social sci-
entists.

If it is indeed the case that we have no reliable figures on the number
of addicts in this country or for any given area of the nation, then several implications should be kept in mind. The selection and use of
given facts to represent the effectiveness of the drug control action is
undertaken to produce a dramaturgical effect. Large busts, successful
"campaigns" or "operations" (Gooberman, 1974), big seizures, the
prosecution of large dealers and associates are used and played up
by newspapers, and narcotics units feed these facts directly to them.
Mistakes are not publicized if possible, and such demeaning facts as
the small average size of seizures, the high per buy costs of certain
drugs, the number of raids that yield no drugs, the number of buys that
are made but are not the basis for prosecution, the amount of money
that "walks" (is given to a person who promises to return drugs, but
does not, and keeps the money) or is not recovered (when buys are
made and no arrests result), rarely, if ever, appear in the papers. Estimates of the numbers of addicts, even when scientific formulas are
employed, contain great margins of error. These scientific formula are
not used by the police for any purpose other than publicity—they are
not used as a basis for policy setting. Changes in public interest in a
problem, usually created by media amplification efforts (see Young,
1972; and Cohen, 1972), tend to make more unstable the estimates of
agencies that do not have files on users or speak only from general
information. There is a very great public tolerance of a range of estimates with very high upper limits being used by some, such as Nixon,
Rockefeller, and DEA, to gain public support for political campaigns,
and with low limits, or gross underestimates, being used at other
times.[11] Lindesmith (1965) has argued that police and federal agencies generally underestimate the number of heroin users if they rely ex-

clusively on arrest figures. Thus the use of the figures on users is a situational and political one and is more a function of the capacity of the organization to arrest persons than of their information-processing capacities (Mandel, 1969). We can best explain why a level of use is claimed by an enforcement agency by asking what they can gain by publicizing such a figure rather than by seeking to identify the social conditions that might have caused such a rate. Vacillations in the estimates of the number of users in an area might be considered a political or intellectual embarrassment to the agencies that produce them. However, since their primary value to the police is dramaturgical, validity is of little practical concern.

Police Assumptions about the Environment: The Bases of Enactment

The absence of precise, empirically valid information does not, however, mean that the organizations do not act in line with a set of assumptions about the environment and the effects of their actions upon it. Nor does it mean that one cannot formulate a causal model on the basis of these assumptions. An analytic list of implicit propositions underlying narcotics law enforcement follows. It is based on interviews in the two units, especially with the command personnel.

The Drug System

1. Heroin is highly addictive and morally reprehensible (although some dealers are both smart and good businessmen).

2. The demand for heroin is inelastic. The user consumes at a relatively constant level from day to day and will pay more to maintain high "high."

3. The drug-use system is closed and based upon opiates as a model of use, effects, spread, and marketing and distribution patterns. Therefore a decrease in the amount of heroin available will yield:

a. an increase in demand for heroin;
b. an increase in price ("retail") of heroin on the street.
Indices of 3a and 3b:
police buys* (number, modes, purity, size) estimated value, qual-

ity, and size of seizures** addicts' reports of drugs used, cost of "habit," availability of drugs**
dealers reports and health of users (for example, hepatitis)
c. decrease in quality (purity) of heroin
d. reduction in the active addict population ("users" or "junkies").
Indices of 3c:
seizure data**   police buy data**
addict reports**
Indices of 3d:
overdose deaths (Baden-Letteri formulae; see Josephson and Carroll, eds., 1975.)*

addicts' reports (either in jail or in treatment, DuPont, 1972)*
surveys of self-reported use (Chambers, 1975)*

extrapolations from in-treatment population (DuPont/Greene)*
Redlinger method (1975b)

Consequences and Correlates of Enforcement and Use

1. Heroin users commit crimes, especially property crimes. They account for a variable but large (varies from city to city) estimated proportion of crime known to the police.
Indices:
nalline tests on jailed populations*
addict reports of ways they support their habits;*
surveys of users with criminal records;
police experience and interviews with arrested users.**

2. More police personnel, money, and equipment (automobiles, electronic apparatus, cameras) will increase arrests.

3. Arrests reduce crime in general and particularly affect crime associated with or caused by heroin use.

4. Arrests and associated seizures disrupt the dealing system and
thus decrease the amount of heroin available on the street (follows
logic of a 3a–3d cycle).

5. Decreased availability of heroin reduces the addict population.
Indices:
increased size of treatment population*

addicts move from "copping" areas (Hughes, 1977)
increased "cold turkey" pattern of cessation of use

6. Police control action in the form of buys, arrests, and seizures and
have no stimulative effects on the drug use/dealing system, nor do
they induce use, maintain the system, or infuse significant amounts of
money into drug markets.[12]

*Data available to Metro Department
**Data available to Suburban Department

The argument shown proceeds as follows. Beginning with properties
of the drug, in this case heroin, the consequences of reduced availability of the drug through police intervention (buys, arrests, seizures,
harrassment) is reflected in increases in price and decreases in purity,
since as it becomes more scarce, dealers will try to maintain their profits and clientele by reducing the percentage in each unit if possible. At
some point these effects act to reduce the addict population. One of
the consequences of an increased price, according to this formulation,
is an increase in the number of crimes that are committed by addicts in
order to support their habits (Silverman, Spruill, and Levine, 1975). On
the other hand, control agencies assume they can cope with this rise in
crime brought about by their effective drug programs by increasing arrests (as a result of better funding), which in turn reduce the aggregate
level of crime. These arrests, in turn, disrupt the dealing-using system
and decrease the availability of heroin (follows the above cycle again
in recursive fashion). It is assumed, finally, that these police actions
have no stimulative effects on the dealing-using system, that is, they
do not induce use, maintain the oligopolistic shape of the market, or
infuse significant amounts of money into the marketing system. Figure
3.1, a causal model of these processes, lays out the same argument. It
can be seen that the system is assumed to be totalistic, complete, and
closed. Changes in one variable will produce changes in the others in
the directions indicated.

It should be noted that although this working model of the dealing-
using system is commonly espoused by police, they do not themselves
have the capacity, information, personnel, or equipment actually
to monitor these effects. First, they do not utilize a causal model

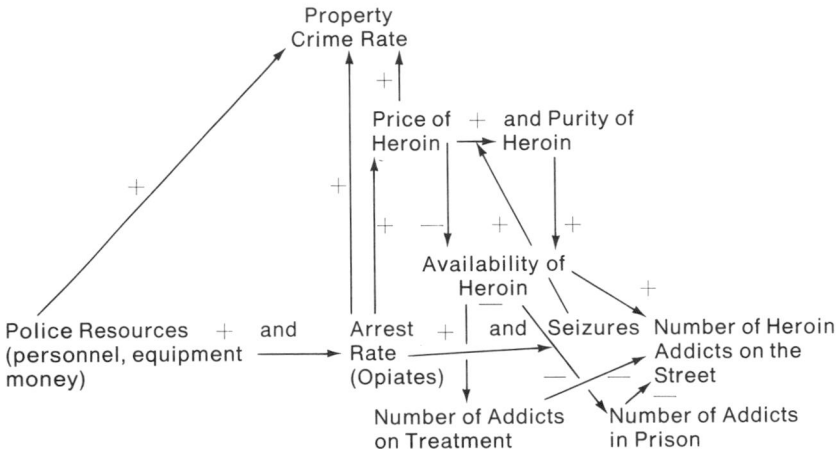

Figure 3.1 Causal (or path) model of the impact of police action on the dealing-using system based on the implicit assumptions in list, pp. 63–65. Modified from Levin, Roberts, and Hirsch, 1975: 58.

that underlies their actions and plans, although this may be their publicly articulated position. They do not act as if these parameters were those they attempted to effect, but tend to emphasize the means used —arrests, raids, buy-busts, buy programs, with their effects, in turn, being assessed by the number of arrests made or the dollar value of the seizures obtained. Second, they do not have the information necessary to verify their public position. Asterisks (see list) indicate the data that is available in the units studied. Third, since they do not have data on all of the parameters of the model, they do not know whether the causal links are strong, weak, negative, or positive, nor can they present data on the percentage of the variance explained in the dependent variable, in this case the number of street addicts, by the various independent variables. What can be concluded from this review of the implicit propositions underlying narcotics policing is that the rational model of drug control advanced by various federal and local agencies and a number of scholars cannot be proved with present empirical data, and it is best seen as a set of working hypotheses. These working hypotheses are a means of making sense of the otherwise arbitrary nature of the world confronting officers, and thus it makes sensible and reasonable what they do, what they attempt to do, and the outcomes that are produced. We can speak of this formulation as an abstracted or sketched version of the enacted environment.

Such is the enacted environment described in abstract terms. As Redlinger has suggested (private communication, January 1978), however, the cognitively perceived environment is real in the sense that it does act to constrain action, is external to the actor, and permits certain actions while making other options more difficult or costly and is contrived in the sense that it is largely maintained by the beliefs of persons who project the reality of this social world and then reify its consequences and characteristics.

The Organization as a Social Mirror

The reality of the environment is not, strictly speaking, arbitrary. It would appear to have been shaped in response to the environment that the agency is mandated to monitor. Other observers have made this claim with respect to other types of organizations.[13] They have articulated an objectivist view of the environment, whereas my argument is based on the ways in which perceptions of the external environment have shaped the development of the units studied. The enforcement units have grown in large part in response not to the actual distribution of drugs, users, patterns of use, and the like but to a projected sense of the problem, sense of its place and character, and a projected imagery of the dealing-using world. To see how this imagery is based to an important degree upon the structures of the dealing-using world, note the following analogies and isomorphism of the enforcement structure and the dealing-using structure.

The enforcement world mirrors the illicit world in the following ways, which make them something like interfacing pyramids. Narcotics dealers must deal; there are pressures to make sales, to be secretive and maintain security against intrusion. Hence they use a personalized mode of dealing. Agents must also produce, maintain secrecy and security, and tend to use a personalized mode of evaluation of their successes and modes of dealing with their informants. Dealers use an entreprenurial model of success, organize their businesses around trusted underlings with whom they have kinship, partnership, local or

Table 3.3 Analogs between the dealing-using system and the enforcement system

Narcotics Dealing Organizations	Narcotics Enforcement Organizations
Pressures for sales and production	Pressures for sales, production of cases, search warrants, and arrests
Concern for security and secrecy	Concern for security and secrecy
Dealings based on personal relationships; trust central to the work	Dealings based on personal relationships; trust central to the work
Entrepreneurial model of success	Entrepreneurial model of success
Feudal loyalty characteristic of organizational relationships; punitive mode of punishment prevails	Feudal loyalty characteristic of organizational relationships; punitive mode of punishment prevails
Pyramidal-like structure of operation; low, flat hierarchy with largest number of actors on the bottom of the organization being exposed to the greatest risks	Pyramidal-like structure varies by unit; flat and low hierarchy with the largest number of actors on the bottom being exposed to the greatest risks
Distrust, lying, misrepresentation, duplicity are dominant modes of interpersonal relations	Trust/distrust, lying, misrepresentation, and duplicity are dominant interpersonal modes. Formalization of relations cross organizational segments
Prices based on relationship to buyer; are negotiated and not fixed	Payment to informants based on relationship to him and case being worked; prices are not fixed, somewhat negotiated but constrained by both the market and the sergeants and organizational policy
Violence, envy, ambivalence, and revenge are dominant emotional themes	Violence and revenge are dominant themes inter- and intra-organizationally, as are envy and ambivalence
Street "rip-offs" of money and dope are common; law does not provide protection for such losses by dealers	Street "rip-offs" of money happen with some frequency; law is a powerful force protecting narcs and sanctioning their revenge actions
Work demands are sporadic and episodic, often nocturnal. Work is overdemanding and must be controlled by manipulation of the clientele	Work demands are sporadic and episodic, often nocturnal. Work is overdemanding and the clientele must be controlled by manipulation
Clientele can be "turned" to be used by the "enemy." Cannot be trusted (yet must be trusted); are viewed as tricky and deceitful, as are agents of control	Clientele can be "turned" to be used by the "enemy." Cannot be trusted (yet must be trusted); are viewed as tricky and deceitful, as are agents of control

Prestige comes from associates; quality of one's clientele, dope, amounts dealt ("weight"), and style of life. Knowledge of the drug scene is a basis for prestige among one's peers	Prestige comes in part from targets and the quality of one's past arrests and seizures. Knowledge of the drug scene is another basis for prestige
Routines and a rationalization of practices is a basis for success in the business	Routines and the rationalization of practices is a basis for success in the business
Both caution and risk-taking are essential to success	Both caution and risk-taking are essential to success
Generally a young man's work, dominated by young men's style of life and interests on and off the job	Generally a young man's work, dominated by young men's style of life and interests on and off duty

racial ties, and base their actions roughly on a pyramidal structure of authority. Agents also work like entrepreneurs, and in fact envy the dealer for his success, freedom, and cleverness; they rely heavily on their partners but tend to distrust others in the authority pyramid within which they work. Partnerships are usually based on similarities of ethnicity, age, sex, and background. Dealers distrust others as a mode of doing business, are shrewd evaluators of others, and use lying, deceit, duplicity, betrayal, threat, violence, and extortion as dominant interpersonal modes. These are also the dominant modes of operation among narcs. The amounts paid to employees or informants for drugs and the prices charged for drugs are based on trust and interpersonal relations as well as monetary considerations. The prices are typically negotiated and are not based on fixed or predetermined schedules. The agent, when working with informants, follows the same pricing pattern, the same modes of interpersonal negotiation and bargaining over prices paid for services, and rests his decisions on his assessment of the person, his relationship to him or her, as well as what the person has done in the past. Because the level of trust is low and the protection of the procedural law is deprived from dealers in their relationships with other dealers and users, violence and "rip-offs" of each other's dope are common. Thus, feelings of revenge, envy, and retaliation are common among dealers. These same feelings suffuse the narcotics agent's world. He envies the dealer and hates him at the same time; he feels a moral distaste for his doings, especially when they involve what he considers to be kids, and for the fact that he seems to be above the law, avoids its pressures, and does not have to respect it as the officer feels he must. He wants revenge for past situations where the user or dealer has avoided arrest, been released on bail, beaten a charge, pleaded-out to lesser charges, dealt while still awaiting trial, and the like.

Dealing work, although based on rational systems of accounting (profits and losses are recorded), is sporadic, having high peaks and troughs, and is full of uneven demands on one's time. Drugs are dealt at all times of the night and day. Opiates especially must be used by at least some users daily, seven days a week, fifty-two weeks a year, year in, year out. Christmas is not excepted. Often, the work spreads out unexpectedly and involves the person in both day and night work. Agents quite clearly operate on analogous schedules. They work sporadically and spend enormous amounts of time waiting for phone calls, for deals to go down, for other people to show up at a meeting place, for equipment, for money to appear, etc. The work then may involve bursts of energy extending for days at a time, around the clock. Although the scheduling of drug units does not appear to be a result of information on the pattern of dealing in cities, it would appear that the flexibility in hours and periods of work is a reasonable approximation of the phenomenon they are mandated to control. The clientele of the drug dealer can be "turned," that is, the user can be made an informant for the control agency or can become a double agent. Likewise, the informant utilized by an agent can be also in the employ of a dealer or can be turned by the dealer using the same means (extortion, threats, money, promises of immunity, or exemption in the future).

The using population is something like civilians in a war: they suffer the indignities of the two warring parties with little of the benefits associated with "victory." Routinization would appear to be more common the higher one mounts the dealing structures. That is, it is assumed that the larger the dealer, the more rational his methods of accounting, business practices, modes of deception, and prevention of arrest (Moore, 1977). It would appear that the more enforcement activities become more systematic and planned, the more they target large dealers, and the more they are aimed at small dealers, the more proximal, spontaneous, and unplanned are the actions of the agents. In both kinds of work, caution and risk-taking are required and rewarded. One cannot survive by being only cautious, and the high-risk-taking officer and dealer will soon be arrested and/or out of the business. The symbolic rewards of the dealing world, according to McAuliffe and Gordon (1974), include not only the respect of other dealers and users, but access to better quality heroin if one uses it. Their view is that there is a prestige hierarchy within the dealing world, and it is based on several dimensions. It is clear that to the extent that these activities are known, greater prestige accrues to the investigator who makes a "big bust" or arrests a "big dealer" no matter what the circumstances. Thus, the prestige of the dealing world is mirrored in the prestige structure within the world of control.[14]

The extent to which these analogs between the market and the control agency, or between any agency and the population it is meant to control, hold true across agencies and markets should be investigated further. It would appear, however, that some complex interplay of agency conception of the environment and the empirically verifiable features of that environment occurs over time.[15] The arguments made by organizational theorists, such as Thompson, may appear to hold true, but not for the reasons they have advanced. The argument is that where an organization must cope with an objectively uncertain environment, organizations and workers will require flexibility to produce and adjust to the unpredictable nature of the events to which they respond (compare Stinchcombe, 1959).[16] Thompson and others have argued that in these conditions one would expect to find ambiguous, tacit, or unwritten rules granting wide discretion to the individual worker. From this we can infer that organizations such as drug enforcement units, faced with uncertain, shifting environments, where demands and pressures change, will be characterized by flexible, contradictory, tacit, or unwritten rules. This combination of a defined-as-ambiguous environment and flexible and shifting internal rules and definitions of goal attainment ("standards of desirability") is conducive to uncertainty for actors responding to concrete rewards (Roy, 1953; Skolnick, 1966:180). Other organizational theorists have suggested

that actors faced with uncertainty while attempting to succeed, or produce, will develop educated guesses (Wildavsky, 1974), strategies
(Barth, 1966; Goffman, 1967; Silverman, 1971; Crozier, 1964) and
rules of thumb good for all practical purposes (Sudnow, 1965; Garfinkel and Bittner, 1967). These accommodations or working bases (Manning and Redlinger, 1978) for dealing with uncertainty or ambiguity
may differ from public statements of goals and intentions, thus creating
a public pro forma description of activities and a privately sanctioned
set of working rules. Modes developed for the resolutions of uncertainties may account for the often mentioned gap between the publicly
stated goals of narcotics enforcement and their operational or de facto
goals and procedures (see Senate Testimony, 1975, especially pp. 16,
46–55; Skolnick, 1966; Hellman, 1975).

These outcomes or characteristics of organizations have never been
shown to be the product of some contours of the external world. In
fact, most of the research relies on subjective assessments of the degree to which managers deal with uncertainty in decisions (see papers
in Rubenstein and Haberstroh, eds., 1966:591–684) or taxonomies of
organizational structure (Lawrence and Lorsch, 1969). The outcome
could be a product of the way in which the environment was defined
and acted upon by organizational managers (Child, 1972), the results
of cumulative historical decisions based on an impression of the future
trends in the market, on political front-work designed to increase the
budget of a unit or department, or a conscious attempt to expand, innovate, and differentiate regardless of the environmental press (Campanis, 1970). In making this argument about the structure of policing,
we have not followed the logic of Thompson and posited the environment as being something "out there" to which agents merely respond.
That is not to say, however, that structural sources of uncertainty cannot be identified, and statistical regularities cannot be produced to
show that the work does contain uncertain features, peaks and troughs
of activity, unexpected outcomes, surprises, and the like. In drawing
out the parallels between the dealing and the control world, it was my
intent to demonstrate that the ways in which the external environment
are perceived and the ways in which one can analytically characterize
it are compatible (Leach, 1965:ix–xv, 1–17). There is both a limiting

reality and a social construction process going on, and they interact to sustain an ongoing milieu in which certain practices are sanctioned and made reasonable. In that context those practices produce results at a reasonable level for those who employ them (Bourdieu, 1977).

Comment

The various kinds of administrative rationality that are employed have some limiting effects on uncertainty. However, the ambiguity in the operation, largely stemming from the ways in which the environment is perceived and enacted in practice and from shifts in political and departmental priorities, produces a working or operative "looseness" within the units and between the units and various segments of the environment (users, dealers, other agencies, city government, the courts, the prosecutor's office). The enacted environment mirrors the world of drug using and dealing and is not empirically monitored but assumed. A loose coupling is thus maintained. This loose coupling ramifies and is amplified in the interaction among goal setting, priorities, strategies, and outcomes. The structural features of policing and this process, being only parts of a larger whole, multiply determine the problem of judging or evaluating the regulatory game in which the drug police are involved.

The information available to narcotics enforcement agencies is limited and largely unsystematic. The information available in some large cities on some dealing-using populations is not used in those cities to direct enforcement, evaluate its impact, or to monitor continuously the actions of the police upon that population. There is no clear link between plans, intentions, and outcomes, and a truncated and incomplete feedback from results to future conceptions of action. In the two units studied, relatively unsystematized agents' information and perceptions of the environment, as well as those of the administrative segment of the organization, are the basis for their current conception of the environment. The actions of the agents are enactments, mirroring what they originally projected.

The nature of the regulatory task makes gathering and using information possibly more complex than is the case for schools, social welfare agencies, or other people-processing, loosely coupled organizations. In this edifice of regulation, the operators must guess about the shape of the market system they are meant to regulate. No theoretically refined conception of the environment that might be used to assess cause and effects exists, nor are there stated goals in the two units studied. The conceptions of the environment are built up through the experience and practice of drug law enforcement and the bits and pieces of interactions with users and dealers that are differentially available to agents.

This conception of the environment, outlined as it was seen by administrators in the two organizations, is an important constraint upon enforcement. The informational lack is abundantly obvious. Predictive or prospective rationality is impossible without accurate available information, and the uncertainty perceived to inhere in the environment adds a social-psychological limitation on enforcement. Certainly the skills of officers and resources provided to a unit are an important constraint upon enforcement. However, the "objective" environment simply cannot be defined without reference to the patterned enactments that the organizational members direct toward that environment.

There is little clear, unequivocal information. The extant information is unsystematic, periodic, uneven with respect to the credibility of the source, and of limited temporal and/or spatial relevance. The level and quality of information when combined with the mandate of enforcement, forces administrators to attempt to control drug use and distribution on the basis of absent or flawed information. They must and do act. We shall see here that they act without stated goals, explicit written policies, priorities, or objectives. Their policies are tacit, their operations largely unexplicated in writing, and their activities embedded in taken-for-granted assumptions about police work and drug enforcement. Agents as a result do not receive meaningful written guidance, and so they create and maintain a great deal of discretion. This chapter discusses what guidelines are provided for enforcement, how cases are defined and made, and what sorts of pressures produce the effort to enforce. In chapter 5 the perspectives of the officers in the two units are shown to be critical in mobilizing them to act. These perspectives make sensible the otherwise rather confusing, discouraging, and complex tasks associated with work aimed to control drug use and distribution by police.

The Environment of Drug Use and Dealing and Policy

Command personnel in both units felt that the use of drugs fluctuated, but in general things were "getting worse," use was spreading to younger users, and although some drugs were considered "race-specific," others were used generally. Heroin was thought to be a "black drug," psychedelics such as PCP, an animal tranquilizer, were thought to be "white drugs," amphetamines and barbituates were in general use, and marijuana was used by large numbers of people of varying ages, both sexes, and in all classes. After stating this set of perceptions, when asked to reflect on the impact of their actions on drug use, command personnel would take the position that the best they could do was merely "hold back the tide of use." They felt that due to limitations in numbers of personnel, budget (especially buy monies for drugs), equipment, and certain legal limitations, they could do very little to affect the market. These two police units accept the mandate of controlling drugs but define that job as endless, somewhat risky, and thankless, and one where they are given inadequate public support, materials, and personnel to accomplish the job, even in the limited fashion in which they define it ("making a little dent in it," or "just disrupting things a little now and then"). These perceptions, not based on systematic data, are utilized to organize rationales for doing enforcement work and are consistent with the modes of targeting used and mobilized within the constraints of manpower, budget, and legality. The perceptions, because they make salient certain drugs, locations, and ways of dealing with the drug problem, are the outlines of a tacit policy. The absence of written policy, when combined with several other features of drug policing and policing in general, means that the aggregated discretionary actions of individual officers in effect set the policy in these units.

Policy as Tacit Understandings

If possible, police departments avoid making public their policies or do not make a policy. Police departments operate on tacit, unwritten policies, and drug units are no exception to this general rule. For a variety of reasons, such as perceived public pressure, desire for secrecy, an occupational tradition that does not honor rational planning and policy (Manning, 1977a, chapter 10), a general organizational crisis orientation, lack of skills and understanding, and no real pressure, inside or out, to have such written policies and procedures, drug units rarely have written policies. Policy in the area of vice in general and narcotics in particular has enjoyed very little public clarification by police administrators (see, for example, PCC, 1967:26 ff; and McDonald, 1973a). Narcotics law enforcement is a particularly problematic area in which to develop, administer, and control policy. It involves crimes without a complaint and for the most part is investigated as a result of police decisions to intervene. Key domains of narcotics enforcement are not explicated by written policies, or the policies are nonoperational. The following areas are those in which decisions must be made and where such decisions will pattern the outcomes that the units produce: level of enforcement; automobiles, monies, or other equipment; choice of investigative techniques; number and types of warrants used; the extent of a search; the allocation of particular charges to given arrestees (associated with violations of federal, state, and local ordinances in most cases); the conditions under which an arrest and/or charge will or must be made; and negotiations with informants. Since it involves a decision allocating scarce resources such as time, manpower, and money,[1] it is inherently selective. The political volatility of issues of drug use and enforcement, however, makes any regulatory agency the target of public moral and political concerns should it develop and make public statements concerning its policies. Any such announcement runs the risk of creating public debate and may open the police to charges of repression, injustice, harassment, and the like. It is precisely for this reason that police administrators have tended to adopt the public position that they attempt "full enforcement" of all laws (Goldstein, 1977; Davis, 1969, 1975). In Metro there were written policies and procedures, but they were not specific in regard to many of the most problematic decision points and were ignored in daily practice except in a crisis. In Suburban the policies were being revised at the time of the study. General orders, departmental procedures, ad hoc advisos, and oral directives are given in both departments, but they are of less directive significance than the informal face-to-face interactions that occur between sergeants and their squads. Through that channel formal outlines of the possible are verbally articulated.

The "outlines" of a policy alluded to previously, with this lack of written policy, produces a dependence on commonsense wisdom about practices and procedures and the nature of the drug market and permits a very high degree of agent discretion. The rational strategy and tactics model that associates goal-setting, rational planning, and outcomes is inappropriate as a paradigm for the study of drug enforcement as it was practiced in these two settings.

The absence of a rational policy is in part a result of the thoughtful unwillingness of administrators of these units to develop and articulate such a policy. The area of drug enforcement, being an area of public dissension, is thought better left undefined. Nevertheless, the officers and the administrators feel pressure to produce and show results to the public and the higher administration in the department. The organization's products are essentially ill-defined, the public disagrees about what they expect, and the agencies mystify what it is they are attempting to do, so certain measures are selectively reified to show results.

These measures, provided they are linked to actual performance assessment, can become powerful inducements to conformity. For in order to show adequate performance, agents feel they must produce
data in line with established measures. It has been argued elsewhere
that internal pressures to produce are found in general in narcotics
units, and the perception of officers and administrators that they must
produce shapes both agent conduct and the tacit rules governing organizational action. The greater these perceived pressures, the more
the conception of the enacted environment becomes translated into
action. These internal and external pressures can produce pressures
to obstruct justice (to fail to investigate and make cases knowing that
violations have occurred) or violate procedural guarantees and constitutional protections. These pressures in general terms and their relationship to corruption have been discussed in detail elsewhere (Manning and Redlinger, 1977, 1978).

The supervision of drug enforcement agents is difficult at best because the assumption is made that they must be autonomous, creative, duplicitous, lying, and must take advantage of events as they un-
fold. This conception of the drug world and the way the laws must be
enforced gives agents the opportunity to create and maintain autonomy within a loosely ordered organization. As Crozier (1964) points
out, segments of the organization that can create uncertainty produce
dependence of others upon them. This is the case in drug units. However, agents do strive for production and to do a good job as they define it. There are a number of general patterns of pressures upon units,
some of which are translated into agent conduct.[2]

These pressures are not directly translated into agent conduct. What
I wish to emphasize is that the translation of the enacted environment
into the organizational project or mandate, what the organization defines as its role and mission, occurs as features of environmental pressure (externally defined) are complemented and amplified by internal
pressures. In the absence of a clear mandate and organizational policy, the interactional processes between agents and supervisors make
durable and lasting constraints on agents' conduct. While idealized
canons provide the legitimating base for enforcement, the activity itself

gives life to the law. It is these departures also that are the base for further discrepancies, some of which take on forms that are labeled "corruption." Corruption and organizational success are linked in an important way. Organizations seek to create and maintain a positive impression or image of themselves. This idealized impression becomes objectivated as a focus of accountability and career success for organizational members. However, in all organizations areas of ambiguity remain that point up by contrast the degree of certainty in other operative areas. In addition these ambiguous areas and the problematic situations they generate reveal the transactions necessary to sustain the formal structure—some aspects of which maintain, for outsiders, impressions of the organization (compare Goffman, 1959; Manning, 1971). All occupations and professions encounter such areas and situations, and as a result they must sustain both practical working arrangements that depart from formal procedure and a fictive front that belies these arrangements. Such internal contradictions point to the practical working base for the actions of officers and place this base within a broader organizational framework. Individual actions shape and sustain structure. Everyday workings of agents and their perspectives regularize, routinize, and make the negotiated procedures through which a social structure of enforcement emerges and endures normatively binding.

By careful analysis of the structure of enforcement, considerable insight can be gained into not only the processes of negotiation but, in addition, into the genesis of organizational departures from idealized standards. The informal working agreements and arrangements made by narcotics officers that contrast with formal, stated procedures are often attempts to resolve repetitive problematic situations. Of course not all the negotiated informal arrangements are attempts to resolve ambiguities and problematic situations; some are pragmatic adjustments that are intended to increase organizational efficiency, ease the strain on individuals, or to promote personal careers. However, in those areas where negotiation of informal working arrangements occurs for the purposes of reducing ambiguity and resolving problematic situations, officers must necessarily depart from official rules and regulations. This is not to say that unambiguous areas and nonproblematic situations are not negotiable and negotiated. In such areas and situations, where the degree of consensus is high, the processes are not as obvious and less time and energy must be spent in negotiation. With concensus, boundaries are more set and the participants involved possess a degree of cognitive closure concerning their areas, know what the criteria of evaluation are, and how they will be applied.

Thus the private modes of negotiation, accommodation, and adjustment, in large part a product of various compromises with stipulated public rules, establishes a dual standard: a publicly announced, or at least administratively stipulated, set of rules and procedures, and a privately adhered to sub rosa set of working arrangements or sanctioned practices. The result of these fragmented means of control over agents' conduct is that there are problematic situations that repeatedly occur that must be resolved in the absence of any formal guidance. General rules, always in conflict, and rules with variable specificity must be applied to particular enforcement situations.[3] The sort of rationality that dominates operations is not a formal rationality associated with the Weberian ends-means paradigm but the substantive rationality articulated by Mannheim (1949:52–57). Whereas formal rationality is defined in terms of goal accomplishment and efficient attainment by functionally related positions and roles (Mannheim, 1949:53), substantive rationality characterizes an act of thought that reveals intelligent insight into the components of a given situation seen contextually. Whether something is considered substantively rational or irrational depends on the contextual surroundings in which it is applied and the accuracy of situational judgments. This concept is most relevant when one deals with decisions taken under conditions of uncertainty. These situations are most likely to be patterned by perceived pressures that "load the dice" in the favor of one or the other of several choices, each of which cannot be clearly linked to a definitive outcome in the near future. The practices of the agents, their situational rationality and modes of accommodation to the environment, are the most significant sources of policy in police drug units. The absence of policy may have some positive effects in protecting agencies from criticism, but it has a number of unanticipated negative effects as well.

Formal Rules

In both the departments studied, organizational charts and formal administrative statements of objectives, intentions, and procedures, provide partial and significant guidance to officers. However, a set of tacit or taken-for-granted understandings, misunderstandings, and practices contextualize and make meaningful "policy" (a word that is not used by officers in either department) and the verbal commands and suggestions provided by supervisors. They mediate the tensions and conflicts just described. Specific reward systems and evaluational modalities in both departments reduce apparent ambiguities to practical matters. These practical matters are determinant of day-to-day operation of both units.

Metro   The *General Orders* of M.P.D. are massive and include *formal* policies (on discipline, use of guns, eyewitness identification), *procedures* (internal handling of complaints, forceable entries), and *court decisions* and legislation (including commentary and explanation). Statute and case law appear to offer the officer no choice once he is made aware of a narcotics violation; he must use all lawful means to investigate it (M.P.D. *General Orders,* series 101, no. 10 and series 307, no. 1). However, there is no requirement that an arrest results. Further, although investigation is required, decisions as to length, type, direction, and level of a given investigation are left to individual officers.

A careful previous analysis of these *General Orders* by a sociologist who was examining the impact of policy on enforcement noted that Metro " . . . was singled out by the ABA for special praise as one of the few police departments forging ahead in the matter of police policy making" (McDonald, 1973a:662). McDonald concluded, nevertheless, that "many matters relating to the enforcement of drug laws are covered in M.P.D.'s general orders and in its training manuals. For the most part, however, they are not specific to drug enforcement, but rather deal with legal issues that cut across the full gamut of enforcement activity" (1973:127). McDonald perceptively observed that "there are only a few standing general orders that deal particularly with drug law enforcement" (1973:127). Duties of the Narcotics Branch are detailed and specify the handling of vice complaints, investigations and arrests, the civil commitment of drug addicts, and the seizure of vehicles involved in the transportation of illegal drugs. In addition, there are three other sources of written policy, although their scope and status as policy are much more variable than the *General Orders*. Memoranda from the chief are circulated from time to time; ad hoc advisos are read at roll call; and a training manual, assembled by one of the sergeants now on duty in the Narcotics Branch, outlines and provides examples of a number of procedures (such as the drafting of affidavits) relevant to narcotics investigation.

Notably absent, then, are written guidelines (policy or procedures) bearing on the objectives of the Narcotics Branch; the allocation of resources to achieve a given objective or end; specific techniques or strategies of enforcement; conditions under which arrests will be made; dealing with informants, especially with regard to reducing, nol-prossing, waiving or otherwise negotiating pleas with them and/or the United States Attorney. If an arrest has not been made but only threatened, or if no charge has yet been made, individual officers possess the power de facto to set the conditions for freedom, and this often entails "working off the beef" (working for the police department in the capacity of an informant, buying drugs, or testifying, in exchange for a reduced, altered, or dropped charge). It should be noted, however, that little or no time was spent consulting written sources for guidance. That is not to say that there was a sense of hesitation or caution about enforcement—there was an air of confidence, good humor, and energy about the office.

The stated aim of the Narcotics Branch, although not stipulated in writing, was verbalized by the three officials interviewed. It was essentially to deal with major violators in heroin and cocaine. Marijuana investigations were left to district narcotics investigators if the amount was small or considered for personal consumption, or if the work promised to yield a small seizure. "We might be interested if it yielded a large seizure—a couple of duffle bags full." Marijuana cases might be mobilized if it was thought that such an investigation would lead to disrupting the flow of other drugs.

This emphasis and approach (or strategy) was devised in 1972, approximately two and one-half years prior to the study, when the present intelligence files (license tag numbers, lists of major violators, investigative reports, nicknames, names, telephone numbers) were established. At that time the previously dominant undercover strategy was almost phased out, and an official emphasis on "major violators" was established. Each of the ten operational squads were to select one or more of these major violators, build up a file, and seek to bring him and his organization to conviction. According to an informant who had been instrumental in establishing the files and the major violator system, " . . . some squads did, and most didn't. . . . [pick a major violator]." The operational and effective mobilizing decisions were made by sergeants. Thus, in an important sense, the nexus of authority in narcotics, as it is in most police departments, is in the squad sergeant's relationship with the four to six men he supervises (Tifft, 1974). The authority of the sergeant and the unwritten procedures and policies, when combined with an "apprenticeship" type of socialization—there is no formal training—means that considerable de facto power to define and set policy lies in the hands of the squad. Thus many of the crucial decisions are worked out between the sergeant and the investigators, among investigators, and by investigators alone without command direction. These decisions and unarticulated emphases occur within an ambience of understanding about a number of key domains or concepts.

Suburban   The written policies of the Suburban Department were as lacking in specificity as those of the Metro Department. That is to say, general instructions concerning the serving of warrants ("raids"), the handling of evidence, and the seizure of property were in written form, but the crucial areas of discretion concerning arrests, acceptable "deals" with informants, and objectives of the unit or generalized strategies and tactics of law enforcement (allocation of resources) were omitted. It was said at the time of the research that written policies were being developed.

The unit at that time was undergoing personnel changes. It was expected that one of the sergeants would be promoted to lieutenant and subsequently take charge of the Narcotics Unit within the Vice/Intelligence Division. The present deputy director, a lieutenant, was expected to be promoted to captain. The captain, although he had been in command of the division for only six weeks, was expected to be transferred.

The unit, according to the deputy director, is ". . . governed by quite firm objectives, even though they are not written." In 1972, two and one-half years before, on the basis of a study made by the lieutenant and the director of the Vice/Intelligence Division, the six or seven undercover officers, who at that time were "living on the street," were brought under new organizational directives. Instead of working undercover, making buys from users on the streets, and building up fifteen to twenty arrest warrants for hand-to-hand transactions until the cases were "closed out" by arrest or because the agent had been "made" or "burned," targets were established. Objections to the previous strategy were that "weak cases" were being made: the warrants would be held prior to being served, and the cases, after arrest, would sometimes be as old as a year and one-half when they reached court. (Thus eyewitness identification could be questioned, facts and dates might be forgotten, etc.) There were no officers assigned to control or "run" the undercover agents, and a self-generated or investigator/informant mode of targeting predominated. Under the new system, assignments were made, and investigators were instructed to attempt to purchase drugs and to continue to make buys just above the level a source could handle, thereby in theory forcing him to contact his source, who would then become the agent's source, and so on until the agent reached a major source. Through these contacts and by establishing informants from other arrests, the agent was instructed to work or "buy up" to a source in the county and seek a search warrant for the residence from which deals were being made. If the address was outside the county, cooperative efforts would be initiated either with DEA or with officers working in surrounding jurisdictions. However, if it appeared that that person's source could be reached, the warrant was to be held until a larger source was uncovered, and a simultaneous raid at both sites would be planned. "The purpose of arrest is to get at a heavy dealer, that's our target," said the lieutenant. To accomplish this aim, money was required:

You need money to get weight off the street. We'd rather have two arrests and a pound of heroin than fifty arrests for marijuana. You've got to have money to fight narcotics; it's a tool for the operation. We want the man who's making the profit, not the user.

The present operation reflected this emphasis, according to the lieutenant.

There is a fairly simple conclusion to be drawn from these materials on the policy and guidance available within the two departments studied. It is clear that guidance is mostly tacit, or based on assumptions about the nature of the work that are sometimes shared and sometimes are not. Most of the guidance tends to be retrospective, or after the fact, which in turn means that it is likely to be viewed by the officers as punitive. Further, it is not likely to have any value in making particular decisions, since all such policy, in the nature of policy, must be generic. As a consequence, the single most important decision to be made, whether to investigate at all, cannot be patterned by the extant written or tacit policies. Thus it must be concluded that the most significant features of narcotic policing are not constrained by policy in the specific sense and that few decisions are effected. Yet practical demands remain; to show activity, "to justify our existence" as one sergeant put it, and "to produce."

Making a Case in Metro and Suburban: Some Contrasting Features

The informal infrastructure of working narcotics is shaped to some degree by developed organizational controls. Perhaps the most important of these controls in the two units are the modes of case defining that have been developed.* To understand the workings of any drug investigation unit, the process of case definition and case assignment must be understood (recall the features in table 2.1). The notion of a "case" is the most important single concept in explaining what agents do and how they operate. Their definitions of "caseness" and of a case will shape subsequent actions with regard to the information at hand (see Moore, 1977:125–147; Senate Testimony, 1976:182–183). The

*The following section is revised from P.K. Manning and L.J. Redlinger, "Working Bases for Corruption: Some Consequences of Narcotic Law Enforcement." In *Drugs, Crime and Public Policy*, ed. A. Trebach. New York: Praeger, 1978, pp. 60–89.

degree to which the organization can control the input of information
that the agent considers is an important variable in making a case. For
if the organization has the capacity to identify information received and
then to review the disposition or action taken in regard to that information, it can attempt to supervise the process of case making. Conversely, an organization like Metro with limited capacity to monitor and
control the input of information and shape the disposition of modes of
working the case has little chance to even identify the dimensions
along which agent work should be evaluated. The organizations vary
considerably in their control and in their capacity to evaluate investigators.

At the center of any drug enforcement organization is the case-as-
signing process. The pressures in narcotics units tend to produce investigator-centered operations: critical decisions on the number and
types of cases worked, cases filed, the ways in which they are investigated, at what length and in what depth, and using what techniques
are largely in the hands of the individual investigator. These decisions
are not reviewed. His action is truly discretionary in organizational
terms (see Kenneth Davis, 1969:96). Metro is no exception to this rule
and is investigator-centered. Suburban, on the other hand, is to a
greater degree organization-centered in its assigning of cases and
their shaping and final outcomes.

The investigator-centered model found in Metro and in many other
departments is shown in figure 4.1.

Figure 4.1 shows that information flows in from a variety of sources.
These incoming calls and informational tips are not tape-recorded, unlike other calls to the main switchboard of the police department, or
otherwise required to be put in writing. No one monitors or officially
records any of the sources. No one can verify or have knowledge of a
complaint except through the official paper generated by the officer
(his buy reports, investigative reports, and submitted vouchers for
reimbursement for buys or information) unless it is independently
brought to his attention by a phone call or complaint made directly to
an official. Officials do not know about complaints unless they happen
to answer the phone. As a result, since an official record is not always
made, few cases are assigned to investigators by sergeants in the

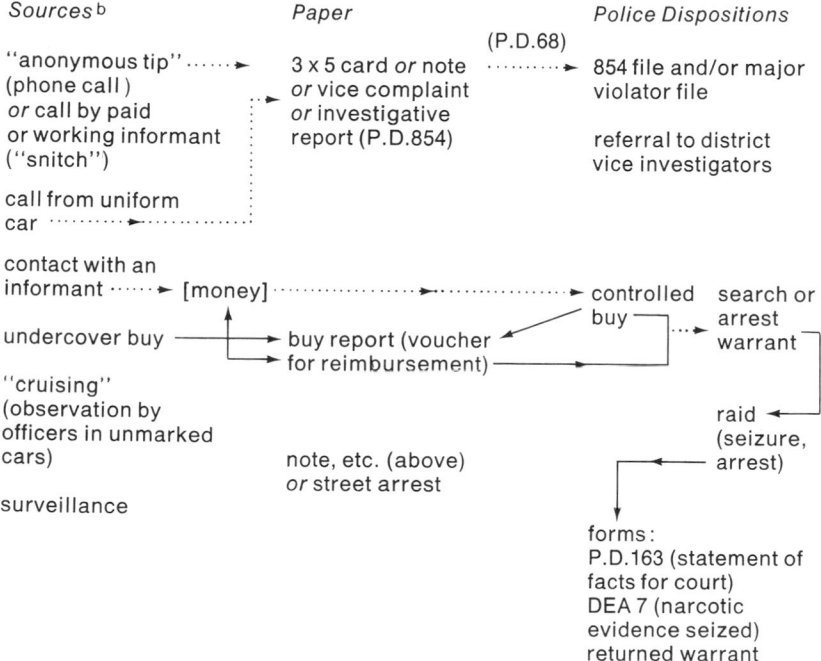

Sources [b]   *Paper*   *Police Dispositions*
                                                (P.D.68)
"anonymous tip" ········►   3 x 5 card *or* note ········► 854 file and/or major
(phone call)   *or* vice complaint   violator file
or call by paid   *or* investigative
or working informant   report (P.D.854)   referral to district
("snitch")   vice investigators

call from uniform
car ··········►··············

contact with an
informant ·····► [money] ··················►··············► controlled   search or
                                                            buy ┐   arrest
undercover buy ───────► buy report (voucher ◄──────   ···► warrant ┐
                      ► for reimbursement) ─────────►

"cruising"   raid ◄──┘
(observation by   (seizure,
officers in unmarked   note, etc. (above)   arrest)
cars)   *or* street arrest   ┌────◄─────
surveillance
                                                                 ▼
                                                            forms:
                                                            P.D.163 (statement of
                                                            facts for court)
                                                            DEA 7 (narcotic
                                                            evidence seized)
                                                            returned warrant

a. Dotted lines show alternatives; solid lines indicate practice.
b. Any source can be written up in any fashion or not at all except for undercover
buys which must be vouchered if the agent desires repayment.

Figure 4.1 Origination and disposition of narcotics information: the
investigator-centered model[a]

manner of other investigative divisions. Most cases are thus self-initiated, self-defined as to promise, priority, and length, and in effect
self-closed. If an investigator keeps a case file locked in his desk, as
many do, rather than in a central file, he maintains almost complete
control over and knowledge of his cases.

Although sergeants are informally given information on cases and
activities by their investigators as a matter of courtesy, sergeants do
not know how many cases any investigator is working on at a given
time. The sergeant's best indices are the buy reports of drugs bought,
expenses and mileage if the officer is working undercover, the monies
he issues an officer for buys, and the investigative reports submitted to
him. The sergeant is usually, although not necessarily, the supervising
and/or signing officer for affidavits, search warrant executions, and

statements of facts for court that are submitted by the members of his squad. In the Metropolitan Police Department, since there is no known base number of cases that have been accepted, or founded crimes, no clearance/closure figures for narcotics investigations are kept. No cases are "opened" or "closed" (except in the mind of the investigator or occasionally by administrative closure) because narcotics cases are infinitely expandable: each seller has a source, that source has another, etc., up the dealing pyramid. An arrest can be viewed as closure or as a mere overture because, as one Metro sergeant put it, "You always try to 'spin' a guy when you arrest him [pressure him to become an informant] and try to go higher." Thus the number, type, promise, and current developments in a given investigation may be known only by the investigator. The further one goes from the street buy-bust situation or observation-arrest to investigations involving a network of employees, secondary level dealers, and sources of dope, the more time is involved in surveillance and background work, and the greater manpower required.[4] Given the opportunity, costs involved in longer term investigations, and the absence of rewards and administrative actions to induce compliance with a strategy of longer term investigations (hopefully aimed at a point nearer the top of the dealing pyramid), most narcotics policemen will seek to reduce the time spent in investigations by quickly closing them out with arrests (see Johnson and Bogomolny, 1973). Since Metro pays overtime for court appearances, this motivates officers to make arrests sooner and more frequently.

In the organizationally centered model, as found in Suburban and shown in figure 4.2, information is more formally handled. All incoming information is classified as one of three types: information for local investigation (anonymous tip, citizen information, informant information); classified report (data on agents' buys of drugs which is also logged in on a master sheet in the safe; amounts taken or returned are reported on a required written form); or special informant file.

If the investigator who takes the call decides it has no promise, he can simply handle it by phone (this is rare), or a lead sheet can be written up. This lead sheet is then given status by the sergeant or the shift commander as "information only" (simply filed), or he can make out a "local investigation" form. Two copies are made—one is kept by the

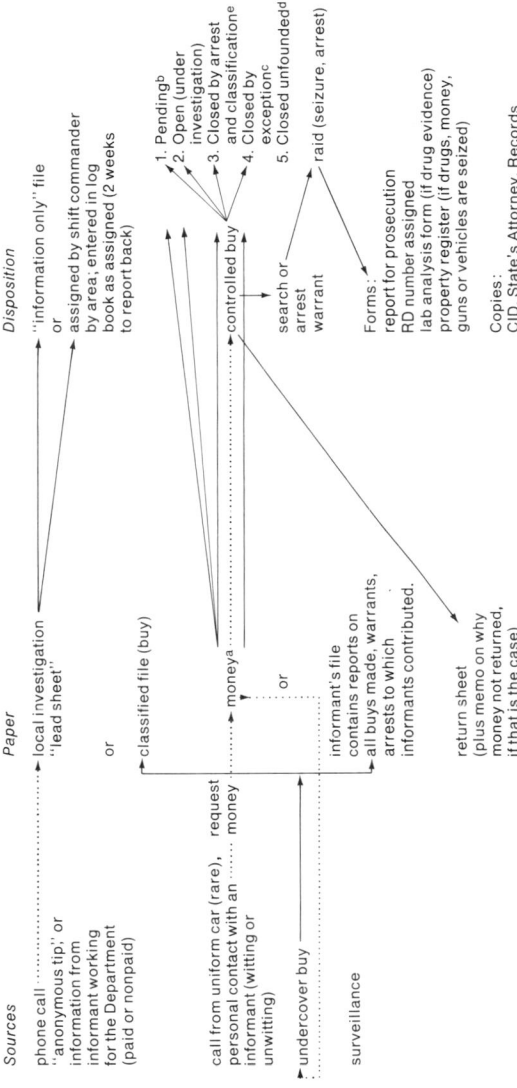

Sources

phone call ·········· "anonymous tip," or information working for the Department (paid or nonpaid)

call from uniform car (rare),   request / personal contact with an ······ money / informant (witting or unwitting)

undercover buy

surveillance

Paper

local investigation "lead sheet"

or

classified file (buy)

money[a]

or

informant's file contains reports on all buys made, warrants, arrests to which informants contributed.

return sheet (plus memo on why money not returned, if that is the case)

Disposition

"information only" file

or assigned by shift commander by area; entered in log book as assigned (2 weeks to report back)

controlled buy

1. Pending[b]
2. Open (under investigation)
3. Closed by arrest and classification[e]
4. Closed by exception[c]
5. Closed unfounded[d]

raid (seizure, arrest)

search or arrest warrant

Forms:
report for prosecution
RD number assigned
lab analysis form (if drug evidence)
property register (if drugs, money, guns or vehicles are seized)

Copies:
CID, State's Attorney, Records
Original remains in Narcotics Unit

a. Each investigator retains about $50 for miscellaneous expenses and on occasion may use this for "buy money."

b. For example, no further information available: information is received that a person is dealing from a certain location, surveillance is undertaken and no dealing is observed.

c. Every effort is made to close a case, whether by arrest, unfounding or by exception. An arrest brought about by whatever course of events, retrospectively generates a lead sheet, a local investigation number, and RD number (radio dispatch, a standard records nomenclature in the department, whether radio dispatch was used or not) and a classification. The classification categories are behavioral, and asterisks are used to indicate the types of violations on which the officer has discretion on use of arrest. The discretionary items are such things as littering and some types of traffic violations.

d. For example, an informant makes a controlled buy, then leaves town or cannot be reached for further work, for example, introducing an undercover policeman to his (the informant's) source for a hand-to-hand buy. The investigation cannot go further without the informant, but might be revived if he returns to activity with the Department.

e. For example, neighbor claims that a field of marijuana is growing next door. Inquiries and investigation reveals that the plants are not marijuana.

Figure 4.2 The origination and disposition of narcotics information: the organizationally centered model

sergeant and one is assigned to an investigator in his/her assigned region of the city. These cases are called "locals" in Suburban. The local must be dealt with in some way within two weeks—closed, closed by exception, pending, or closed by arrest (see figure 4.2). When an arrest is made, the incident is assigned an RD (radio dispatch) number, even though it was not radio dispatched, so that it can be processed through central records. It is classified under a set of available incident/crime categories and given a general departmental arrest number. When this works "backwards"—when an officer simultaneously opens and closes an investigation with an arrest—then the relevant numbers and classifications must be assigned retrospectively. Because this is possible and is frequently done, it is difficult to know precisely what each investigator is working on, as is the case in the self-initiated model. However, sergeants do have a rough index of what investigators are doing because they have access to and must sign all requests for buy money, have a list of "locals" assigned to each officer, and must approve any special informant file prior to its being established. Finally, each officer must write in on each lead sheet the time spent on each investigative episode and must call in to the communications center for messages at least once an hour.

Even in such administrative systems the same structural problems of accountability and invisibility found in the individually centered model are present. In part, the difficulty arises because no one considers "locals" to have much potential. As one Suburban investigator remarked, "We do better on ones we instigate ["investigate" was probably the intended word] ourselves." "Locals" status is problematic as well because some investigators do not do the paperwork on them, others hold them as if they were pending although they are not; extensions are allowed, and when someone is working something "big," he is either given no "locals" or is allowed to let them go. Nevertheless, this assignment is made by the sergeant not the investigator.

Based on the features of the two organizations, one can compare and contrast what I have called the investigator-centered (Metro) and the organization-centered (Suburban) models of organizational control along seven dimensions, shown in table 4.1. The figure should be read in conjunction with table 3.1 contrasting information flow in patrol and narcotics, where the essential features of narcotics crime that underlie these two organizational adjustments are found.

Table 4.1 portrays the central dilemmas of drug law enforcement because it illustrates the interplay between drug crime, organizational adaptions to the market, and the perceptions and actions of agents. The ways in which the organizational administrators perceive the environment in which they operate rationalizes the flexibility that is viewed by investigators as essential to the control of the market. In Metro, where supervision is not close, there is little attempt except after the fact to control the course of the vast majority of investigations. There is little tension between administrative controls and investigator decision making. This develops over time because administrators do not apply sanctions for violations of relevant procedural rules except in crisis periods, and prefer on a day-to-day basis to defer to or accept the informal or tacit rules used by investigators to guide their decisions. Punishment after the fact is common enough to be well known in the Metro unit and is a part of the basis for secrecy and concealment among investigators. On the other hand, in Suburban, some forms of control do operate in advance and reduce the capacity of individual agents to fully control their work. In this sense, the organization creates through its rules a different sense of the environment in which the investigators work. Once the administrative control on certain decisions are abrogated and informal accommodations are made acceptable by this acquiesence, the actions of officers directed to the environment serve to define the environment. In the extreme, one could imagine an organization in which telephone operators monitored all calls and assigned them randomly to investigators, giving them a number of days in which to dispose of the cases. This would be complete organizational control on casework (if no self-initiated cases were allowed) and would be the basis for a conception of the environment as monitored through the calls. The patrol-assignment model would bear a close resemblance. On the other hand, a completely random-individual model is the situation found in Metro, where any clues can be worked with no organizational screening (to a certain point, called the "axial line" of investigations). In the latter case, individual modes of resolving the ambiguities of the work determine outcomes.

Table 4.1 Organizational control of drug investigation: two contrastive types

Type of Control	
Investigator Centered[a]	Organization Centered
Little information can be independently verified. A written record is not required on the receipt of information	Some information (clues) is recorded on special investigative forms
Few cases are assigned by supervisors to investigators (these are "special assignments")	Cases are routinely assigned
No cases are officially "opened" or "closed"	Assigned cases must be closed within a specified time
The number, type, promise, and estimated "pay-off" of cases is defined almost independently by an investigator (or with his partner(s)	Frequent check is made on the number, type, and promise of cases (e.g., discussed at a squad or section meeting)
Arrests, charges, seizures, search warrants served, and buys serve to indicate investigator's activities to supervisors only after they have taken place	Prior approval by supervisors of buys and raids is required
No clearance rate can be calculated since: crimes are not "founded" after an allegation, and cases are, in effect, self-initiated, self-defined and self-closed	A partial clearance rate can be calculated (for assigned cases)
Informants are known only by investigators, not evaluated by supervisors, and may not be placed in official files or given an official number	The establishment of an informant requires sergeant's approval

a. Metro squads vary from this model: Pharmacy and school squads and those on special assignments are under closer control.

Comment

Working bases are developed and serve to reduce the uncertainty, the overload, and the conflict between various rules and values. Since in both organizations there were attempts at administrative control of the cases worked, the tension between modes of targeting developed by the organization and informal or working bases of case investigation, which tend to reflect investigator's interests, reveals the dynamics of these organizations.

Recall the kinds of uncertainty that are associated with the enforcement of narcotics law from the abstract or organizational perspective. Although to an outside observer, who might assume that critical decision points and domains would and should be fully bureaucratized, the day-to-day operations of any narcotics unit appear to be rather unstructured; in fact, they are not. Policies are not written, and key domains are unexplicated by written rules. However, an outsider's perception may be very misleading, for the work does not contain ambiguities from the perspective of the investigator and the supervising officers. Only when torn from the context of certain assumptions, behavioral routines, and taken-for-granted matters that competent narcotics policemen are expected to know and practice, do events and options become ambiguous. From the occupational perspective of the officer, the decisions made are not fraught with uncertainty. However, the occupational perspective of the officer operates when other modes of guidance are least visible. In the absence of some guidance, he will act in accord with his own best interests as he envisions them at the time. The officer's perspective is used here as a kind of baseline against which to contrast modes of targeting.

Given this conception of organization action, one must understand the organizational reality, or assumptions made about all that is good practice within the organization, in order to uncover the context of investigator's decisions and actions. Some of the features of police organizations hold true for narcotics organizations, as do the features that are found in organizations with a high degree of lower participant discretion, that is, conflicts between rules, between rules and personal preferences, and between interpretations of rules across units, persons, and situations. The shared and nonshared bases for negotiation in organizations are of operative importance. The interpretive contexts within which rules in a police organization will be understood are not fully shared between the segments of an organization. Although shared understandings flow from common experience and the identification with the role and concepts, "policeman" and "policing" serve as linguistic glosses for these shared experiences, shared misunderstandings also embed organizational segment relations and bear directly on the interpretation of organizational rules and procedures. Shared misunderstandings provide a fictive sense of agreement, and disputes are actually resolved by the power of the administrative segment. Fictive or apparent consensus is thus a tool of more powerful organizational segments. Integration and schism and degrees of uncertainty are found in both units.

Nevertheless there is a tendency in studies of organizations and in studies of social structure in general to reify the organization and encapsulate the choices of individuals in that structure.[5] Leach, in one of the classic critiques of this tendency in social sciences wrote:

Any particular individual can be thought of as having a status position in several different social systems at one and the same time. To the individual himself, such systems present themselves as alternatives or inconsistencies in the scheme of values by which he orders his life. The overall process of structural change comes about through the manipulation of these alternative means of social advancement. Every individual of a society, each in his own interest, endeavors to exploit the situation as he perceives it and in so doing the collectivity of individuals alters the structure of the society itself (1965:8).

The particular choices that are made appear to be those giving the greater advantage of the person as he defines this in context or situationally. The constraints that emerge from the organization may or may not be consistent with the actor's perspective. Friedson's important work on social control among physicians echoes some of the themes discovered among narcotics officers. He argues that the informal or indirect social controls that bear on the organizational actor's behavior spring from values and norms, and these are frequently in conflict with the formal rules that are derived from a utilitarian rationality (Freidson, 1975:7, Mannheim, 1949:274-275; Crozier, 1964:8). The assumption that has been made is that the formal rules, such as those described in the last section of this chapter, are the actual operative rules within a system of work control. A focus on prospective guidance and proscriptive rules may blind us to discovering the relevance of retrospective guidance and operative rules. Further, these errors are compounded by a failure to see how contradictions between the formal goals and structures are associated with certain segments of the organization. This tension produces constant vacillation of the meaning of social structure and of the work itself.

It is not immediately clear at this point in the argument how the day-to-day decisions of officers are made, but it would appear that rather than being an aggregation of individual choices, they are based partly on a perspective that develops within particular segments of the organization. Freidson has argued similarly, noting that the way in which the work is organized and controlled influences the nature of the work itself (1975:94). The rationalizing forces represented by the standard operating procedures, general orders, and even the day-to-day bulletins and advisos tend to convert the perspective of the officer to the control system of the organization on one level. Standardized units are needed, tasks and work loads are considered as units in accounting systems, and measures of efficiency and effectiveness are derived on this basis (Freidson, 1975:94–95). The perspective of the officer, on the other hand, develops as a means to deal with the reflected problematic situations of the work, and he sees these problems in terms of his own skills, abilities, limits, and opportunities. The choices made reflect a fusion of rationality and these matters of personal style and ability. The symbolization of one's personal feelings, obligations to the ritual order of the organization, and the technical demands of "doing the job" cannot be separated in the acts of enforcement. The technical and the ritual meanings of action, as Leach writes (1965:13), are not separate but are aspects of any kind of action.

For example, officers may focus on black street dealers in an attempt to clean up a street scene (which is composed of people who use and deal on street corners, block traffic, disturb neighbors and non-users and is the source of many citizen calls). This is an instrumental act intended as a means of "cleaning up" a street scene (an end). It also has ceremonial or expressive aspects because it differentiates a group for pressure and makes a statement about its character; it emphasizes the dominance of the police (who are predominately white), a racial group, a preference for styles of life and drug usage, and a whole variety of messages about the selves of the victims and the enforcers. Thus, any enforcement of drug laws always contains or manifests a political, an economic, and a ceremonial component, a set of messages about the groups, selves, and identities of participants. This is the case regardless of the self-conscious intentions of those involved. I am concerned here with the form of the drama as much as or more than with the players.

When one does attend to assessing the attempt by organizations to control and guide actions and the ongoing resolutions of problems, the irony of seeing all measures of effort as precise and valid measures of organizational aims or rationalities must be appreciated. The roots from which the evaluation of organizational effects grow and those of the actor are not isomorphic. The more elaborate the attempt to take facts out of context and use them as measures of organizational or individual motivations or intentions (the organizational project), the more the "facts" will become yet another form of modern propaganda (Altheide and Johnson, eds., 1979). Facts taken from their context and placed within a frame of reference that sees them as issuing exclusively from the prospective rationality of administrative plans, intentions, and evaluations, are converted to organizational purposes. When the organization uses these facts in a cynical fashion to convince the public of organizational effectiveness, as the police do with crime statistics, they are propaganda. On the other hand, officers are inclined to see all of their actions and decisions as being wholly contextual, almost idiosyncratic in form. From a sociological point of view, this is also a misleading perspective, for they do alter their behavior and adjust their actions in line with their readings of social situations, personal advantage, and organizational rules and procedures. Although they operate with a limited means-ends rationality, it is not the rationality of the organization, and it is not the rationality that is attributed to actors by such theorists as March and Simon (1958) and the open-systems theorists discussed. It is situational rationality.

5

Modes of Resolving Uncertainties: The Investigators' Perspectives and Organizational Targeting

Thus far, the structure in which drug enforcement is mobilized and some aspects of the enacted environment and its relationship to organizational action have been outlined. This somewhat abstract view of organizational structure and environment must now be complemented by a detailing of the perspective of those who produce, in day-to-day fashion, the behaviors that are seen as constituting organizational structure and function. The concept of a perspective is evoked here because it captures the view of officers as they interpret, make sense of, and carry out actions based on choices that make visible the attempt to eradicate drug markets.

At the beginning of this chapter the working perspective of the officer in the two units is described, and then it is contrasted with analytically defined means by which organizations might systematize enforcement. The officers' working perspective, the means by which the officers mediate potential or actual conflicts between rules and organizational demands, and personal interests, values, and commitments are in conflict with attempts by the organization to shape and guide, albeit in a limited fashion, the enforcement effort. The various possible modes of targeting, or setting of goals and objectives, and those actually found in the two units are described. They are ways that the organizations attempted to control individual officers' discretionary actions. The organizational capacity to control agents was exercised more consistently by Suburban than Metro during the period of the study.

A tension existed in both units between the informal perspectives of the officers and administrative attempts to reduce and control their actions. Each of the targeting modalities contained in itself a degree of conflict and contradiction, as well as a potential conflict between officers' intentions and organizational plans. Much discretion exists, whatever the targeting mode. Where discretion exists, so will problematic situations requiring the invoking of the perspective within which they can be viewed, delimited, worked out, and finally resolved in some routine fashion. As will be abundantly clear, neither targeting nor the perspectives of the officers can resolve the frequently encountered problematic situations. A tension is sustained. There is continuous interaction between organizational authority as represented by attempts to reduce agents' discretion and by the perspectives of the officers, which are means to deal with the same uncertainties and maintain the autonomy of the agent segment within the organization.

The Investigators' Perspective in Metro and Suburban

Perspective is a concept that integrates thought and action. A perspective is "a coordinated set of ideas and actions a person uses in dealing with some problematic situation . . . a person's ordinary way of thinking and feeling about and acting in such a situation" (Becker, et al., 1961:34). The problematic situation may not be seen in the same way by the actor as by the observer, so one must provide concrete details and reasonable grounds for labeling an act or idea as a part of a perspective (Becker, et al., 1961:35). A person develops a perspective when he encounters a situation that calls for action not easily defined within the context of prior beliefs or the requirements of the situation. A situation will not be seen in the same way by every person. At the extremes are persons who drift and glide through situations without being aware of making choices, and those who are always guided by a firm set of values and clear awareness of choice situations and decisions. Becker defines the utility of perspective for guiding choice.

. . . In other words, perspectives arise when people face choice points. In many crucial situations, the individual's prior perspectives allow him no choice, dictating that he can in these circumstances do only one thing. In many other situations, the range of possible and feasible alternatives is so limited by the physical and social environment that the individual has no choice about the action he must perform. But where the individual is called on to act, and his choices are not constrained, he will begin to develop a perspective. If a particular kind of situation recurs frequently, the perspective will probably become an established part of a person's way of dealing with the world (Becker, et al., 1961:35ff).

A perspective guides choices and is rooted in certain assumptions about the organization, about the environment in which the organization functions, and about the sanctioned and allowable practices that are tacitly acceptable within the organization. In this way, in all organizations the broad conceptions of the enacted environment and the mandate of the organization are translated into action. (See Strauss, et al., 1964, and the papers in Blankenship, ed., 1977.) The way in which this translation takes place is important, for it arises as situations that are undefined in the written rules of the organization are made sensible and reasonable. The tacit bases of decision making are the working rules that make enforcement possible. In narcotics the working bases are made sensible or integrated by means of the perspective. When organizations permit a high degree of individual discretion, the perspective of the actor will be critical in determining how they adopt to the organization, and in what ways the organization adopts to the environment. It is not organizations that act, but actors in organizational roles, working out the daily basis of conduct. The particular content of the perspectives of officers in Metro and Suburban is important in patterning ways that they act out the enforcement drama.

The Perception of Overload in Drug Work   ∂0H395

As a result of the perceived environment in which they envision themselves, officers see themselves as being "overloaded." They see the environment of drug use and trade as one they cannot fully control but only regulate. They see this as an environment that is characterized by secrecy, duplicity, and clandestine planning and marketing. They view themselves as being limited not only by their own energy, imagination, and skill but also by the law, constitutional guarantees, and levels of available money, personnel, and equipment. The consequence of this perspective is that over time officers develop a sense of "overload." (This sense is similar to that felt by the medical students studied by Becker, et al., in *Boys in White,* 1961.) "Overload" exists when " . . . people believe there may be more work than they can do in the time available. A potential overload may be more difficult to deal with than a real one" (1961:90).

In what sense are drug police overloaded? Like medical students, drug police are not bound to their work by fixed hours. They must decide, outside the eight hours for which they are normally paid, if and when they will work. Since they are considered to be working at all times in a sense, any variation from perceived "full effort" is not well thought of by supervisors. On the other hand, if they work overtime they will be away from their families, their own leisure interests, and in

some cases from second jobs. Second, the limits of information required by work are vague in the sense that they know they must know
about the law and procedures of the organization and the "drug
scene," but they do not know in what detail, with regard to what drugs,
in what areas of the city, nor at what level of dealing. Further, the daily
requirements are vague and undefined, unless they are assigned
cases in the fashion described below. Third, the informal suggestions
they receive from sergeants are not specifically tied to case actions
and decisions but to general kinds of cases, amounts of money spent,
and negative sanctions about mistakes or miscalculations. It is hard to
say whether one has done enough toward developing any case. Since
the cases are expandable, even an arrest cannot be easily said to
close an episode or investigation. Finally, if there are specific monthly
reports of arrests, there is no perceived relationship between "doing
well" and arrests. Many arrests may not mean quality investigative
work is being done, while a few do not indicate great skill either. The
hours of work are shift-based and rotated but are open to constant situational redefinition by the sergeant, lieutenant, the work group itself, or
by the individual. Friends and family pressures usually act in the opposite fashion, to reduce the available "extra" hours of work given to an
investigation. One is always expected to be willing to help when called
by a fellow officer. Being willing to help a colleague any time of the day
or night is thought of not only as the basis of being a "good cop" but
also is the basis of day-to-day acceptance in the unit. Individual definitions of the limits of a case also serve to make the working time flexible
—one can always argue that an informant ("a snitch") will not call, that
one should call it a night, that "you can't push these things. . . ." On
the other hand, if one refuses to come in to the office or to a raid planning site to assist others when one is technically "off duty," takes too
many days off or vacation time, one is labeled as "lazy" or as letting
other people down. The level of work expected from officers is never
clearly defined by administrators or even by immediate supervisors
but is most strongly patterned by the interpersonal demands of partners and squads.

The perceived potential volume of the work available is based partly
on the shared perception of officers concerning the presence of drugs

and the levels of use in the area. It is felt by most officers that "drugs are everywhere," that "nearly everyone smokes dope (marijuana)," and that "anyone can buy drugs on any busy street in the area." (This last phrase is sometimes uttered sarcastically when young "rookie" officers are having difficulty in making buys or in obtaining informants to make buys for them.) Officers share the perceptions of the administrators concerning the pervasiveness of drugs, for they see the flow of drugs as a "never-ending stream" that is outside full police control.

If there were clear decision points at which it was to be decided either by the officer or partner, by immediate supervisors, or higher administrators that a case would be initiated, pursued in a particular fashion, or dropped, then the sense of overload could be reduced. Officers could anticipate the kinds of cases that would not be supported or that would be defined as outside the interest of the unit. This is not the situation in either unit. Only a few decision points do exist where organizational controls can be exercised. They surround obtaining a search warrant, mobilizing unit support for a buy-bust or a raid, securing permission to advance money (to "front" it, in street terms) to a person as an act of good faith so that the drugs will be delivered, and persuading a sergeant in Metro to sign an affidavit for a search warrant. At these key points, however, there are no rules to provide prospective guidance. Guidance emerges in and grows from the collective interaction between officers and partners, officers and citizens and informants, and to a lesser degree between officers and their squads. The sergeant plays a role in this latter form of interaction. In order to understand how the investigators' perspective guides them, one must understand that it is primarily rooted in the context of informal interaction in squads. The perspective grows, is nurtured, and is sustained in that context.

Perspective and Supervision in Metro and Suburban

The degree and type of supervision exerted by the sergeant, and conversely the loyalty and fealty of his men, shape their perspective and investigative focus. Sergeants are, in many respects, the axis around which enforcement rotates, standing as they do midway between the administration and the investigators (Tifft, 1974; Cain, 1973). They consequently adjust and mediate the demands and expectations of the men and the expectations of the higher officials, sometimes appearing to be on one side, sometimes on the other—"Their role is to crucify or justify," said one investigator. The men under the sergeant are beholden to him for official evaluations or "efficiency ratings." These ratings, along with examinations, are one basis for promotional decisions. Men also depend on a sergeant's good will for support in defense of decisions taken on the street with regard to payments for information or reward for a "good seizure"; for amounts of money handled by the investigator and whether he can use IOUs; for approval of mileage (in Metro), daily expenses, and buys made by undercover agents; for support in request for larger buys or longer investigation requests; for signing off on search warrants and affidavits; for use of cruisers in Metro; and for the setting and enforcing of the rules of the game, that is, especially how closely the use of money, time, the kind, and length of an investigation are supervised and how much pressure is applied for "meat on the table" (arrests).

Sergeants grant leniency or overlook infractions, and this provides great power for supervisory personnel in both units (Gouldner, 1954). On the other hand, investigators owe the sergeant respect and loyalty, are expected to use discretion in their expenditures (since approval is after-the-fact for virtually all buys), in their "goofing off" or converting resources and time to their personal use, in striving for success in the sergeant's terms (having to do with level and direction of effort), and "making him [the sergeant] look good in the lieutenant's eyes" (thus efforts are made to keep "star investigators" in squads by sergeants).

These general characterizations of the authority and control of the sergeant are important, but they perhaps overemphasize the formal aspects of their control and do not bring to light sufficiently the relative salience and importance of other informal, historical, and biographical matters. By and large, the officers under a sergeant in the drug unit are not beholden to him because of their fear of his giving them lower efficiency ratings (since these are viewed as ritualistic paperwork), but for his tolerance and informal rewards. Such mundane matters as granting time off, overlooking tardiness, sloppy work, absent reports, and

mistakes that endanger others or lead to loss of money are the resources of the sergeant. Rating of efficiency and even promotion rec-
ommendations that might issue from the sergeant are of differential but
mainly peripheral importance to the officers. Since sergeants have
much to say about acceptance of an officer into the unit, and whether
he will be assigned to his squad, a clever or shrewd sergeant will work
to orchestrate entry and exit from his squad and maintain working relationships among the partnerships that he has accepted and/or created
(sometimes officers will request to be made partners, but more often
they are assigned to a partner). To some extent, sergeants will attempt
to recruit officers with whom they have previously worked in patrol or in
other specialized units. Other informal bases can be fostered or are
already extant, such as playing together on sporting teams, or hunting
or fishing together. Solidarity is not solely based on the present work-
based relationships of the officers but on a variety of work and nonwork
bases. Each of these social ties or identities are sources of links as well
as divisions, and they are rooted in both biography and history.[1]

All of these forces or pressures passed on from sergeant to men and
from men to sergeant tend to differentiate individual members of the
squad, acting as they do to "increase production," "put something on
the books," or lead to "having something to show." But these pressures for individuation are to some degree balanced by other, differentially operative pressures that tend to induce solidarity between members of a squad. One category of pressures is informal interactions,
which result from the rotation of squads together through turns, the arrangement of desks in the investigator's room (squad members desks
are clustered together), the interaction and gossip at the beginning
and end of turns (when the morning and afternoon turns overlap), and
when charges are being made by a squad in the investigator's room.
The second is cooperation on raids, which are usually carried out by
five men, an official, and at least two uniformed men. Raids are the dramatic high spot of the work and a source of solidarity, risk, and mutually cooperative efforts. The third is the allocation rule of arrests on
raids. The affiant (the person who has developed the case to the point
of being able to write the affidavit for the search warrant) gets first
choice and his partner is given credit as the assisting officer. Other

members of the raid party are often "given" an arrest, and those who want an arrest so that they can appear in court and be paid for overtime or to make a better showing on the monthly "scandal" or activity sheets are often accommodated (see the list of principles). Racial identities and solidarity bind together some members of a squad. A squad may work collectively on a single large investigation—some will carry out background investigations, some will do surveillance, some may work undercover, some will gather intelligence, etc. This same principle works when one or more squads work together, when members of one squad assist another in a raid, in working-up charge paperwork, supplying a name or piece of information on a case. These bind men together across as well as within squads and reduce loyalty to a single sergeant.

Following is a list of some principles for arrest allocation on narcotics raids in Metro based on interviews with three key informants in June 1975.

Rule 1:

The principals (the most important persons who are arrested in the raid) go to the affiant and partner who are listed on the arrest form as arresting officers. The affiant is the person who usually has worked the informant for the evidence for the affidavit; writes the affidavit for the warrant; has it signed by his sergeant and a judge and thus generates the search warrant; plans the raid with sergeant's participation; and makes major decisions about when and where the raid should be carried out.

Rule 2:

Arresting officer, if officers other than the affiant and partner are listed, is distributed by a set of subrules.

Subrule 1:

Arrests are assigned to officers who actually participated in the raid.

Subrule 2:

Arrests are assigned to officers in the narcotics or vice unit unless there are extenuating circumstances:

a. A fleeing person is captured by a uniformed officer. This is rare because " . . . they [uniformed officers] don't know what is expected of them . . . " and . . . "aren't in a position to capture people since they secure doors after the raid party of drug officers is inside." It does happen when a uniformed officer has been sent to the back of a place to watch a rear exit for drugs.that may be thrown out or for fleeing occupants. In Metro, narcotics officers always covered the back because they anticipated this contingency and wanted to catch the drugs or the person attempting to leave.

b. The uniformed officer served some critical function in setting up the case itself (got evidence for the affidavit). Giving the uniformed officer an arrest under these circumstances is considered "good PR" by drug officers. They make a special point in Metro of thanking uniformed officers for coming and for their assistance.[2]

Subrule 3:

Remaining arrests almost always go to the squad members participating in the raid; the squad of the officer and partner who obtained the affidavit and are the arresting officers for the principals. Arrests are not assigned to officials (sergeants or above) unless there are rare and extenuating circumstances.

a. A sergeant grabs a man rushing for the toilet or sink with the dope, intercepts him, and thus prevents him from destroying evidence by flushing it.

b. The sergeant is written in by the squad because he has to go to court anyway.

Subrule 4:

Any remaining arrests go usually to affiant and partner.

Subrule 5:

After these categories of persons are given arrests, any remaining arrests may be allocated to "those in the squad who want or need court time" (most people do, so this is not a very strong rule) or "need an arrest" to keep up their stats.

Subrule 6:

Others on the raid who need an arrest.

Subrule 7:

People in the office who need an arrest.

Rule 3:

Assisting officer is allocated according to the following subrules:

Subrule 1:
First such arrest goes to partner of affiant.
Subrule 2:
Allocation follows subrule 2.2 above, but extenuating circumstances
do not appear here.

Rule 4:
Informal credit is given to other participants in the raid, whether in the
squad or not. A set of subrules deal with subsequent obligations and
credits:
Subrule 1:
Squad members expect assistance in raids they subsequently plan.
Subrule 2:
Non-squad members expect a "return favor" in the form of assistance
on their subsequent raids.
Subrule 3:
Subrule 4.2 does not apply as strongly to officers from vice, pornogra-
phy, prostitution, or gambling units.
Subrule 4:
Rule 4 for arrest allocation does not hold when narcotics officers par-
ticipate in gambling raids when they are assigned to assist.

In addition, a structural feature of the organization of Metro leads to
solidarity within squads and across squads and thus reduces pressures for individual success striving. Day-work squads, which are on
days only, work specialized tasks: there are four squads carrying out
these functions, the schools, pharmacy and compliance squads, and
the administrative squad. In all, these total some twelve investigators
and two sergeants (although one sergeant supervises undercover personnel and the school and pharmacy squad, his interest is in investigation, and he takes little interest in the activities of the schools and pharmacy investigators). These groups do not compete with the other
people in the Branch.[3]

The squads in Metro tend to specialize in their investigative activities: some focus on longer term investigations, others on shorter term
investigations, others on shorter term street work. The net effect is to
"keep some arrests trickling in" as well as "keeping something else
going." Thus, another basis of solidarity derives from the functional in-

tegration required by the tasks involved in maintaining and operating with a given focus of enforcement. In addition, given the natural drift of investigators toward compatible partnerships and sergeants, there is an attraction potential of a given focus or member-as-potential-partner. The focus of the squads, defined in terms of their level of intervention (street work, long-term investigation, or the specialized day-work sections), bears on the degree of integration of a squad and its relationships to other squads within the branch. On the basis of interviews with a key informant who designated the focus of each of the investigators, my observations, and interviews with each of the sergeants, the squads, and their members were classified by their level of intervention (focus). These results are shown in table 5.1.

The classifications in this table are based on the orientation of the investigator, not by partnerships (some partners differ in focus). Several points about perspective can be inferred from the table. The first is that roughly 29 percent of the Metro unit is oriented to major investigations (they were so classified at the time of the research); that the remainder of the squad, excluding day work which is largely assigned cases, works the street. Second, there is a tendency for squads to cohere as

Table 5.1 Investigative focus of squads in metro: major investigations, day, work, street[a]

Squads	Major Investigations		Street		Day Work	
	(N)	Percent of squad	(N)	Percent of squad	(N)	Percent of squad
1					5[d]	100
2	5[b]	100				
3	4[b]	67	2	33		
4	1	16.6	5[c]	83.3		
5	2	40	3[c]	60		
6			5[c]	100		
7			5[c]	100		
8			6[c]	100		
9	2	40			4[d]	60
10					5[d]	100

a. Persons allocated by orientation and squad, not partner.
b. Majority (60 percent or more) of squad works major violations.
c. Majority of squad works the street.
d. Majority of squad works day work.

units in their focus. The least coherent groups socially are those who are focused on street types of short-term investigations. There is a kind of solidarity by aggregated individualism rather than the shared and collective action achieved by squads two and three, in which the majority of the officers work on major violators. Third, the bases of collective action are different in these two kinds of conditions: Squads where the focus is on street work and short-term investigation are always available to work a case, take a phone call and follow it, run out and jump in the cars, hassle street dealers, serve arrest warrants, cruise the streets and "head hunt," and the like. The major violator groups are not so free to give up ongoing investigations. Thus they are penalized in short-term cases, and there is a higher risk that future cases will not pay off. They depend on the squad to a higher degree and in turn owe more to their sergeants and to each other as a result of their division of labor. On the other hand, the integration of the street groups comes through the rotation of arrest rule, the shared help in serving search warrants, and informal interactions.[4]

The ways in which sergeants control the officers under their supervision are important in shaping and maintaining this perspective on integration. The degree of control exerted by the sergeant over his investigators varies in two ways. If the group is striving to carry out a major investigation of a large violator, the coordination of effort required is major, the tasks complex and interconnected, and the solidarity is of the integrative sort; the role of the sergeant in this case is central to the enterprise itself and representative of authority in a fairly direct, consistent fashion. If, however, most of the investigators are focused on street work, the coordination of the sergeant is likely to yield symbiotic integration based on occasional assistance in raids and the serving of warrants. These can often be accomplished in a partnership, as in the case of a street rip-off of an observed deal or serving an arrest warrant. Coordination is discrete and individualistic, and the work-focus rewards the ambitious, fast-working agent. The rewards are more individualistic, since only the affiant and partner may go to court and receive the associated pay or compensatory time, and are not collective in the sense that a wire tap that has failed to yield useful data or affidavit for a wire has an impact on an entire squad not just the individuals. Street work, in short, is less risky, quicker, entails better pay, requires less investigation and supervision, and results in higher arrest rates. (This focus has an impact mostly on the lowest levels of the market — on the street hangers-on, "jugglers," and small dealers.) The sergeant in a street-work squad can supervise either in a cooperative style or in a rigid disciplinary style patterned on the supervision found in the patrol division.

These supervisory styles are more pronounced in Metro because it is a larger unit, serving a more diverse population and more stratified community. It has also accepted greater responsibilities in terms of enforcing compliance with various facets of drug laws. The division of labor can be seen as a function of the size of the unit itself. In addition, the money available and the emphasis on the buy-bust strategy in Suburban has allowed them to work largely undercover. (This is also to some degree a result of the fact that when the unit began, it was entirely an undercover unit.) This mode of operation makes the kind of supervision required of the sergeant more informal and is based more upon his expertise and authority as an investigator (Tifft, 1975). As a result there is less concern about arrests as an indicator of success, less pressure from the sergeant about arrests, and more emphasis on "making cases" or on the quality of the investigations, as well as on closing out the assigned cases.

The sergeant in Suburban left supervision of the assigned cases to a corporal on the evening shift and to an investigator on the day shift, thus making the sergeant's job more an informal supervisory one. The second sergeant of the unit was, at the time of the study, recovering from a serious gunshot wound so was not permitted active work where danger was involved. He was soon to be promoted to lieutenant. Respect for him and for the major supervising sergeant came from their long street-work experience, their reputation for fairness and "understanding," and their knowledge of narcotics investigation and the county. There was no differentiation by perspective in Suburban and no major differences in the styles of supervision employed by either sergeant. Since there were no extra monies to be made by court time, arrests per se were not sought. Rather, operational overtime was sought, but this was closely monitored by the officials, and they did normally sign-off on requests for overtime (officially grant the request by signing). They would sign prior to an operation that was expected to require overtime. The sergeants always signed in my observations, usually accompanying the signing with a joke about the planned operation ("you set this up just at the end of the shift, nice way to get some overtime in"). The investigators, on the other hand, never requested overtime pay for the actual time spent unless the investigation yielded a felony arrest or a "good seizure."

These conditions of supervision and style of operation tended to make the perspective of the officers in Suburban unitary and make them loyal to their sergeants. They shared the same view of the aims and objectives of the unit: to make quality cases that do not involve small amounts of marijuana. There was no latent division between street versus major violator orientation in the unit, although the assignment of cases tended to go to the younger and inexperienced officers, while those who were more capable of buying dope and setting up buy-busts were rarely assigned cases. This is another example of the leniency pattern referred to previously.

These perspectives and informal relations embed the targeting modalities. The targeting modalities should be considered as organizational or administrative variations upon the dominant informal infrastructure. That is to say, the extent to which any formal means of control can exercise prospective guidance is very limited.

In the following section and in subsequent chapters, the investigator's perspective is viewed as the fundamental basis for or grounding of action, while the degree of formal organizational constraint is viewed as variable. The primary question asked is, To what extent do organizational policies and procedures constrain the investigator's choices made concerning investigations? An example of two extremes that might be found may be helpful. If the organization assigned all cases and did not permit officers to develop or act on any case without prior approval by a supervisor, the degree of organizational control would be high. If, on the other hand, investigators were given freedom to investigate any case they chose, were not required to seek approval for any decisions made in the course of the investigation, and could pursue the case choosing their own method of investigation, the degree of organizational control would be low. There are other options that lie between these extremes, and in fact both organizations studied exercise some control at key points in investigations. Neither organization has full control. The cases worked, the ways in which they are worked, and the manner in which they are resolved are all negotiated. Supervisors and officers, from time to time, and not on every point in every case, bargain over the aims and potential of the investigation. Expediency, information, resources available, and the investigator's skills are all taken into account. In order to discuss more systematically the degree of organizational control over cases, a typology of targeting has been developed. These types of targeting describe the essential features of the patterns by which agents receive and develop their cases.

Five Modes of Targeting

Targeting, like strategy, has several meanings. First, it can be defined operationally: One can extract from available records the social characteristics of the persons arrested or charged (age, race, sex, and education), find the correlates for these characteristics and numbers of arrests by unit, and then typify the units on this basis (see Johnson, Peterson, and Wells, 1977). The difficulty posed by such profiling activity is that the resulting arrests are seen in this context as intentional or as rational outcomes of organizational decisions, when in fact a whole series of other variables affect the arrest rate for given groups. For example, such things as how frequently the persons have been arrested before, the visibility of the street dealing scene, the race and sex of the investigators, and the decisions that occur during an investigation are not revealed by such profiles. The profiles reify organizational intent and the organizational project because they obscure the ways in which these cases are defined and worked by agents in course of investigations.

　　Second, one can seek to uncover the rational plan by which an organization intends to accomplish an objective or end. In the two units studied, there were generalized approaches outlined by administrators but not a plan in this sense. Third, one can look at the organizational capacity to act in certain ways as an incipient strategy, and by so doing, see strategy and structure as isomorphic (Chandler, 1962).

At least in part, I have adopted this third approach in describing the skills, roles, and resources of the various units. These provide important constraints on the sorts of investigations both units can mobilize. The fact that Metro had a diversion-pharmacy squad and Suburban did not gave them a different capacity to investigate and make such cases. But in addition to these limitations of structure, the idea of targeting is used to examine the sources of the cases that are developed in the units. Since the administrative segment of the organization cannot maintain control at every point over all the cases worked in their respective departments, differential capacity to control cases always exists. Cases can result either from externally or internally generated information. Cases vary by the extent to which the investigator controls the parameters of the case, which is in large part an inverse function of the external source dimension. The level of the market at which such cases potentially make an impact is also a means of characterizing organizational capacity. The units can be arrayed by the mode of targeting used, level of the market at which such a mode can be expected to have an affect, and the degree of organizational control.

Precise distribution of the numbers of cases that come from each of these sources is not available and could not be available given the nature of the files and records kept by the officers and by the units themselves. The assignment of units and the modes of targeting are logical and ideal types derived from close interviewing with informants, from administrative interviews and records, and from the elaborations about practices given to me by my key informants.

The most important correlates of these modalities as they were observed in the two units are identified and described here. The first dimension ordering table 5.2 is the level in the market at which such investigations can be expected to be located (using heroin as the model here), the possible scope that the investigation might take (defining a conspiracy case involving a large number of persons or important dealers as being broad in scope and a single arrest of a user as being narrow in scope), and the possible market impact (changes in price, purity, or the number of dealers). The level at which it is possible to

Table 5.2 Modes of targeting ranked by degree of organizational control possible, frequency of use, and role of users, by unit

Modes of Targeting[b]	Level, Scope, and Impact on Market	Degree of Organizational Control of Choice of Targets	Metro	Suburban
Mode A Militaristic	High, wide, great (dealer focus)	High	Rarely used	Rarely used
Mode B Goals-Meanings	Variable, narrow, variable	Medium	Non-street-oriented and non-day crew, officers	Rarely used
Mode C Agent-Informant	Tends to be low, narrow, little	Low	Street-oriented squads and others not on day crew	Used by all officers
Mode D Citizen-dominant				
1 "Big Issue"	Variable, narrow, variable	None	Commander determined	Commander determined
2 Citizen-response	Low, narrow, little	None	Officer determined[a]	Cases assigned
3 Organization, Citizen-response	Variable, narrow, medium-low	None	Handled by schools and Pharmacies Squads, day crew	Cases assigned
Mode E Patrol-created	Variable to low	None	Patrol arrests for drugs credited to morals division	Patrol arrests for drugs credited to patrol

a. One clerk, available 8–4 P.M., takes phone messages for officers.
b. The modes are ranked by the degree to which the organization can exercise control over the individual officer's choice of targets. Militaristic targeting, since it is based on command decisions, is the most controlling. The goals-meanings mode, using some guidance based on predetermined types of acceptable targets, is the next most organizationally controlled. Citizen-response targeting, if cases are assigned, is less controlled, but when cases are not assigned, it is equivalent to the agent-informant mode, in which organizational control is lowest and in fact minimal.

work, the expected scope, and impact on the market are very roughly related to the degree or organizational control possible. Organizational guidance is a neccessity for generating complex cases. However, as has been repeatedly emphasized, any mode can produce the arrest of a high-level dealer or dealers, any case is infinitely expandable in theory, and the impact on the market is almost impossible to measure or at least to definitely establish. It is even more difficult to predict in advance the outcome and impact of undertaking an investigation.

The second correlate of the modalities is the degree of organizational control exercised when such a modality is employed. The most controlling of the five modes is the militaristic mode and the least is the patrol mode. In the patrol mode there is essentially no control whatever of the targets chosen since, for all practical purposes, drug arrests by patrol are random events; the basis of the arrest is rarely, if ever, a result of information received concerning use of or traffic in drugs. The other three modes are ordered in decreasing extent of organizational control, and increasing individual control of targets. The third dimension ordering the table is the unit and the practices found there. The final and most central dimension is the modality of targeting itself.

The remaining chapters in the book are organized around three of the five modes of targeting found in table 5.2. Two of the modes are not relevant to the ongoing operations or selection of targets by drug investigators because they do not control the patterning of patrol (mode E) and in neither organization was militaristic targeting used (mode A). The goals-meanings, agent-informant, and the citizen-dominant modes account for virtually all the cases made by drug-unit investigators. The majority of drug arrests are made by patrol in both departments. Each of the five types are described in this section. The central or core meaning of targeting comes form the militaristic mode, so it is discussed initially.

In military terms targeting connotes a systematic planning, identification, rationalization of choice, and some estimate of the political-economic consequences of eliminating or neutralizing that objective. Such an approach requires intelligence and the application of intelligence to operations if it is to work. The militaristic mode of targeting (A) is rare in policing. One infrequently sees the development of targets

derived from unit goals and objectives and associated strategies. Ideally, targets are set clearly by command and they are worked until im-
mobilized, arrested, in jail, on trial, under investigation by IRS, or the
like. This procedure would require a set of files, ways of supervising
the units, and persons involved and making them routinely accountable, opening and closing cases, monitoring information received, frequent staff meetings, and the other preconditions for rational strategic
action outlined. This was not done systematically in either unit. Although there were targets developed, these targets were not based on
the intelligence provided to the Metro Unit by the Intelligence Division
of the department, but came as a result of fortuitous coincidence of
several investigations occurring simultaneously within the unit itself.
Thus, although it is an ideal option that could be the basis for the mo-
bilization of collective enforcement action, militaristic targeting is not employed.

A second mode of targeting is an analogous approach that uses
general terms or categories of persons to guide action. This mode is
called the goals-meanings (B) approach because ti sets analytic definitions of targets or goals. Major violators are defined as goals. However, the definitions and meaning of the term "major violator" and other
key terms are not administratively constrained. Investigators assign
meaning to the terms and determine the choices they view as being
required by the investigation. This is the most common mode found in
the Metro Department and the most complex to discuss.

A third mode of targeting is the agent-informant mode (C). In this
category, the investigator and/or the informant, with varying amounts
of supervision, set the targets. In a sense the full determination of ac-
tion-choices is the product of an interaction between the informant and
the investigator, with a few key domains patterned by supervision. This
approach is the most common one in Suburban Department.

A fourth mode is in a way a mixed mode in which citizen complaints
(D) determine the cases to be investigated. This is called the citizen-
dominant mode of targeting. There are three variants on this mode.
The first is the "big issue" or politically volatile issue that requires a
publicly acknowledged police presence or attention. A target chosen
in order to ease public concern or demands (short-term alleviation of

pressure) may mean a case is assigned on that basis for investigation. The source may be the result of public outcry or concern, or private demand, such as phone calls asking police to "do something" about activity in a neighborhood or location. Since the concern of all narcotics units was with reducing public concern and outcry that might be embarrassing to the unit or to the department, the operating rule in both units was to respond to all demands, public or private, that might lead to embarrassing incidents should they become more public. Thus the unit commanders pointed out, when discussing goals of the units and the process of targeting, that the unit had to deal with the public's concerns and respond to citizen's requests. They rarely led to what administrators or investigators considered a "good case." Responses to short-term crises were not easily resisted in these units. They were vulnerable to pressure from the public and political groups like the city council and citizens groups. It should be noted that heroin and the first priority drugs are consensually defined as being a community threat; and thus enforcement success is viewed as an important source of community support. The less condemned drugs, especially marijuana, are least likely to generate public support and are viewed officially as something that one investigates if one has to, but something that agents prefer to investigate only if it leads to a big seizure. The drug unit has to respond to internal or self-defined pressures for enforcement also. If, for example, the head of the vice unit, who was also the head of the drug unit in both organizations, decided to mount a gambling raid or stage a "round up" of prostitutes, then he would assign personnel from the drug unit to that temporary duty.

The second variant of mode D is the citizen-response when phone calls are assigned by the unit for investigation on a routine basis. These are considered in this context to be calls that are not seen at the time as politically volatile or potentially big issues, but routine matters. Examples would be the woman who calls to say that there are marijuana plants in the window of the next apartment and she wants the police to investigate, or the parent who wants a police officer to destroy "some strange weed" found in the bureau drawer of their son or daughter. The organizations vary in the extent to which they can monitor and investigate these calls.

A third variant is the organization-citizen targeting approach, a mixture of the military targeting approach and reactive targeting based on a complaint. It resembles the military conception of operation because the targets are chosen from intelligence, information received in the course of other investigations, or from reliable sources in the community (physicians, dentists, pharmacies), and then informants are developed in order to "get next to," "infiltrate," "work your way into," surveil or otherwise penetrate the "operation," "target," or "conspiratorial group." In Metro a pharmacy squad worked on a reactive basis, that is, on the basis of complaints brought to them by the citizens. They kept files of suspects and pictures of previously arrested persons as well as a set of possible perpetrators and locales to which they could direct their attention. A similar squad, supervised by the same sergeant, worked schools in much the same way. Because of the perceived political sensitivity of school busts, there was much reliance upon the cooperation of school authorities in these investigations. Often, the narcotics unit was called by the school authorities and asked to investigate. Both units had "infiltrated" schools, made dope buys undercover, and mounted "busts" of high school students in the spring of 1975.

A final mode of targeting (E) is in effect a non-targeting activity, for routine work of patrol units produces the case. Patrol-created targeting yields arrests without the allocation of the resources, time, and effort of unit personnel. This mode occurs when a patrol unit, either responding to a complaint or dispatch, stops a person or vehicle in the course of routine patrol, has probable cause, and in searching finds drug evidence in the possession of the person or persons stopped. In a sense, then, the case is opened and closed simultaneously with the arrest. In both units, records of arrests made for drugs were kept separately by patrol and by the narcotics unit. In both organizations and in others (Williams, Redlinger, and Manning, 1978), patrol officers made the vast majority of all drug arrests, usually incident to routine traffic stops.

There are a number of functions that patrol units performed with regard to narcotics enforcement in the two sites. These general functions can be briefly listed. To greater or lesser degrees, all units used patrol officers for assistance on search warrant raids, for transporting prisoners, for security on the raid site, and for some surveillance. Patrol officers may be asked to check a suspect in a bar or in a neighborhood because police believe that drug dealers do not fear or suspect patrol cars as much as undercover agents or unmarked cars in their areas. These contacts can be a means by which officers are identified as possible candidates for working narcotics.

The two units subsequently use patrol-generated information in various fashions. In Suburban, officers only saw the arrest and charge sheets and did not question persons arrested by patrol unless patrol officers brought the persons to the unit or called for a narc to interrogate the persons involved. In Metro, although the sheets were no less visible (hanging on the wall near the investigator's office), officers did occasionally go down to the jail and interrogate prisoners. These prisoners were not always arrested on drug or drug-related charges, but the officers suspected that they might be willing to serve as informants; if they lived "in the right area of the city," if they were known for previous drug activity, if they were not under a "heavy charge," that is, assault, rape, homicide, or attempted murder, they might be good informants. The prosecutor would probably accept a deal if they plead guilty. They might, in other words, have information on drugs, the drug scene, or certain dealers of interest, and further might be willing to make a deal, plead guilty, and "turn" and "work off their beef." "Working off" a charge by making buys, informing on drug dealers, or introducing police to dealers can result in a dropped or altered charge. The informants obtained in this way are not many, and this practice is only continued by a few narcotics officers, although it is a common practice among detectives in other units.

The degree of cooperation between the drug unit and patrol is variable and characterized by ambivalence. The following reasons tend to reduce cooperation. Drug officers are protective of their special domain of enforcement and their freedom to explore cases. They do not always welcome "go-getters" in patrol who seek to make cases routinely in narcotics and in effect "steal" cases from the drug unit. They do not want to see a developed capacity for drug investigation spring up in intelligence, in juvenile, or in patrol. This would mean a countervailing organizational location of drug knowledge and enforcement capacity, which could be threatening to the resources and opportunities of the drug agents and their unit. This distrust is somewhat recipro- cated by patrol. Routine arrest reports are not read systematically in the units and checked out with patrol officers and neither are intelli- gence reports. This means that patrol and narcotics units do not rou- tinely cooperate on programs, functions, or objectives but only on an ad hoc, case-by-case basis. In this sense patrol is essentially an inde- pendent mode of enforcement not controlled to any appreciable de- gree by the command of the drug unit. This is ironic in light of the pro- portion of the arrests that they make and the resources for enforcement located in the patrol division of any department. This empirical finding does not mean that in an organizationally centered agency, coopera- tion could not be developed and mutual programs and strategies could not be articulated and implemented. Such programs could only increase the overall arrest output of he department and the informa- tional input to both organizational segments.

Since there is little that the unit can do to either induce, reduce, or produce such arrests, this mode of targeting only names the source of arrests or cases. The organizational guidance exercised by the unit in determining how and when they are made is essentially nil. This mode is mentioned only in passing and will not be discussed further.

Comment

In drawing the characterizations of these five modes of targeting, some of the major constraints on agent action, and the sources of their cases are outlined. Some final qualifications are necessary. When the agent- informant interaction mode dominates an organization, then the extent of the impact on the market, level at which the attack is launched, and the kinds of cases made are problematic and not controlled by the or- ganization. Likewise, rhetorical statements about the drugs focused on in the unit and the level of the market attacked are more an evocation of administrative interests or wishes than an operative strategy. Under this approach whatever the stated goals, the operative goals are deter- mined by what the informant knows, can do, and will do. Also, dominance of these strategies varies over time. The capacity of either of these two organizations to achieve stated goals using modes of targeting is a function not only of the stated intentions of the administrative component of the organizations but also of the capacity of the organizations to achieve or implement these goals. Kaufman, in a classic study of a kind of public bureaucracy, claims that policy is articulated as rhetoric at the "higher levels," but must be enacted at the lowest level of organizations. Until it is enacted, all else is intention (1960:34).

It should be pointed out in this context also that there is always a temporal dimension to the use of these strategies. They virtually always involve an informant at some point. The reasons for this reside in the aforementioned character of narcotics crimes. Thus the degree to which one relies on informants depends on the point in the investigation one wants to examine; even the most preplanned targeting of a well-known dealer in town will still require the acquisition of an informant to get next to him. Very rarely are arrests made as a result of lengthy investigations based on planned targets and systematic agent infiltration, however, many do result from luck or chance. Some chance cases produce large seizures. These kinds of very satisfying outcomes tend to reinforce the belief that one can never tell when a good case will come along, that drug enforcement is a matter of luck in many cases, and that in effect one must attribute much of the success to luck or chance.

All three modes can coexist, and they do in the two sites studied. This difference in mode of work, in kinds of cases received and investigated, is correlated, as mentioned in the chapter on evaluation, with such things as age, race or ethnicity, and years or time in the unit. As with all such static depictions of the activities of the two units, these modes do not capture dynamics very well, the relative salience or predominance of the strategies over time, the actual capacity of the organizations to achieve results, nor the mixture of strategies that one finds in the units. The effects that are pointed out here hold true to varying degrees across the units studied and are not characteristic of one. The modalities are found in both units to some degree. Although they are not mutually exclusive, the extent of one or the other being used does vary.

III

Ground

6

The Goals-Meanings Approach to Targeting

The goals-meanings approach, the agent-informant mode, and the citizen-dominant mode are found to varying degrees in the organizations studied. Each mode has a differential capacity to constrain or alter the perspective of the agents. The perspective of the officers, growing as it does from the enacted environment conception and providing the action bases for enactment, in both units is always the dominant ground against which any modification, administrative plan, or strategy must be seen. *Agents' perspective on the work dominates and controls what is done in the name of police control of the drug markets.* The more precise and exact the plan and mode of targeting, the more agents have embedded it in commonsense meanings that rationalize their own practices. The significance of the formal rational schemes, militaristic targeting, and the goals-meanings approach is twofold. The first is that the absence of the militaristic approach suggests that rational systems-theory views of organizational action do not describe very well what is done in these two organizations. Second, absence of these approaches shows that administrative control in drug units is likely to be weak, inarticulate, non-constraining, and operates in the breach and/or mainly after the fact. Although this assertion is made on the basis of a close study of two units, the generic features of enforcement lends support to it. Often police departments or drug units launch major new campaigns or operations intended to make significant impact on the drug trade, and will accompany these campaigns with public statements of their targets and perhaps even objectives. The rhetoric is a thinly veiled hope, since the organization typically has so little capacity to guide and direct its agents. When organizations do attempt to bring their agents' behavior in line with intended policy, as shown in this chapter, the results are produced more by agent discretion than by the constraints of the formal policy.

The Goals-Meanings Approach Defined

The metaphor of planned targeting and objective and goal setting is based on the presumption that the meanings associated with the key terms involved in such a planning exercise are not contextual, not temporal, and are relatively clearly understood by all participants in the ac-

tion. The most important key term used in the two organizations studied was one they differentially adopted from the Drug Enforcement
Administration, "major violator." The adaptation of this term was an attempt by DEA and by Metro, in particular, to guide investigators to
higher levels in the market and encourage the development of more
complex cases, especially those involving conspiracy charges (White
Paper, 1975; see also appendix 6A).[1] The term "major violator" and
several others that cluster together in the investigation of drug crimes,
"seizure," "case," "good seizure," and "skills," are not defined uniformly within these units. The terms, when used, refer to different action
consequences and concerted lines of action. The situations in which
they are used determine the meanings that the terms will have and the
actions that are touched off. We cannot predict the actions and decisions investigators take by saying that they are oriented to major violator investigations because that means different things, that is, implies
different goals and outcome measures, in different situations. The most
critical decisions in both units are not made on the basis of considered
administrative judgments or written orders, directives, or procedural
manuals (SOP). Significant decisions are made by investigators in line
with their tacit understandings and interpretations. Such understandings are context-bound, that is, specific to the given organizational situation in which they arise.

The term "goals-meanings" is used to indicate that targeting or goal
setting is based on a situational definition of what is a meaningful priority, objective, or goal. A number of key concepts are thus situationally
specific in their meaning and implications for action in both settings.
Thus problematic meanings and the context within which they are
understood must be examined. Since "major violator" is key among
the several terms used to guide case investigation, it will be analyzed
in more detail in Metro following an overview of some of the problematic meanings associated with key terms in each of the two units. In a
final section on the uses of "major violator" in Metro, it is shown how
organizational location, the history of the relations between the persons involved in a decision of the term, and the horizon of investigative
possibilities pattern the investigators' understandings and subsequent
choices.

Metro

• The term *"major violator"* can be formally defined in at least six different overlapping, but competing ways: (A) operationally in terms of the "big cases" of a particular investigator; (B) the squad or sergeant's definition of the target of their investigations; (C) the defined target of the one squad in the branch that is said to be concentrating on Latins and "major violators"; (D) the names found in the major violator file kept in the department—said to be around 425 according to the chief clerk in the captain's office; (E) the analytic definitions used by the Drug Enforcement Administration (see appendix 6A). Since the amount of dope a dealer has changes from day to day, and it can be calculated in a variety of ways (how fast his turnover is, how many buys are made from him, the quality of his dope, a single purchase of one ounce, or two "halfs"), it is easily seen that his "weight" changes over time. One solution (used in Phoenix) is to use the size of seizure as a retrospective basis for labeling a major violator. (F) Textbook definitions; style of life, levels of insulation of the dealer from the street, weight he deals in, and the sources of his dope.

• Investigating marijuana and other drugs shifts in meaning given court decisions, attorney's rules, the interpretation of the investigator or sergeant as to whether or not it will *"pay off*," and the interest one has in adding an arrest to his activity sheet for the month. Several investigators told me, and it was a common understanding, "I'll take a street arrest anytime."

• Definitions of a *case* and associated terms like "good informant," "good seizure" from a raid, and "adequate payment" of informants (which is personalized and based on wide limits depending on the service rendered, size of the violator, size of the seizure) are all contextual. They change in meaning from situation to situation. For example, one investigator told me, "If you ask me, or if you ask A, or if you ask B over there how much he pays his informants, you'll get a different answer from each one."

• Definitions of *success* vary. (A) They vary by the level of focus of the investigator. For example, if one's focus is on "the street," an arrest or so in a week is "doing well." A person or squad whose focus is major violators may not make an arrest for six months. These very different definitions of success mean that persons who work the street tend to see major violator investigators as "the biggest bunch of bull-shitters around," while those who prefer long-term investigations and have lower arrest rates tend to see the people who work the street as "door kickers" and "vice squad officers." (B) Definitions of success also vary by the degree to which the officer is *oriented to making money*. More arrests mean more court time; court time (through an elaborate system of rules about pay) yields overtime (time and a half) pay (see appendix 6B).[2] (C) Definitions of success vary by level of group identification. They may be *individual* or *collective* (squad or unit). Thus, although one may personally bring in many "bodies," it may reduce the chances of other investigations being successful (either by making dealers jumpy or cautious, or by arresting persons who were under surveillance so that their source could be traced). On the other hand, a person who makes few arrests, but facilitates other people's investigations or raids (by acting as surveillance coordinator, doing paperwork or records checks, assisting on raids and arrest-warrant serving) may be viewed as contributing to the success of the squad. Some squads work only together or in partner-teams within their squads, others do not. In the latter, success tends to be individualistically defined; in the former, collective or squad or unit definitions predominate. On the whole, however, there was no sense of "group pride" or loyalty to the unit per se, only to the squad, one's partner, or one's self. (D) Definitions of success vary as a function of whether or not one wants to achieve success as an investigator within narcotics or work to make sergeant. All promotion involves transfer. To be successful on the street will result in numerous court appearances, while seeking success via formal promotion requires one to avoid court (especially on days off) and the street in order to study the regulations on which the sergeant's exam is in part based. Further, the more time one spends in specialized investigation, the less familiar one is with the regulations that are emphasized in the exam. The test focuses on the problems and enforcement knowledge relevant to the work of the uniformed patrol officer.

• *Levels of skill vary, as do definitions of appropriate skills.* Those skills useful for street work, for example, interaction with street people, inter- rogation of arrestees and "turning" them to work for the officer, build- ing a quick case and "ripping him off" (getting a search or arrest warrant and executing it) do not contribute to developing long-term patient investigation of major violators. Longer investigations may in- volve camera, videotape, recording, and sound equipment skills, care- ful paperwork and background investigation and lengthy surveillance. Furthermore, they may require skills of role-playing as a "Big man" or "heavy dealer" able and willing to front the money for a large deal in order to get contact with those higher in the dealing hierarchy. The per- son who tends to specialize in or seek the cultivation of one set of skills is not likely to possess or desire the other. Skill acquisition tends to be somewhat asymmetrical in that those who have skills to work long-term investigations can, in fact, develop or often have skills necessary for short-term investigation. The opposite is not true. While the skills re- quired for street work are in part culturally "derived" (blacks born and raised in the city have "natural street skills") or can be learned in ap- prenticeship relationships with other investigators who are experi- enced, skills needed for long-term investigations are possessed by only a few officers. Skills such as use of telephoto lens, photographic expertise with a number of types of cameras, and use of electronic equipment are exclusively possessed by a few men who have been sent to specialized schools. They are either unwilling or unable to teach other officers those skills. Further, the activities at issue were performed in private—at the sites of wire intercepts, on surveillance, or at raids. For example, the sergeant in the Metro unit who is in effect the technical consultant to the division on electronic and photographic equipment is very reticent to teach other officers these skills. Thus most of them have difficulty using a Polaroid camera, and errors in use routinely occur. Evidence is thus lost. The same problem of lack of knowledge hampers the use of electronic equipment (for wire inter- cepts) and body transmitters (used to maintain contact with under- cover agents during negotiations or potentially dangerous interactions where the undercoverman needs a back-up unit ready to intervene on his behalf). Although the FBI operates a camera school and DEA holds several schools in which camera and surveillance techniques are taught, few of the agents had attended them (one sergeant had been to the camera school, and less than ten officers had attended the DEA 10-week school in which camera techniques are taught). Only four investigators of the sixty-one officers in the unit had experience with wire intercepts. If such a strategy were chosen, it would be difficult to staff it, given other obligations of the officers. Many departments (not Metro) do not possess the equipment needed for a wire intercept or for extensive surveillance using cameras, telephoto lenses, or night vision devices.

• Actual skill level varies, and the skills are not randomly distributed among the several squads. Thus beliefs and actual skill were inconsistent. It should be further emphasized that the definition of what skills are required for a given case vary and that these *definitions* provide the limit and boundaries of the case and how it will be worked. If one deems the appropriate skills for investigation to be short-term skills then those are the skills thought to be appropriate to the investigation. On the other hand, if one deems that long-term investigative skills are required, then those are the skills that will be applied to that investigation. In other words, the case or the features of a case do not intrinsically provide those features that are read as requiring certain skills to be applied. Rather, the officer's skills and his definition of the requisite skills provide the mode of investigation in a given case. Believed skill and skill utilized are functions of the definition of what the case requires, not of essential features of the facts of the case. To a lesser extent, the actual available skills possessed by squad members will pattern the approach taken to a case.

• The problem of *evaluation* is made more complex by the fact that the *indices of activity* and success are multiple and crude. Investigators are likely to reject the principal modes of formal gathering of data. Activity sheets totaling their arrests, court appearances, and the like are called "lie sheets." The lieutenant and sergeants likewise view them as misleading, and the lieutenant told me that he "rarely read them." However, there is a consensus about the outstanding investigators in the narcotics branch and this includes some with long-term skills and some with street skills. Further, there is a problem obtaining information on the activities of a given investigator other than from his reputation for general skill. Investigators do not as a rule talk about their cases with anyone except their partners. They may not actually do that. The information they provide to sergeants is sporadic and truncated, often something as elliptical as, "I'm going out to check on that business with Slick." Therefore, investigators are unaware, except on occasion when a raid goes down or persons are arrested and brought into the squad room, of precisely what other investigators are working on if at all, how they have resolved various cases, and what the disposition of a particular case is. There is much small talk about what happened to people who were locked up. However, investigators rarely keep track of cases other than their own, and information on their own cases, if they are not called to testify, is often highly variable and inexact.

• Although the Metro Department is authorized to make arrests, they do not make the charge against the accused; this is the domain of the U.S. Attorney's office. Although by the presentation of evidence and negotiation with representatives of that office, the police can have an important effect on the resultant charge, there is a constant exchange and negotiation of cases between the narcotics branch and the U.S. Attorney's office. If an arrest is rejected, or "no-papered", it will not be sent forward for prosecution. A further complication is introduced by the fact that drug offenders can be charged either under federal or local law; violations of federal laws carry felony penalties, whereas local laws treat many drug offenses as misdemeanors. The investigators view the federal court as more problematic even though they would prefer to prosecute under federal laws. Most charges are reduced to lesser charges and are tried in local courts. As a result of the ambiguity of charge and legal systems in which it will be adjudicated, that is, what is acceptable to the courts and prosecutor's office, *arrest, charge, and conviction are seen as almost independent phenomenon.* Any one can be used as evidence of "success" or "failure"; however, compare the strategy of defining success in terms of "making cases." Several "characteristic" attitudes of narcotics policemen result. They tend to view the narcs' game as being one of building up convictions against a person, even on lesser drug offenses, thus discrediting his testimony in court, increasing his "back-up time" (the time left to serve which must be done on parole and which, if he is convicted again, will more likely result in a prison sentence), and conversely, raising the credibility and authority of the officer, both in court and with the defendant. Whether the person pleads guilty and serves time, or "works off the beef," additional charges against him are always welcomed by officers.

Suburban
The strategy of buy-bust that predominates in Suburban Department creates a number of ambiguities not only behaviorally in terms of the range of outcomes possible but in terms of defining the meaningful limits of an investigation. Ambiguities surround the key terms "source," "target," and "good seizure." These ambiguities persist because of the vicissitudes inherent in arranging a buy-bust sequence. An agent will attempt to make one or more buys in an undercover role. First the agent has an informant "walk him in" or "cut him in." Then the agent attempts to buy a slightly larger amount from a seller than the seller is holding at that time, thus forcing the seller to arrange a buy with his source. The agent will then attempt to arrange a face-to-face transaction between himself and the source. If and when the later buying situation occurs, it may be possible to make the purchase and then arrest ("bust") the seller and the middleman and seize the money and the drugs. Of course, this pattern of buying up without the arrest-seizure episode can be repeated, each time buying larger amounts and rising in the dealing pyramid. Ambiguities are implied by the terms that partition and make meaningful the process of buy-bust.

• "Source" is a problematic term. Each seller has at least one source and that source has at least one other, etc. Logically it should be possible to reach the end of the chain were it not for a number of practical limitations. One set of limits has to do with credibility. Drug dealers, especially in opiates, are cautious about accepting new customers. For an agent to rise in the hierarchy beyond the kilo level, he almost certainly would have to deal in drugs himself and to have substantial

backing from other dealers who have known him or previously dealt with him (compare Heller, 1973:397–398). It is possible to circumvent this if the seller is greedy. In the drug world, like any other business, money is power and brings out lust, which can destroy caution. Another set of limits devolve from the amount of money available. "Flash" money or front money is needed to make large buys and to convince potential sellers that the buyer possesses the money for a deal. Further, in order to work up to a source, a considerable number of (or a few expensive) buys must be made for which no hope of recovery is entertained—his money must be considered "investment" capital. A third set of limits issue from political boundaries and the limits of cooperation. If a source lives outside the county, cooperation with other counties is needed if that source is to be arrested at his residence, or if his source in turn is to be arrested. All such cooperative ventures, whether with other counties, state police, or federal agencies, are problematic and a source of constant concern and irritation. Often an arrest of a small dealer will be made in the county rather than attempt a cooperative bust of his larger source, since it would mean sharing evidence, publicity, and credit with adjoining county or state personnel.
• The term "target" is also ambiguous. In part it takes on many of the implicit meanings attached to the term source and some of the same practical limitations. In addition, the target of a given investigation, especially if it is local, need not fit the criteria of "major violator" or "dealer in weight" simply because organizationally, every local that is founded must be investigated. Occasionally, locals eventuate in a search warrant. In one case, for example, the evidence retrieved from a raid, one marijuana plant, was taken to the judge who signed the warrant.

Because all but two of these investigators were inexperienced and none had received formal training in narcotics investigation, and because, organizationally, all locals must be investigated, "targets" are not always major violators or anything approaching that (by any definition). A target can be seen as any person arrested. Since in many respects narcotics enforcement is a continuing game in which each arrestee can produce other leads, or "do" (buy from) others, an arrest is seen as easily as the beginning as the end of an investigation. Targets themselves are always subject not only to redefinition as the level of an investigation shifts but to retrospective-prospective redefinition; events change the previous meanings of the target, and future intentions can alter a previously investigated target.

• "Good seizure" can be defined in several ways. The first is to consider any seizure a good seizure—especially since there is always considerable fear of "coming up dry" (seizing no drugs). A second definition is to view the seizure in the context of the amount of drugs previously bought. One investigator, for example, bought five pounds of marijuana and eventually seized only two. In the context of all seizures made that would be a good seizure, but not in comparison to the weight that was dealt by the persons involved. Good seizure is relative to the type of drug involved: an ounce of heroin is thought of as a good seizure but anything under fifty pounds of marijuana is not. Good seizure is relative to the expectations held of the warrant—one disappointing raid yielded less than a gram of heroin, when it was understood from informants that the person was holding twenty bags the night before. The interconnectedness of the concepts of "target," "source," and "good seizure" make their meanings a function of the associative connection in which they are seen. If a dealer is seen as a source, reached after several buys of a given size and considered a major target of an initiated investigation, then a good seizure will tend to be something of weight. The reverse is also true; an investigation of little promise, with failure indicated (failed buys, misinformation provided, inability to reach a larger source), will lead agents to expect very little of a raid (an affidavit may never be written; a warrant, once obtained, may never be served).

Major Violator as Rotor: Targeting and Investigating

The term "major violator" is used to establish for practical purposes a person of investigative significance.* Recall the overlapping and competing six meanings of the term major violator elicited by observation of its occasioned use in the two settings, mentioned previously. The

*This and subsequent sections of this chapter originally appeared in P. K. Manning, "Rules in Organizational Context: Narcotics Law Enforcement in Two Settings," *Sociological Quarterly* 18 (Winter, 1977);44–61.

fact that these uses and definitions are overlapping is significant. Outside a particular context, patterned by the history of speaker/hearer relationships, their organizational location, and the horizon of investigative possibilities, the term floats abstractly. As an abstraction, it cannot precisely guide organizational action. The context within which the term is used provides the tacitly assignable features that make possible investigative decisions and their sanctioning by the appearance of · consensus between supervisors and investigators. Let us discuss these contextual matters, one at a time, recognizing they interact in any given case.

History   If members of a speaker/hearer dyad are strangers to each other, and one is outside the organization, then textbook definitions are employed. In initial interviews I was told repeatedly by sergeants, lieutenants, and the commanding officers in both units that the aim of the organization was to attack major violators defined either in DEA terms (E), in textbook definitions (F), or in terms of the file (D). Thus outsiders are given abstract, neutral terms unrooted in the exigencies of investigation, since it is assumed that as strangers that they do not share detailed tacit knowledge about investigative work. On the other hand, when two persons who have spent more than a year in the unit discuss investigation of major violators, other defining matters come into play. A shared history is insufficient explanation for the meanings assigned to the term.

Organizational location   If a sergeant intentionally focuses his squad on trade at a given level of the market (in Metro, nine of the squads had a focus or orientation), two meanings could be assigned to major violator. If term is used by a member of the squad, of the two squads oriented to major violators oriented to "Latins," who are thought to be big dealers, then the term refers to them on occasioned use. It refers to whomever is being investigated at that time by that squad. If, on the other hand, the squad is one of the five primarily oriented to the street (table 5.1) (to the arrest of smaller dealers on a high arrest basis), then the term refers to what the other squad is doing (namely, the "Latin squad," or the other squad that was at the time of my research working on a "big case"). If there is not a single focus agreed upon by sergeants and squads, that is, if sergeants do not closely supervise their officers, whatever the investigator is working on at that time can be defined as a "big case" because as one investigator told me, "everyone likes to think he has a big case always going." This is possible because the sergeants do not have reference to the data on which that judgment might be made; most investigators, for fear of having a case "ripped off" (stolen, investigated, and perhaps brought to prosecution) by another investigator, keep files locked in their desks or keep notes privately and clandestinely. Some cases are not written up until after arrests have been made. Thus, the autonomy of lower participants and lack of close supervision allows a shifting and unverifiable set of definitions to come into play. Thus, definitions A, B, or C can be invoked by investigators depending on the sergeant's orientation to the term.

Horizon of investigative possibilities   If the term major violator is used when persons are known to each other and when the sergeant does not officially define the level of target sought by his squad, then operative exigencies come into play; terms like "you know, anything can come out of that sort of thing," "it's one of those things," or "they'll get over on you" serve to imply consensus on an intractable ambiguity. These working terms may initially be based on analytic definitions (E) but soon are rationalized in terms of "doing the best one can under the circumstances." Like all work, narcotics enforcement is constrained by conceptions of what is thought to be a "good job." This idea contrasted in Metro with the term "cash register" (an officer who "rate-busts," makes numerous arrests, frequently appears in court, and consequently earns overtime pay). Thus definitions A and E become unspoken meanings assigned to what one is actually doing and by transition, they refer to work on major violators. The investigator can escalate the level of his investigation and then label it as one centered on a major violator. He does this by making a series of buys such that he can request that the dealer provide him with a buy of an ounce or more. In time, it can become an investigation of a major violator by DEA standards since he has made a buy of an ounce or more. This does not mean the dealer usually sells such weight, only that the investigator was able to persuade him to sell an ounce to him. As long as there is very loose control over the actual targets of investigations, as opposed to what officers describe as being their targets, the same term means or indicates very different symbolic conceptions of the role of the narcotics officer. The actionable targets of the unit shift. Depending on the history, organizational location, and their perception of the horizon of investigative possibilities, it indicates different meanings of the term major violator and thus makes it possible for shared misunderstandings to develop.

The features of these six definitions, as they are recognized within the specified speaker/hearer dyads, become prospective as well as retrospective bases for investigative efforts. However, since the actual basis on which a case is initiated is unknown in detail to sergeants and supervisory personnel, sanctioning for failure to investigate major violators will only result when an account or justification (referring to the relevant situational features of the term) cannot be offered and/or is not honored or found acceptable by the hearer.

These formal ambiguities are made complex because the facts about investigations are not fully shared between organizational segments, yet one segment is required to initiate investigations and to justify them, while another level has responsibility for the evaluation of the success of these investigations. Patterned ambiguities concerning the term major violator and the basis on which accounts will be accepted by supervisory officers maintain the appearance of consensus between segments, while allowing the uncertain and often fruitless job of enforcement to proceed. Axial terms meant to focus investigative activities, such as major violator, are actually like rotors, pointing first to one connotation of the words and then to another. When additional sources of information are utilized, for example, expenditure vouchers for payments made for drug buys or for services rendered, the same ambiguity remains. It is solved in the same practical manner, that is, implicit understandings serve to sanction certain specific practices associated with rules governing payments and definitions of success.

In general, for practical organizational reasons and to reduce the endless uncertainty in the work, investigators and supervisors play a game in which each assumes the other is evaluating him, but withholds those questions and data that might make a close and critical evaluation necessary. Furthermore, evaluation is not made on the basis of expenditure patterns but on whether a case is "made," or whether in the eyes of the sergeant or the lieutenant, the case "might have paid off if other things hadn't interfered." Thus "success" in controlling major violators is a judgment made by supervisors from data unrelated to major violator's arrest, capture, harrassment, conviction, or imprisonment. We have come back full-circle to the term major violator.

The targeting in this mode is thus dependent not on the formal definitions of major violator that have been developed by administrators and planners, but on the meanings that are negotiated between investigators and sergeants when a case of this kind is discussed. Since not all cases are discussed, not all of them contain the potential for being defined as involving major violators, and sergeants rarely advise on the actual substance of a case, the modality is marginal to everyday affairs in Metro.

Appendix 6A

Some narrative from Senate testimony at the time of the research will contextualize DEA's use of the DEA-G-DEP objective.

BNDD'S Approach

Considerable interest has been expressed in the Federal approach to fight drug trafficking, BNDD, believing that most heroin was smuggled into the United States by organized rings of traffickers through extensive national and international distribution systems, committed its resources to breaking up the major organized rings. In 1969, it initiated the "systems approach" to arrest and prosecute those major traffickers whose immobilization, BNDD felt, would most help reduce the availability of illicit drugs. It identified ten major and seventy-five secondary drug distribution systems.

By January 1972, BNDD recognized that the systems approach was not producing the desired results. All ten major systems were still operating, although two had been severely disrupted. BNDD modified its efforts into the geographic drug enforcement program (G-DEP). This program has been continued by DEA.

The G-DEP objective, like that of the systems approach, is to direct priority enforcement action against major illicit drug distribution organizations. The principal difference is that under the systems approach traffickers were identified as members of specific illicit drug distribution systems whereas under G-DEP they are identified according to their importance and are classified by the type of drug they traffic in and the general area where they traffic. Class I and II traffickers repre-

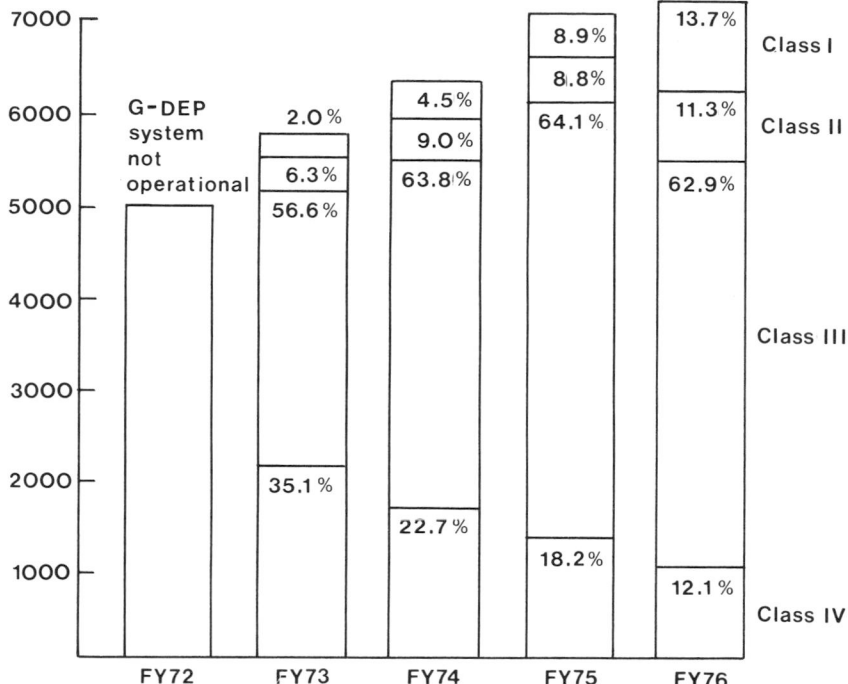

sent the most important violators in the drug traffic and their designation must be approved at the headquarters' level. Class III and IV traffickers are less important, much more numerous than I's and II's, and their designation does not require headquarters' approval. A general definition is shown as attachment 7.

The DEA policy under G-DEP provides for allocating 70 percent of enforcement resources to arresting and prosecuting class I, II, and III traffickers.

Our December 1973 report to the Congress discussed BNDD and DEA's difficulties in immobilizing major traffickers. Our [DEA] current work indicates that although improvements have been made there are still difficulties in this area (Senate Testimony, June 1975:100–101).

DEA G-DEP Violator Classifications

Generally the four classifications of G-DEP violators can be defined as follows:

Class I; Those violators who are major illicit laboratory operators, heads of criminal organizations, smuggling heads, and those who consistently deal in volume quantity of high-purity drugs.

Class II: Those violators who, through the volume of their illicit activities, are identified as significant wholesalers of illegal drugs supplying various other traffickers.

Class III: Those violators who are active distributors of illegal drugs in quantity at the sub-wholesale levels.

Class IV: Those violators who do not meet the criteria established at the I, II, and III levels (Senate Testimony, June 1975:123).

In Senate testimony in 1976, Peter Bensinger, the administrator of DEA, presented data on the arrest pattern of DEA for the previous five years, using the violator classifications described above (from House Testimony, Oversight Hearings, 94th Congress, 2nd Session, September 1976:336) (see figure A6.1). The difficulty in defining these violators is discussed in this chapter. The validity of DEA's classification of their arrestees will have to await future research on their decision making and investigative decision-making. Moore suggests (1977:chapter 3), as does Senate Testimony (see Interim Report, "Federal Narcotics Enforcement" 1976:182–187) that the undercover strategy favored by many of the "old hands" in DEA is likely to produce low-level focus and a lack of administrative prospective control of the initiation and closure of investigations.

Appendix 6B

Comp time could be received by making a written request to one's sergeant 24 hours in advance (by rule), but in practice it would be requested almost any time up to the time of the beginning of a shift. (People would call in a few minutes before they were to report and ask for comp time and the request would be approved verbally by the officer's sergeant or by another official of sergeant's rank or above). If the requesting officer makes a request for time off and this request is denied twice within ninety days, he must be paid for the time. Since the request is virtually always granted within the alloted time, this is not an actual source of income. On the other hand, one had to be shown on the book for any comp time granted or taken, since if anything happened while you were on comp time (accident, injury, etc.), you would have to be "on the book" to receive payment. Most officers accumulate so much comp time in Metro that they lose it at the end of the year.

They are expected to work extra hours as a part of the job, yet are not paid. If they take too much comp time or do not accumulate it in the first place, they are not thought to be doing the job.

Paid overtime on the other hand, could be routinely obtained under certain conditions for court appearances. Both courts were across the street from the police station so going to court did not involve travel time, parking problems, etc. Officers were not paid for travel inconvenience, or the like, as is sometimes the case. If one is on duty on days, 8:00–4:00 P.M., when the case is set for court, then one is not paid for the first appearance but gets comp time. One is paid two hours court (regardless of the actual time spent) if one was not on duty (days) at the time. One is also paid if court runs after 4:00 (end of day shift) on the first appearance. In addition , if the case was called a second time, if there was more than one court session, whether or not the officer is working days, he is paid time and a half. The conclusion I draw from this is that officers are rewarded monetarily for court appearances because this is the only legal way to make extra money that does not require special approval (grudgingly given in Metro). Arrests are the way to get into court. If one is oriented to making money, then arrests will be a high priority in one's goals and working perspective. One informant summarized this position well in an interview with me:

Lyman: Sergeants may want to get major violators, but they have to show that their squad is getting arrests. You have to get arrests. If you get arrests, your unit's looking good. If you're not . . . doing. . . if you're doing major violators, you're not showing arrests. So, the sergeants are in a dilemma. Some guys like to—naturally, some guys like to work using search warrants and working street rip offs and arrests because they get court time. The more court time you get, the more dollars, the more possible money you can make. If you're not going to court, you're not going to be making any dollars. So the more arrests you get, the more chances you have for making extra money. Any guy's going to really want to make a few extra bucks.

PKM: How does that work?

Lyman: [You have to get yourself into court.] What this means is that short-term, high arrest work leads to a greater number of court appearances, which, in turn, make it possible to earn more overtime pay. If you ask around any other jobs—bricklayers, bus drivers, or any other kind of work, they've always got overtime pay. Policemen can't get it in the same way. All you can get is comp time.

The goals-meanings strategy is based on assumptions about the extent to which named targets and associated procedures and priorities are defined and acted upon uniformly. They are not uniformly defined and are discussed primarily after the most significant and determinant decisions have been made. Targets are sought on the basis of situational or contextual understandings of key words that guide enforcement action. In a sense, the agent is able to maintain his own perspective on what is needed for a satisfactory closure for the case. The cases that come to the agent's attention in this way are rather few. The most important source of cases are those he constructs himself or develops in concert with or as a result of interaction with an informant. These cases are produced by the agent-informant mode. The goals-meanings approach can be distinguished from the subject of this chapter: in the goals-meanings approach the organization has made a prior decision to allocate resources and to guide agent action by naming major violators as targets. Recall, however, that once the case is produced by this modality, a variety of means can be used to pursue it. These means could include the use of informants, but the information given would not be pursued at that time unless the informant could direct the officer to one of the named groups, persons, or someone who dealt in an amount of heroin that exceeded a certain weight, for example. Constraints on the agent to operate in this way are fairly weak and are dependent on sergeants' attempts to monitor activities, especially at key points. One key point is the assigning of money, at which time he might be able to prospectively guide effort.

If the sergeant does not employ a major violator modality or attempt to control agents to such goals, then the agent-informant mode of targeting will characterize the way that the agent obtains cases. Cases resulting from this mode are those in which an informant provides the lead and the major violator term has not been employed to constrain choices. In these cases the agent is able to produce information leading to a case through interrogation by systematically interviewing a person for information about certain neighborhoods, persons, groups of persons, or events, or when an informant brings such information to the attention of the investigator. The informant may be on salary to the department, be a volunteer, or be working off a charge under the officer's direction but must stand in some formal relationship to the officer when the information is provided. This relationship distinguishes "citizens" from "informants."

The agent-informant mode is significant from the perspective of the officers because they have learned to see their possibilities for success as dependent on identifying, cultivating, working, and maintaining their informants. They assume that this is the most fruitful way of working, in large part because they have never done anything else, have received little or no formal training because they have not seen other modes used, and because it is part of the traditional lore of the units that informants are the sine qua non of narcotics work.

This chapter outlines the informant-agent mode and shows how the necessary elements in producing a case of this kind are only occasionally patterned by administrative or supervisory decisions. In the absence of other guidance or information that is shared and systematically made available to all officers, the agent-informant mode operates almost entirely based on what the agent perceives as being in his best interest at the time he makes decisions. Detailed cases or narratives show the organizational chaos this produces, whatever the intent of the investigator.

Actions, Elements, and Outcomes in the Agent-Informant Mode

When there are no guiding precepts such as major violator, and there are no universally shared sources of information such that each investigator might weigh his options against a set of known case-making opportunities, expediency will rule. Of course, it may rule anyway. The weighing up of options is accomplished in terms of rewards as they are perceived by investigators at the time, the informal or formal pressures applied by the sergeant supervising the squad, the number of informants available to him at that time, and the level of their knowledge. Where these conditions of expedient action rule, a set of elements of any case must still be present. Table 7.1 shows these elements. The more complex the probable outcomes are (table 7.1, col. 3), the more elements are required in the scenario (col. 2). In a complete scenario for the most complex case, four elements are involved. This scenario

Table 7.1 Actions, elements, and outcomes in drug investigations

Type of Action[a]	Needed Elements	Probable Outcomes[b]
Cruising/hassling	Information	Deterrence; no case
Street rip-off	Information	Arrest-possession case
Head-hunting	Information and informant	Arrest-possession case
....		
Informant/search Warrant/raid	Information and informant Money (small), personnel (for raid), some flair (planning, organizing)	Arrest, seizure Sale/possession case
Working up the dealing system	Information, informant (usually), money, substantial flair	Sale, possession, possible conspiracy

Note: Dotted line indicates the axial line where money and flair become critical and where external (supervisors, primary and secondary, attorneys and court system, other organizations) constraints are progressively more likely to operate.

a. Roughly arrayed by time involved, complexity of case involved, expense to organization and individual agents, and number of problematic or unpredictable aspects of the case.

b. A possession charge does not necessarily carry a heavier penalty than a distribution or intent to distribute charge but is considered less effective in disrupting a network than a distribution or intent to distribute case. But the latter, like conspiracy cases, are more difficult to prove in court since they may not involve buys or a large seizure (implying that those arrested have the capacity to deal/distribute to others).

involves the presence of a tip or informant, information that is credible and relevant to a case, (that which is seen as evidence in the context of that case and as legally substantiated if the officer intends to make an arrest), money, and imagination or "flair."

"Flair," a term used to describe to me what was expected of a good narcotics officer in Metro, has a special meaning in the context of drug policing. Flair does not refer to specific details of performance because it is said to be difficult to describe precisely. It is used to distinguish a good officer from a bad one. There are pressures to produce, but what is produced is not clearly stated and can involve arrests of various kinds, good seizures, assistance to other officers, or diligence in the assembling of evidence or completing paperwork. Flair refers to the ability of the officer to put together the elements of a case in an intellectual fashion, to anticipate the problems that might be involved, to check out and systemize what is known and what might be known about a person or target, to carry through the investigation and execute the closure that is appropriate to the case at a given point. As shown in table 7.1, flair is also contextual with respect to the kind of case that the officer attempts to make, but specifically it tends to be used to refer to more complex cases that require the use of a search-warrant-raid strategy or an "agent ascendent" strategy (working up the dealing system). Because the term is used loosely to refer to all types of investigations in spite of the fact that it most specifically has relevance only in more complex ones, its use creates a patterned ambiguity in evaluation. Although officers are expected to be self-starters and to produce, neither of these qualities alone distinguishes competent or good officers from bad ones; flair does. This is so because the elements in cases that are more complex require more persistence and are more problematic in the sense that the more complex the scenario or imagined plan, the more likely that elements other than those under the control of the investigator will have a bearing on the outcome of the case.

The subtle rewards that flow to officers with flair are perhaps an attempt by administrators to encourage those few officers who do take the risk of making more difficult cases. The sequencing suggested in table 7.1 does not always occur as listed for the elements may appear in another order. The elements do not have to appear in this order, but in the absence of any one, the case will not develop in the intended fashion.[1] In other words, information is a requirement for any case, but an informant is required for a head-hunting operation. One may have the informant but be unable to get him to produce the needed information. One may have an informant, find from him that a major dealer is operating in a certain area but be unable to conceptualize how to make a buy from him, etc. These variations in case making are discussed in this chapter.

In the following examples, an informant is initially available, and information may or may not be present, as is differentially true for money and imagination. The agents tend thus to be constrained by the information of the informant, his position in the market, the informant's age, race, and sex, and his drug of choice. Conversely, the skills of the agent or the agent and his partner will be very important in producing cases. The perspective of the officer in Metro is always shaped to some degree by the pressures placed upon him by his sergeant. The formal structures of reward and the squad and partnership relationships between the investigators within squads interact with the investigative focus or perspective of the individual to produce the level and direction of effort within the Metro Unit. Pressures in the units that are street oriented (squads and investigators) are very much in the direction of immediate action in the situation in which an informant comes forward.

Decisions made after the fact, usually by sergeants and other higher supervisors, concerning rewards to be paid to an informant or the altering of a charge if he is working off a beef, or the approval of a raid, do have controlling effects. Prospective decisions involving the amount of money that is fronted or flashed and agreements made between the sergeant, the informant, and the officer about what is considered good work and between the defense attorneys, the prosecuting attorneys, and the lieutenant will also have some effect on whether and to what extent a given case is pursued. Wherever possible, examples of when the planned scenario does not happen are given: when the deal does not "go down" as planned, when the informant does not provide the necessary information, when the legal basis for the investigation is shaky, and the like. Successful cases are also included. The concepts of a good case, or having a flair, or even making cases does not pertain exclusively to arrests made, but to cases that, if all other things had been constant, would have materialized in the desired form.[2]

Metro

There are five different types of actions within the agent-informant mode. They are basically distinguished by the degree to which they require elements in addition to the informant and/or information (see table 7.1). Since the notion of the informant-agent dominant mode is based upon either information and/or the informant being the basis of the agents' choice, one of these two is present by definition. However, the line that changes the types of cases made from straight, street rip-offs (arrests made quickly on the basis of "hot tips") or head-hunting (working the street with an informant and making arrests either by "eyeballing" a dealer from whom there is an arrest warrant or observing him in the act of dealing) to more complex cases involving money, imagination, or planning is a thin one. The thinness of the line is indicated by the fact that only investigators can decide whether they want to exceed the short-term arrest scenario. If the investigator does decide to make the case something more than a cruising, street rip-off, or head-hunting, he then must have two things: money and flair. To some extent the latter two items, in turn, require either the cooperation of other investigators or supervisory support, mainly in the form of willingness to front the money for the buy or whatever to the investigator. Finally, one must be able to work an informant, which largely hinges on being able to judge his credibility. Several cases of agent-informant interaction follow:

Cruising, Head-Hunting, Rips, and Hot Busts

We drove to Fairchild Lane. As we went by, I saw that there were large numbers of people out on the street. Most of them were gambling, playing craps, drinking, laughing. They were mostly young and middle-aged men (very few women). There were a few men in their twenties, and a lot of young children. As we drove down Fairchild, the children began to shout and then chant, "olleray," "olleray"—which is Pig Latin for "roller"—the local slang for policemen. These cries and the chanting alerted people down the block although we were about one-quarter of the way down the street before the call was issued. It was repeated and echoed by children along the way. It was agreed by the others that it was a relatively mild reaction to our presence and that it is often much worse and their response a lot more active. In fact the day before, two officers had tried to take a man out of the area and were confronted by a crowd of some thirty-plus people who tried to take the prisoner. One officer fell to the ground in a scuffle with the prisoner, and the other had to draw his pistol to escape. This occurred after a note had been posted in the office concerning the fact that a snitch had informed Sergeant Stop that "there may be a retaliation by the residents against people being arrested in the area." It had occurred to one of the same officers on July 9, and to him approximately two weeks before. On the way out, there was a discussion of this problem of arousing the crowds in this area. It was argued by Titus that if one tried to make an arrest in the middle of a crap game, the people in the circle·could intervene quickly. But it was his contention that drugs were in the ring between the players and available for people who wanted to purchase them. Sergeant Roy said that when he was walking a beat around the Coliseum that there had been a number of incidents. He claimed, at that time, that it was told to the people that if the incidents continued, that a double patrol would be assigned to the area, that is, each half-block would be patrolled by two men. They would be ordered to arrest everyone in the area who was on the street and perhaps call out the whole turn [all the men on duty at that time in the area] and arrest everyone they could. They used this strategy of arrest for a few hours and according to him, it solved the problem of harassment in the area. Sergeant Roy then said, "If they want to fuck with the police department, then they'd fuck with them." Since the police had been ignoring the crap games in the area, they would now begin to enforce the law and take in everyone who was playing craps on the street. He said, "Yea, we ought to come down with the whole turn, the whole 4–12 turn, and just arrest everybody — lock them all up." They all agreed that it would be a good idea.

The next case is a more obvious instance of investigator's discretion of even less focus or clear intent than the hassling of street people on Fairchild, because there was no interest in making a drug arrest or deterring drug dealing. It was intended simply to establish the police presence in several areas of the city. It is even more significant because the officer who was doing this was assigned that evening to pick up the drug evidence from the various substations of the city and bring it into the central station depository; he was not required to initiate investigations.

After we left the district station, we drove to an area of the city where V.N. said we might see some street dealing or some whores. When we arrived and began slowly cruising through the area, there were several attractive women standing on the street in tight skirts, semi-open blouses, and wigs. They looked seductively toward us until they caught eye-contact with V.N., who began to laugh at them. He called out, "Hey Jim, you still sellin' that stuff cheap?" The person glared and turned away. "He hates to be called Jim, his street name is June. He's out here every night trying to hustle men." I asked if he was a "man." It was explained that he was a cross-dressing man (transvestite)—a homosexual whore who stood on the corner to be picked up mainly by whites. We went around the block and came back, but Jim had moved on. We then drove up Sweet Street and spotted a few of the prostitutes standing in front of various large motels on the circle. Then we travelled south on Sweet, took a U-turn, and came back up Sweet. We spotted a man who was slowly cruising and eyeing women on the curb. We came up behind his car as he parked illegally at the curb by the corner. Our lights illuminated the interior of his car, and the conversation between him and the young woman, who had come over to his car when he gestured to her. As we stayed there, he began to glance back nervously and to look alternatively at us, at her, and in the rearview mirror. After a few minutes she pulled her head out from the window, and he swung out into traffic. We drove on. V.N. was chuckling as he pointed out to me that we had made the ol' boy nervous, and that he might have to pull around the block a couple of times before he "got up his nerve" enough to come back and proposition her again. He then took me to the same scene I returned to a week or so later (Fairchild Lane) [reported in the first case]. A third scene I was shown was called the "most dangerous place in the city," a place where it was said, "a police car cannot go for fear of being shot at, firebombed, or stoned." Earlier in the summer this short dead-end street had been the scene of a fire bombing of a cruiser, and the police had decided not to go in unless they were certain that a crime was being perpetrated at the time. V.N. did not enter the street but simply showed me the place and mentioned that some street dealing goes on here.

A second type of street cruising is a street rip, a failed example of which I observed in Metro one very hot July morning.

I was engaged in a fairly interesting discussion with Detective Bert when Sergeant Roy went out of the room and came back and asked Bert if he would like to go on a street rip-off. Bert was due in court, but it might be continued until 2:30 he said, and he would like to go along. Then Roy asked me if I would like to go along, and of course, I eagerly assented; then Tanner said he wanted to go along. This meant that five men, Roy, Titus, myself, Sergeant Tanner, and Bert would go on a street rip-off. Sergeant Roy explained that a snitch had said that a man was going to be walking up Ramada Avenue with some 200 pills on him and that we could rip him off at that point. There was no planning and no discussion of the details. We simply got a cruiser and went out. All five of us got in the car. Titus, the only black man, began to laugh about the fact that if he was seen in the car with a bunch of white policemen, they would figure that he's either locked up or that he's a snitch. We laughed. Bert said, "I hate to bring this up, but since I'm driving, I'd like to know what the situation is." As we approached Ramada Avenue, Titus filled him in very inexactly, not saying what side of the street, what the people looked like, which way they were headed, except that they were going up to the Vista Hotel [presumably to sell the pills there]. So we went up the street trying to decide whether to park on the east or west side of Ramada Avenue and where along either of those sides to park. Meanwhile, it was getting very near the time that the snitch "Bill" and the two other men were supposed to be walking up the street. At this time we spotted a person who Roy and Titus knew as Bill. Two men were walking along Ramada Avenue at this time. Titus said that perhaps the one was Bill. Bert didn't know what was being said. Finally they stopped. He blocked traffic. Then Titus said, "Go on up so I can see what he looks like." He drove the car up and decided that it was Bill. Roy said it didn't matter because they had no probable cause anyway. Then it was asked whether we should go down and stop in front of a carry-out that was down the way, or up further. It was decided that we would stop on Ramada Avenue and wait at the bus stop. While we were waiting, a middle aged black woman, who was drunk, came up and said hello to Titus who was in the off-side back seat. He said "Hello, how are you doing?" She said she had seen him around. He said, "Yea." She asked, "What are you doing with those police?" Roy answered that they were locking him up for wife-beating and beating his child. A couple of the officers echoed that he was a wife-beater, and they were taking him in. She looked us over quickly and said, "Oh yea?" Then as she turned, she kind of half spat at him and said, "I knew you were a snitch," and she looked at Titus. We all chuckled and laughed because it had been his fear before. He said it was an insult to him to be called a snitch. We all thought it was ironic that she didn't think of him as a policeman at all, but in her scale of values, much lower; an informant. Titus read the sports page and commented off-handedly about the seven-foot-five-inch wrestler who may be signed by the local professional football team. We all engaged in a conversation about the merits and demerits of size and speed on the football field and the possible utility of such a giant, his cost, his relative use compared to the present quarterback, and so on. It was now about 95°, and we now steamed in our own sweat. Meanwhile, no one was carefully watching the street, and it was obvious that anyone who wanted could identify the car and the occupants as police. Certainly anyone coming up the street from the south would have noticed it and cut into an alley and avoided the scene if at all possible. It was finally decided by mutual agreement that nothing was going to happen.

A third type of street cruising is head-hunting. This can be employed when an investigator has no current targets or persons of interest nor any informant who can make drug buys. In one variation of head-hunting, one simply goes into the street with an informant, has him point out dealers, and waits until a deal is observed; drugs may be passed from hand to hand, be concealed in newspapers, or they may be placed near by the dealer—under a garbage can, under a rock, or in some other public place where it is difficult for the police to prove possession. If the drugs are placed in a stash or secret spot, the purchaser hands the money to the dealer and then is told where to find the dope. If a deal is observed, one can jump out of the car, attempt to seize the dealer and the dope if he has both, and make an arrest on the spot. The eyewitness status of the officer provides the probable cause for the arrest.

A second variation of head-hunting is to have an informant attempt to make a buy from a street dealer and then arrest the street dealer at the time in a sort of "hot bust" action. In this situation the hope is to seize the dope and the money and to use the officer's eyewitness account as probable cause. This action may or may not "burn" or expose the snitch as a police informant to street people.

A third variant is based on a call concerning an imminent deal; one goes out and makes the buy. Such events can be generated entirely from unanticipated undercover action. Consider, for example, this story provided by Sergeant Roy.

An undercover man was walking down the street and was asked by a dude "Hey man, want to buy a pink bam [Preludin]?" The undercover man bought it and arrested him on the spot. So we asked him then if "he wanted to help himself out a little bit." He did. He said he knew another guy across town who was dealing in Quaaludes and who was holding about 800 tabs. The guy was trying to "wholesale" them in large lots at about $3.00 a piece [they were being sold on the street at that time for $5.00 a tab]. We went out the next day and picked up the dealer, and he had, you know, in Crayola can with about 650 Quaaludes on him. We picked him up early in the morning, and you know, he'd been dealing since earlier that evening, and he had only 650 tabs, so we figured he'd sold about 150 tabs in those few hours. One hundred fifty tabs times $3.00 means he had made about $450 already. If he'd sold the full 650 more, he'd have what, $1,900 or so. But we picked up about $3,000 in cash on him. So you can never tell. You just pick up some little guy and he turns into a big one like that, you know. That guy is big money. That's big people. Course, I'll take anything [arrests]. I'll take all I can get. A guy can't show goose eggs forever. It doesn't look good on the scandal sheet.We don't really see big dealers, you know. I think . . . we don't see really big dealers; probably a guy who's really successful   [can avoid us   ]. We don't see the really successful ones.

Search Warrants

A more elaborate pattern is found when a buy is made and it becomes the basis for a search warrant. The search warrant, when served, can be the basis for an arrest or arrests, and/or seizure of illegal substances, paraphernalia, stolen property, or guns. The raid described in chapter 8 is one such case. Another example of the search warrant raid approach follows. The choice of this approach is said to be based on "an investigator's style," according to officer Acumen:

Acumen: It's a matter of the investigator's style. He'll do it his way unless he's given a direct, unless a direct order is given—and that's just not done.

PKM: Could you give me an example of an investigator's style?

Acumen: Well, we get a call. Say a guy's dealing out of his store. We'll go out to Southeast, we'll go out there and get a Special Employee [SE] and make a buy. We'll check out the address, go to the office, get a search warrant, go out a couple of days later, rip it off. Now, whether we get anything with a search warrant or not is pure chance. There's a lot of luck in it because you don't know when he gets his drugs in, what time, or when they might be there; you're not sure about the time of the raid, and you might even investigate it for eight months, and still not, you still take potluck when you go in. But you've got one arrest and you can close out a complaint. Now the alternative is to sit on it. Maybe go out for a couple of weeks, watch it, sit in the car and watch it. See who's going in and out. Get a few tag numbers, get some names if you can. Find out if there's some other major violators around. Check out the guy's house—say you find out it's a $60,000 house somewhere out in the suburbs with an El Dorado out in front. And maybe you'll get something out of it. You might go and check the files. The files don't get anybody arrested, but they'll help in investigation. You might want to check with homicide; you might want to get an informant who might give you two or three addresses. Then you can tell the sergeant, and he can take it or not. He can hit him with a search warrant, close it out, rip him off if he wants. But nothing is really spelled out. Nobody ever gives a direct order.

A search-warrant raid crosses the axial line separating investigator discretion and organizational control as exercised by a sergeant. Even this control can be subtle in form, as the investigator who told me the previous story commented:

Maybe you go . . . the higher you go (in the department), the more crime prevention emphasis there is. Even there, there may not be a belief in long-term investigation. When you move away from, when you get away from, when you're interested in long-term investigation, you are in effect moving away from drugs. You're getting, you're focusing on people associated with the distribution of drugs and use, but not with the crime of drugs itself. . . . Investigators just have to figure out where the sergeant draws the line. It's never very clearly laid out. It may just take the form of implicit threat about keeping up your arrest statistics. There's really no direction provided. You might get something okayed, some procedure, or warrant, but the sergeant doesn't necessarily know where it is or where it's going down.

Constraints in Complex Cases

When moving from the purely investigator-controlled activities of cruising, street rip-offs, and head-hunting into the kinds of techniques and actions that require some supervisory approval, such as search-warrant raids or working up the system, one becomes increasingly dependent on supervisors, on other investigators, and increasingly constrained by the law (see table 7.1). A supervisor, a sergeant or above, must review and sign all affidavits for search warrants, must accompany all raids based on such warrants, and is responsible for the conduct of the raid. The line at that point becomes a major line of demarcation in the unit. It separates officers by squads and by individual investigative focus and also indicates the kinds of impact the unit will have. The essential features required for working up are listed in table 7.1. Note that when one intends to use the search-warrant technique or attempts to work up, that one requires not only information and an informant (usually), but also normally requires money and substantial flair. Supervisory accord, if not knowledge and approval, is required. Since such strategies often require complex planning and investigative actions, legal constraints become more important. They may be involved in getting an informant, in making arrangements for his charges to be modified, for him to be released on lessened bail, for his trial date to be set back, etc. Other constraints come with attempts to surveil and/or to use pen registers or electronic communication interception devices. Finally, even if all these elements are present, or in the case of legal constraints, if they are absent, the investigator has to have flair. This may also involve the coordination of a group of people to assist him on surveillance, raids, in getting informants, or in checking out leads.

Money, Flair, and the Law   The previously illustrated types of investigation are possible because they are very short-term; do not tie up the investigator when other members of the squad may need him to help serve a warrant, make a street rip-off or serve an arrest warrant, or when his sergeant wants results; and are very cheap in dollar terms. When one does develop an investigation where a supervisory decision is taken, even by a sergeant, the use and availability of money is critical. An investigation involving only $100–200, initiated with a sergeant's approval, can still be controlled prospectively if it doesn't yield results. This is noted by the lieutenant (Manning, 1977):

A sergeant had found a "dynamite" informant who was making two and three buys a night for him. He gave him $60 for three buys he made last week. He claimed a good snitch such as this one "can make a couple of buys a night, maybe even three and can earn himself $40–50 a night, tax free, maybe work five days a week." Last week he was able, on the basis of the snitch's work, to obtain six to eight warrants and expected to get twelve to fifteen more warrants "in the next couple of weeks" as a result of his work. [The SE had been working about two and one-half weeks.] Only two of these warrants had been served, and the expected warrants had not yet been drafted as affidavits. It appeared that he was paying the snitch over the standard payment if he was paying $60 for three buys. [They were small buys of $5–15 worth of heroin or Preludin, totaling $35. Twenty-five dollars of the sixty was a "bonus" for the work and for the six guns seized in a raid the SE had set up with controlled buys.] Subsequently, at the end of the month, the lieutenant reviewed the payments and found that only about "ten pills had been seized." The SE had been paid some $330 over a twenty-day period. The lieutenant had been alerted to this expenditure and results by the operations sergeant who processed the vouchers. The lieutenant spoke to the sergeant about it.[3]

If the investigation begins and is not curtailed by examination by supervisors as the above incident was because it extended over several weeks, it may still be truncated because the department refuses to: front a large amount of money so that either an agent or informant can

make a large buy, flash a large amount of money to prospective buy-
ers, or let the money "slide" or walk so that even larger amounts of
dope can be bought. This would permit an agent to work up the dealing structure to larger dealers, make a possible larger seizure in a buy-
bust situation, or make more cases by accumulating more hand-to-
hand sales cases. An officer in Metro provided examples of several
cases having these features:

I asked Redmon what his biggest seizure was. He said a quarter of a
pound of cocaine and another quarter of a pound that could have been
seized but the uniformed man at the door turned him away. He was
the man who was securing the front door. He considered "two-three
ounces to a pound a good seizure." Once he paid $3,800 for four
ounces of heroin and made a sale case. LEAA fronted him a $8,000
"flash roll" for the purpose of making that buy. He had made this
$3,800-buy as the result of a chance event. When he was working mid-
nights driving the narcotics cruiser [picking up drug evidence from the
precincts], he got a call from a uniformed man who had made a routine
traffic stop. The patrol officer wanted a narcotics cruiser to take a look
at the man. The person stopped appeared to be on drugs and was
shreaking and yelling at the top of his voice not to search his car. It was
very easy for Redmon to search it because he had just hit six parked
cars and the car was pretty well ripped up. He searched through the
car, looked in the air conditioning vents, under the seats and so on. He
found several kinds of drugs: cocaine, TCP, many kinds of pills, heroin,
and marijuana. It turned out that the driver was a student who was one
of the main dealers at a local university. He was able to spin him. The
dealer got to his middleman. The middleman was buying from "Reds,"
one of the big dealers in town. Redmon was able to set up a four-ounce
buy from Reds. He closed the sale case with the four-ounce purchase.

PKM: What happens when you reach a point where you might be
asked to deal?
He said when he was working undercover in "Hippie Center" he used
to buy four or five spoons a day. He played the role that he was only a
"go-fer" for a guy who lived out of town who was using the stuff or dealing in it.

PKM: That must be one of the problems of working undercover — that
you would become embedded in a set of social relationships at one
level that makes it difficult for you as undercoverman to move up to a
higher level.
He agreed.

Redmon: If you're trying to get at a guy who's smallest deal is $1,200,
and you want to buy $50-bag off him, he'll laugh at you. The problem is
that the people across the hall [officials] don't ever want you to spend a

lot of money on buys and they want a search warrant with the lowest possible cost. In the case of the four ounces of heroin [above], I wanted to make a $125-buy because that was the smallest deal the guy would make. I didn't think the officials were going to approve it because it is too expensive for a search warrant, but they did. We had this problem with a man who was dealing and we were able to get him with $30,000 worth of acid, but the smallest deal he'd do was about $500. When you're talking about LSD at $0.45 a tab, that's a lot of material.

In these stories the first evidence of patterning by administration is noted. But it should be appreciated that in the "dynamite snitch" case it was only an issue after the fact when the administrative sergeant brought the spending of Sergeant B to the attention of the lieutenant who, in turn, spoke with Sergeant B. In the case precipitated by a call to Investigator Redmon, the patterning came as a result of administrative control over large amounts of money. The amount was more than could be accumulated by a sergeant in his kitty, or in the reserve that individual officers might have built up, or could be created by using their own money for the buy. But the transition point from discretion to prospective/retrospective control comes at the point of a large amount of money or after-the-fact expenditure.

Other constraints upon investigator discretion, even when the case is investigator or informant initiated, are legal. These typically come after an arrest, except in the case of wire taps when prior permission in the form of an approved affidavit is required. Thus the legal controls on investigative tactics in particular are very weak and for the most part occur after the fact; examples are the use of the exclusionary rule to suppress evidence in hearings after the arrest; or refusal of the prosecutor's office to accept or to paper a case. These legal constraints work in some fashion to pattern future action, but I cannot say how. Consider the following examples:

Sergeant Roy gave me an example of a case that was "no papered" by the U.S. Attorney: They had information from a snitch, who'd made a buy on the premises, that a furniture store owner on H Street was selling dope out of the office. He had a guard at the front door who would let in one person at a time to look at the goods, and a secretary who sat at a desk outside his office. Roy explained, "After the snitch had made the buy, we got a warrant. We sent in a couple of officers in street clothes, a man and a woman, so that the owner would think they wanted to look at some furniture. When we served the warrant, we had a uniformed patrolman come in with us. When we entered the inner office, we found and seized one ounce of good dope in the safe. We asked the secretary if she ever went into the boss's inner office and she said, 'No, no, she didn't ever go back there.' The only file that she had anything to do with was the one file where she locked her purse up. The guard said, 'No,' that 'the boss had told him that he didn't want him ever to go around that back office.' " When they took the case to the U.S. Attorney's office, he no-papered it, saying that there wasn't proof that the dope belonged to the owner: The owner wasn't there, and it couldn't be proved that it was his; anyone could have put it there. Roy's argument was that it should have been papered because the people should have decided whether the man was guilty, not the prosecuting attorney; that is, a jury of twelve people should have decided. He gave the following reasons in a fairly rambling session: (1) Maybe there'd be a chance of "work him" between the time of the charge and the trial. "Maybe we could bend him a little," he said (2) He might plead later anyway. (3) Let the jury decide, let twelve people decide, whether or not there was sufficient evidence for the arrest of the person.

This case presents a somewhat different perspective on the purported "anticourt" bias of the police because it suggests that under certain conditions the police view a court trial as valuable. In this case it might have meant that the person would plead out the case, that he might have been willing to work if the charge had been made against him, or that he would have provided other evidence prior to a trial. If he does go to trial, of course, it is often expensive and may create financial hardships for the defendant. This is considered part of the game and is viewed with some amusement by officers. In some senses, Sergeant Roy was taking a rather "philosophic" view when, on another occasion, he said that he was guided by what he felt people wanted him to do and what the courts would allow. He was rationalizing the arrest of a small dealer:

If people want us to go out and drag them in by their hair, then we'll do it, but they gotta pass the law so we can do the job. But, if they want to have legal controls on us and the courts and all, well, we'll bring them in, and the courts will just release them.

People don't know, you know. They really don't care about something like Quaaludes. There may be fatties on the jury for all you know. People are really not worried about something like that — a diet pill, they think. All they really care about is coke and heroin, that's all. Well, you know, they care about their kids on a tricycle getting in trouble using that shit. I'm worried about this myself: My kid getting into that marijuana stuff and going right to heroin. You know, somebody was telling me about how these other countries, they use—Jamaica, India, and places like that—they use marijuana, and how it's not bothered them. But how do we know? I mean, do we want to be like Jamaica? Jamaica's not living up to our level of productivity, and why do we want to be like them, anyway?

Working an Informant   A third constraint results from the relative skill one had in being able to "work" an informant. This is a most important form of constraint upon the working of cases in both units. The following discussion utilizes interviews gathered in Metro, and primarily outlines the problematic features of working a case in Metro in which there ·are crossracial nuances to informant-agent interaction, competitive aspects of the relationships between the district vice units and the central vice, and in which in general officers are much less trusting of information they receive. The level of tolerance of persons is lower, and the level of "paranoia" is higher in Metro than in Suburban. One way to examine this process of working an informant is to note to what degree information received is embedded in a context and how this context makes the credibility of the source a crucial issue in pursuing the case. The linear development of a case is implied by these features: from information to informant or vice-versa, hence to money (controlled to some extent by supervisors), and then to flair, which is itself constrained or controlled by supervision, by the law, and by those of working informants.

Situational features of information-evaluation are extremely salient in the agent-informant dominant mode. Most of the important or actionable information is received by narcotics officers from informants. Therefore the context within which the information is presented is important. Prior to an assessment of any actionable consequences of decisions and the prospective evaluation of the meaning of one's action comes evaluation of the information. Narcotics information cannot be separated from its source. Thus the investigator's problem is that of assessing the credibility of information and the informant. This is so because although there are endless possibilities for manipulation of the paper associated with a case, the matter of face remains a salient issue. Officers seek to maintain the appearance of capability, honesty, credibility, and responsibility with their peers and their informants. Failures or errors such as a controlled buy that falls through, a buy-bust that leads to a shoot-out, a surveillance that ends in a wild goose chase, hitting the wrong door, or "coming up empty" on a raid (no drugs or principals arrested), failing to properly interrogate an informant to get adequate information about a house, and the like are all sources of embarrassment. They demonstrate publicly that the officer's claim to valid status as a competent officer is unstable or problematic. Maintaining self-esteem, then, is not simply a matter of adequate performance of uncertain tasks, but depends on the symbolic meanings attached to failure and situational competence, especially in work with informants.

Information relevant to a drug case is always embedded in a context or situation in which the agent involvement is typically high and the outcomes are problematic. Two issues gain centrality: the credibility of the information received and the indicators of manipulation.

Credibility can be damaged or established by one or more of several indices that would be of concern to a good narcotics agent.[4] First, if the informant is discovered to have lied to the agent, revealed either by information provided by another agent, by other informants, or by arrestees, his information is considered malicious, and it will cast doubt on subsequent information he provides.

Second, if the informant exaggerates or tells nonmalicious lies particularly with regard to where he can make buys, from whom, of what size, and with what frequency, then he is viewed as less than credible. Sources of contradictory information are also characterized as potentially deceptive but must be sought and used by the agent desiring confirmation of an informant's information.

Third, the informant may provide "old information" that is already known to the agent or to his partner, or information that is insufficiently precise to permit an affidavit for a search. The informant may not know when, in what quantities, and from whom a person obtains his dope.

problem of prediction remains complex. An officer must be able to work with relatively high degrees of uncertainty with respect to a given domain (information on which an affidavit can be filed, buying abilities, information concerning dealing activities, buy-bust trustworthiness). The officer frequently must assess the relevance of second-hand information and base his next move on the information received. Since the credibility of the source of the information itself is always the primary question, the level of information or the content of a message is a secondary or even tertiary concern.

A second set of concerns are the indices of informants "trying to get over on you." There are abundant indicators that are used by agents to detect the honesty and integrity of the informant and, by extension, his information. Manipulation, as well as reduced credibility, is indicated if the informant is caught giving erroneous information. This is indicated, for example, if he tells the officer that there are no guns in a house and guns are found when a raid goes down, if he says someone is dealing who everyone knows is dealing, or claims he can buy from a large number of persons and then refuses to do so, equivocates, or is vague about what he knows. Manipulation is indicated when a specific task is agreed to and the informant does not carry it out, such as making a buy.

Similar problems of controlling the informant arise when an informant does not arrive on time for an appointment or does not call when he promises to do so. These reasons are indicative of the degree of control the officer maintains over an informant. Almost anything can be asked of an informant by an officer, although it may not be legal or proper; therefore, any refusal can indicate that the officer is not in control, that "the snitch is running him, he's not running the snitch." Certain rules may be used to set the initial conditions of employment of informants who were working off beefs.[6]

There are several issues bearing on the conditions of employment which also suggest credibility. The first is the nature of the state of, or the quality of, relations between the narcotics unit and the district attorney (D.A.). If the narcotics unit has a good working relationship with the D.A. and it is such that no investigators report having any problems when "dismissal in the interest of justice" is recommended, or when certain types of probationary sentences are recommended because of "help received" by the defendant-informant, the current working relationship between the narcotics unit and the D.A. serves to reinforce the credibility of the bargains made by individual investigators. The second consideration is the "contract" between the investigator and the informant. Unlike the first contract, this may be written, but it is usually an oral agreement between the investigator and the informant.[7] There is some pressure on the investigator to act credibly, and the credibility of the investigator is based upon a tacit agreement with the D.A. This agreement is reflected in the expectations narcs have of their informants.

As is implied by this discussion of the conditions of work, there is pressure from the informant upon the officer to clarify his status. The informant also seeks extension of his trial date by procrastination, failure to show, failure to call the officer after promising to do so, etc. In each of these cases a dilemma of trust emerges, for although the officer depends on the information an informant supplies he cannot appear to allow the informant to manipulate him. This is true not only because it is a matter of face, but because the information may insure self-protection or reduce the uncertainty of the work.

There are great pressures to form collusive relationships with snitches in order to frame or "flake" people (plant evidence) or to use violence against the snitches to control them, to allow expendiency to rule and work informants for small cases, and to permit lateral snitching. Lateral snitching, a common practice, involves turning in people who are smaller than or equal to one's self in terms of access to dope, thus maintaining an ineffectual impact, in most cases, since informants are generally at a low level themselves. Informants, in turn, attempt to alter the timing of their court appearances, want protection for themselves or others, and may ask for small loans and protection from minor charges they may have been hit with between their first arrest and trial. The officer, on the other hand, wants to maintain the mystique around precisely what his obligations are and use this vagueness to manipulate the informant.

Two of the most damaging activities suspected of snitches by agents, which are signs of manipulation, are use and/or dealing in drugs. If the snitch comes to work (to make a controlled buy) "dirty," then he is a suspect. Since he is high, he is assumed not to be motivated to work to get the money to buy the drugs he needs. Second, when high, he no longer cares about getting accurate information. Detail is helpful in planning and executing raids and may insure accuracy of the affidavit. One cannot subsequently tell, if he does not bring out the bag of dope, whether he has shot up inside after making a buy or not. If not, he may be pocketing the money without working. It should be emphasized that using drugs is assumed; if you are working someone because of their knowledge of the drug scene, then it is naive and not very strategic to deny that they are or to expect that they are not using drugs if they can. Informants would be of little use if they were not using. Thus use has to be a highly situated matter that is denied while being essential to the success of narcotics law enforcement.

A final indication that the snitch may be manipulating an agent, is evidence that he may be dealing drugs while working for the police department. This means that he is using his status as an informant to carry on a business and that he may be informing to the police to reduce his competition. This is serious insofar as he is seen as being in a position to make a profit from drug dealing using his informant's activities as a "cover." The police department in this way is not only keeping the dealer in business but supplying force to reduce the informant's competition. Making money from informing is assumed to be a legitimate motive, but business success is not an intended consequence of informing.

Other Constraints

These very complex matters of money, supervision, the law, and working informants are a set of formidable constraints on drug law enforcement. The most carefully developed plans of officers have a way of going wrong even when the conditions I have outlined do exist because there are other more powerful forces that work against the development of a successful case involving either a search-warrant raid or working up the dealing system. These constraints are of the following kind and are so complexly interrelated with the job that the elements or propositions from enacted environment notions frequently become explanations for failure. Included is the irregular behavior of the target groups, which limits the capacity to plan, to observe, intercept their messages, or catch them at crucial times when they are holding dope; the uneven nature of the dealing activity of target persons—the fact that drug enforcement must depend on "doper's time" means that there are enormous periods of waiting for something to happen: for someone to call, for someone to appear, for someone to contact someone else; the uneven capacity of officers and supervisors to think, plan, and coordinate others; absolute limits on the numbers of persons, money, and time that are available, no matter what the intent of the organization; the aleatory aspects of the situation of arrest itself —peoples' plans change, they misunderstand, they are ignorant, they become frightened, equipment fails: batteries fail, buildings obstruct transmissions, cars run out of gas at critical times, guns misfire or jam, radios fail to function, etc. Above all, of course, only partial information is available to officers because they must rely on the word of informants so frequently.

The limits of this secondary evaluation problem cannot be overly emphasized for it is one of the most important constraints facing both units. Unlike other mechanical processes, which depend only on the system's technical or informational capacity to operate at a given level, investigators must work within these limits and, in addition, must evaluate the quality of the information that is entered into the system. Because this evaluation in Metro and other drug enforcement units takes place only in the head of the investigator, subsequent decisions can be premised on an unvalidated assumption: the initial information was as it is reported and came from a credible source. This is the unavoidable basis of almost all drug enforcement and as such is the basis of those sequences of action that are captured in the official statistics issued by agencies of control. Enormous energy is thus generated on the basis of a thin texture of information gathered by an individual investigator or by him and his partner. The interconnection of dealing and enforcement worlds outlined in chapter 3 and the paradox of enforcement that "you can't trust anything a junkie tells you," and "you have to rely on the informant" for virtually everything one undertakes come into play. They are undesirable and yet unavoidable constraints.

Suburban

In the Suburban unit, the conditions of interaction between agents and their informants are rather different. These conditions, matters over which the individual agents have little control, pattern the types of inter-actions that are found in the unit and the prevalence of certain strate-gies and tactics. In table 7.1, the first three types of actions, cruising/hassling, street rip-off, and head-hunting are rare events in Suburban. They may not happen at all there. This is true for at least three reasons, all of which are functions of the political, ecological, and social struc-ture of the areas in which the two groups work.

Ecological, Structural, and Organizational Constraints

Suburban does not have a street-dealing scene within the county; there are no traditional "copping areas" for buying heroin or other drugs (Hughes, 1977). The closest functional equivalent would be shopping malls in the several large cities within the county. Officers do not choose to work cases from shopping malls because they view it as almost insulting or degrading to buy marijuana from a fourteen-year-old. Further, it would not yield an adult arrest and might involve the son or daughter or an important business person. Any young person can buy grass in any shopping mall in the county. This ecological factor is complemented by the availability of heroin and other drugs just "over the line" in Metro City and the legal limitations that make officers hesi-tant to make arrests in Metro City or in a nearby county, although they do. Thus there is no copping area, no local knowledge of users who "hang out" there, and no concentration of pads, dealers' places, or dealing scenes in Suburban. There can be no hassling or cruising or street-rips. Head-hunting takes the form of serving arrest warrants or picking up people on indictments after buys have been made from them and cases are being closed out.

There are also several matters of organizational structure that limit the options of the individual agents. When the unit began, it was almost exclusively an undercover dope-buying operation that used arrest warrants and buy-bust strategies. Informants were used to "cut in" the officers so that they could make buys and possibly buy up. This strategy is well described by a sergeant:

PKM: Tell me a little bit about how you try to investigate a case once you get some information.

Sergeant: We first get some information; we find out somebody is dealing. Then we get the background information on the subject. We might get his bank account, tag numbers, friends, even the clothes he wears, we might stake out his house. Put some surveillance on him and watch his goings and comings and who is visiting, etc. We then try to find out who we know that knows him. If we have an informant who knows him, we hope that maybe the informant is under the gun or working off a beef. We may threaten him. We try to find out who he is getting it from. If we can get a buy or two off him, then we try to get the informant to cut one of our men in with him, to make a buy from him. Then we try to arrange a meeting after he is in to eliminate the informant. We might start with buying a gram and then go to a quarterpiece, then ounce or pound buys if we can.

Another sergeant further explained their strategy:

We prefer that we get a man cut in for hand-to-hand buys. This avoids the snitch's having to testify in court or questions about the credibility of the informant in court. . . . I feel that we are not pushing our snitches hard enough, that we should just walk in with them — say that we're going to go right on in.[8]

This strategy continues, with most of the officers having been in the unit more than twenty months at the time of the study. There were no rules about entry or exit, and there was some concern at the time of the study that these officers may be "burned out," getting too close to the street people, or becoming too well known in the area. Also, the organizational structure and the environment are somewhat consistent because the use of young white agents (all were in their twenties and thirties, and all but one was male) working undercover made it possible to buy dope in the area where the principal problems were defined as heroin, cocaine, and PCP (animal tranquilizers that act as a psychedelic drug).

It is interesting that in an affluent county that is politically sensitive and has a police department that maintains its image as a "service" department,[9] they should have developed a strategy for falling on big dealers and using the buy-bust, working-up investigative strategy. This is a politically acceptable position since it leads to dramatic seizures, involves "falling on" black and Hispanic people, and leads to publicly very visible enforcement. The events and statistics, including the street value of drugs, are utilized for publicity purposes, and the strategy is predicated on the availability of large amounts of front money and flash money from the county and from DEA. The strategy is compatible with the political milieu of the county since it deals with minority populations in a dramatic way, which substantially affirms the upper-middle-class notion about drugs and drug dealing, and it is made possible by the upper-middle-class population in the county, who strongly support the police. This political centrality of the county probably led to the $25,000 grant for use in drug enforcement and the $200,000 organized crime grant from LEAA. The strategy is also compatible in that it virtually obviates concern with marijuana arrests. Marijuana busts would be politically controversial in the county. Furthermore, the state's attorney made the announcement in 1975 that he did not want to prosecute personal possession or small seizure cases.

The sergeants now working in the unit had long experience in drug enforcement. Sergeant Jones began the unit around 1968, and recruited Sergeant Smith shortly thereafter. Both had worked the streets and were known and respected in Metro and in their own units. Smith had been shot in the most important event in the history of the unit: the murder of an undercover agent, Officer Wilson, in a planned buy-bust that collapsed into a shoot-out in a motel.[10]

The similarity in class and backgrounds between investigators and their quarry is in distinct contrast to the situation in Metro where 61 percent of the investigators are white, the city is nearly 72 percent black, and the heroin-using population on which they focus is entirely black. The number of informants is small in Suburban, no more than "25 or so at the present time" was the estimate of the supervising lieutenant. (But he told me he did not know how many informants there were in the files, that he did not ask the men, and they were more comfortable if he did not ask about or know who or what was in the informant file.) It was not possible to find out how many were actually in use at the time or how many were on file in the unit. Ironically, although the unit had a large informant-miscellaneous information buy fund of $25,000, the officers preferred informants who were working off a beef to those who were paid. They would not pay a person who was working off a charge, except in special circumstances when the person they were after was large enough to justify the payment as an additional motivation for the informant. Unlike Metro, they paid for seizures other than of marijuana at approximately 10 percent of their value. They had paid nine rewards in the previous six months, the largest being $1,700 dollars for information that led to a successful raid on a PCP lab. These conditions, the political and ecological structure of the county, the strategy and tactics of the unit, its sociodemographic composition, and the availability of money, work to over determine officers' options. These conditions, as well as the use of "locals," or case assignments, reduce the officer to working either toward buy-busts or search-warrant serving outcomes, with the possible consideration of conspiracy cases involving surveillance, pen registers, or communications intercepts (wire taps) (see figure 8.1).

The size of the unit and consensus among the sergeants, as well as the tradition within the unit of working undercover, also makes supervision somewhat closer qualitatively. In several instances when I was observing the unit, full section meetings were called. In one meeting, the strategy of hand-to-hand buys was discussed at length, with Sergeant Smith emphasizing that too many cases were being lost because people were not making out arrest cards for hand-to-hand buys. They were hoping to work up to a buy-bust and file possession, intent to distribute, and conspiracy to deal charges, rather than prosecute only on a sale case. It also involved more paperwork to make out the arrest cards after each buy when one was planning to buy-bust a person, charge him heavily, and then have him negotiate out of it. But at least a sale charge could be filed, and the case would not be lost if the buy-bust failed.

In another meeting I observed, discussion of a strategy for "getting" a notorious dealer in the local area, Hampster Gerbil, took fully an hour. A number of people contributed to the discussion volunteering tactics of surveillance, who might be able to buy from him, costs and benefits of renting an apartment in the unit in which Gerbil worked in order to maintain surveillance on him, arguing about his volume, who works with him, and other miscellaneous facts. These group discussions were never held in Metro, and it was even rare for a squad to discuss an immediate matter at hand—a raid on which they were all going to participate.

These ecological and organizational features are the context within which the following cases were worked. The outcomes are ordered by the extent to which they require organizational control and collective action or, conversely, the extent to which the agent is constrained by persons, rules, and groups outside his control. To show that not all cases work out or produce as planned, examples of failed operations are also provided.

Watching, Hassling, and Confronting

The closest thing to "street hassling" that took place in Suburban was simply watching certain kinds of people ("colored"), in certain places (around the Metro line). One investigator told me:

We drove by a downtown area and the officer said, "See all these colored people? You can sit here all day and observe them, and everyone of them looks suspicious. You could spend the whole day checking out suspicious looking colored people right here. Because I've done it before working [here]." To this officer virtually any "colored person" is suspicious and therefore cause to be concerned and watchful.

The same frustration attends making buys in an area where one does not know the people and does not have informants to identify them later, that is, if one does not have a traditional copping area within one's district: one can attempt to make sales cases on "cold buys" of small amounts of marijuana from people, but the sellers are so young that it makes prosecution unlikely, the drugs are sold in such amounts that the case would not be prosecuted or are bought from people known only by a nickname or a street name. Without a name arrest warrants would be difficult to serve even if issued, since the person could not be subsequently picked up in a given area or located by name or address. Viewing people smoking joints of marijuana in cars is common in any large city, and it was common in the county. It was frustrating, one investigator said, because there was so little evidence and so little one could do:

He claimed that he could have copped five ounces of marijuana by now but he wouldn't have known the names of people whom he bought from anyway. It would not have been bought from a large source, according to him, so would not be worthwhile. "That's why we can't jump on people who are smoking joints. When Gun and I were coming back from an investigation the other night we looked out the window of the car and saw people in the car next to us smoking a joint. But we couldn't do anything about it."

It could be argued that another functional equivalent of "street hassling" in Suburban was calling people on the phone and "shaking 'em up a little." This was done by a young officer in Suburban while I observed:

Then Pete Collage got on the phone with a man. He asked him if he had been at one time employed by Tiger Tool Company. The man said no. Then he asked again what Pete's name was, and how to spell it, and what police department he worked for. Pete asked him if he had ever known a certain man, whose name he gave him. The fellow denied knowing him. Pete told him that the second man had used the number of a medical society to purchase chemicals, such as lactose, from Fish Chemicals Company. He asked if he'd ever known him, his present address or phone number, and the subject denied any knowledge. Meanwhile, I was looking at Pete. He was giving me broad winks. I wasn't sure what was going on. He then asked him if he knew about this lactose and explained to the listener that lactose was used to cut heroin and that the man whose name he had given him was suspected of dealing in narcotics. The person on the other end asked how he had gotten his name and why he'd called him. Pete replied that "he was not at liberty" to tell him what the nature of the investigation was. Pete asked him if he'd be willing to testify to a grand jury of this ignorance. He denied knowledge of any of the details of this person's activities, although he did say that he was a friend of this person. After he'd hung up, Pete began to laugh and explained to me that this fellow was the best friend of a major dealer in narcotics and that he knew that the two of them were dealing. He had apparently intended to frighten them because they were under investigation. Pete further explained to me that the other fellow had been denying that he knew the person, that the person had said that he only knew him through his wife, he didn't know his address or phone number, and knew nothing about any of his activities that might involve lactose. The call was simply a way of scaring him, and he assumed that the guy would be, at that minute, calling his buddy and telling him that they were under surveillance. Apparently, frightening him was expected to have some slight deterrent effect.

Another functionally equivalent alternative is what is called in Suburban "confronting them with Plan A or Plan B." This was Sergeant Jones's term and was always a source of some amusement when it was suggested as a solution to a case. It is discussed in more detail under citizen tips in chapter 8 because it often issues from a citizen tip that is not itself legally actionable but leads officers to observe the scene. For example, if a citizen calls to say that marijuana plants are being grown in the window of a house, officers may go and investigate it, and then talk to the people inside, suggesting that they get rid of the plants and we "forget about it" (Plan A), or that the police will have to come back with a search warrant and "tear up the house a little" and seize all the evidence of manufacturing of illicit substances. (It is also mentioned that this carries a fifteen-year federal sentence (Plan B). If the same situation is produced by an informant tip, or if the informant claims he has made a previous buy from the person, knows the person has a record or previous arrest for drugs, or is on parole, then the same strategy will be used to coerce him to surrender his drugs. Usually, as Sergeant Jones told me, the evidence is an insufficient basis for obtaining an affidavit for a search warrant, so the intent is to scare or extort the drugs from people. Such actions are not written up since no arrests are involved, and unless they resulted from a local, there is no need to close the case.

Buy and Bust

Buy-bust is the dominant strategy within the class of cases determined by agent-informant interaction in Suburban. One cannot determine or calculate what percent of cases are buy-busts, what percent of those are successful (how defined?) or unsuccessful because no file is opened or made on a case that falls through or doesn't go down. Thus there can be no question of establishing the representative nature of the cases presented. The best that can be made of such a situation is to present both successful buy-busts and unsuccessful ones and compare some of the essential features.

In the Able case, Jones [an informant] had offered to take Jim Cohen and Fred Fisher to cop from Able, in this case an ounce of cocaine and an ounce of heroin. Jones and Cohen went to the shopping center; Fisher followed in another car. They assumed that the dealer might try to rip them off, so Fisher took the money in his car. Then it was agreed in the shopping center that they would go to another house to make what turned out to be a heroin buy. They suspected that the dealer suspected that he was being followed by a sergeant of the Organized Crime Section [he was], and therefore asked to stop by a house. He stopped by the house, but he didn't go in; he went around back. They decided to arrest him on the spot, and they did. They had a search warrant for his house, but not for the second house: the first had been the location of a previous bust. They recovered a lot of implements, tools, and marijuana plants, but no large amount of drugs was seized. I suggested that some police departments might have gone in and hit the door of the house at which he had asked to stop. Jim patiently explained to me that they didn't have the evidence to do that; that Jones had not gone in, that he had only gone around the side of the house, and that they weren't sure that he actually handled the dope, or that he *ever* possessed any dope. They did not attempt to get a search warrant for that house. I suggested that, for example, it might have been possible for Fred to claim that he had seen the fellow go into the house and that there was probable cause to believe that there was dope in the house.

A second case of buy-bust was more successful.

Fred and Pete discussed a case in which they had bought from a guy and then executed a buy-bust. First, they bought one ounce of heroin for $2,000. In the course of this, the man who sold it said that "his man" [connection] would be in the basement, but he would not show himself. They were able to check the license tags of the car parked outside in front of the house and discover who it was. Then they ordered a second ounce-and-a-half of heroin, which would cost them $3,000. They came back later for the second buy and subsequently created a buy-bust situation. They were able to seize the $3,000 and the ounce-and-a-half of dope. Then they arrested the guy who sold them the dope and his source, who was again in the basement waiting. They returned to the station, at which point a sergeant talked with them. They convinced the guy to allow them to make a consent search of the house under the agreement that they would not charge him with any of the dope they found there (Plan A). They returned to the house, with him and recovered $1,500 of the $2,000 that they had paid for the first ounce.

The following examples suggest some of the vicissitudes of buy-busts (recall Officer Wilson, note 10.) They are considered to be among the most volatile situations.

PKM: I asked Officer Fox if he had ever participated in a buy-bust situation.[11]

1. The example given was nearly a buy-bust. He had the arrest warrant for one person. Then they put in a slightly bigger order from him so he would have to buy from his source. He and his partners had put in an order for three pounds of grass. What they had planned to do when the bigger order came in was to get his source with the three-pound order, get a search warrant, and hit the house. However, they were following the fellow they wanted to bust (he had the marijuana in his car) to his place to make the transaction, and got caught in traffic. They decided that they better jump out and make the arrest. They got on the radio and asked the uniform car who was in traffic in the third lane and up to the right to assist them in stopping this man. Then his partner jumped out. According to Fox, if your partner jumps out at this point, you've got to go. Fox had to follow him. They arrested the guy with the arrest warrant on the street. He said this is a very dangerous kind of situation because if a "nervous" cop, say an off-duty policeman going home, or a federal policeman or FBI man, or whatever, on his way out of town, had seen this, he would not know what had happened. He might draw a gun and try to intervene since all he sees is people rushing out of cars and dashing around in traffic with guns drawn. It was fortunate that the uniform car was there to help.[12]

2. Fox told me of another case. He had an informant from another county who took Fox to cop five pounds of marijuana. The plan was that after he had copped the five pounds, he would take the bad buy home, and come back to serve the search warrant on the house from which he bought it, and seize the remaining grass. He had, in other words, the source—the informant had cut him into the deal and he had seen the deal go down. Fox had paid $700 for this marijuana. When they served the search warrant, they seized only two pounds of grass. A supervisor took him aside and said, "You don't buy five and seize two." He noted, "It's tricky to ask for just above what he's holding so he has to go to his source." It is also tricky to buy an amount that forces him to get extra poundage or extra weight from his man, yet not overestimate the amount that he has in total. In other words, if you order five pounds thinking that the man is holding ten, that's not bad; you might get a five-pound seizure and a five-pound buy; however, if, as in this case, the man is holding seven and you buy five, then the seizure is only two, which is the reverse of what one hopes for.

3. Another of Fox's cases involved a situation where one investigator

had been cut in by an informant to make a buy. He made the buy — a fairly large one of grass. Then Paul Gun went back and did a $1,700 buy-bust on the same man. In the buy-bust situation, as he pointed out, they didn't have a search warrant. They wanted to make the buy-bust. He had to come back in this previous case in the seizure of the two pounds and ID him because they only had an arrest warrant. Apparently they talked their way in, and after the buy served an arrest warrant on two guys. A search warrant was based upon a previous buy, which is the basis for a distribution count; there was also the buy of that evening; and there were two counts that were the result of arrest warrants. In this case, the search warrant was the basis of the seizure, and the arrest warrants were used on the two other people involved in the distribution.

4. We waited in a bar between 6:00 and approximately 9:30 for the call. The situation was this: Fred was awaiting a call from a fellow who was going to sell them one hundred pounds of grass. The man was driving down from New York. The informant was someone that Fred and Jim had busted. He was supposed to call between 4:00 and 5:00. He didn't. They finally called him. He said that he understood his man was on the way. They continued to call approximately every half hour over the next three hours. Various information was given, and it was speculated first of all that the fifty pounds had arrived and he had gone back to get the thirty pounds. They were debating whether or not to buy the fifty pounds or to wait and get the extra thirty and seize it all. They didn't know where this other thirty pounds was or what the situation was. The snitch speculated that maybe the person had been busted on the way down. They wondered if they did wait to buy the dope, whether somebody else might buy it. Or, if they put it off, they might lose the arrest. Therefore, they could not decide whether to buy the smaller amount, try to make a buy-bust, wait for the larger amount, and if they waited, run the risk of having someone else buy it, and then having to wait until another large shipment came in. So there was a question of how strongly they wanted to push this informant to bring the deal in. In effect, we spent the entire three hours waiting for calls that never came in, and finally decided about 9:30 – 10:00 to go home. We went back to the station, locked up the station, and·there were jokes made about "going out on locals."

We spent the late afternoon of the next day waiting for the same person to call. The information was that the fellow had had an accident, and the second man had to drive 120 miles or so to pick him up. He was said to have left around 4:30 P.M.

I went out the next day, arriving about 3:00 P.M. The entire narcotics group was seated in the investigators' office talking about various cases. I discovered later that this was because paychecks were coming. A sergeant discussed the buy that Fred, Jim, and Pete had been attempting to set up for the last week. The latest news was, according to Fred, that the guy didn't want to deal until after he'd attended a funeral. [I think there was general concensus among them, which I noted by the way they shifted their feet and cast their eyes down, that they assumed that the deal was in fact off or, more precisely, it would never go down in spite of their work, planning, and persistence. Nevertheless, they made plans.] The sergeant instructed them that there should be no more three-man undercover operations. [I think because it can "burn" them, and with a small unit, that reduces workable personnel. Their names or faces may get around to users in the area.] No more than two men at a time should work undercover on a case, according to the sergeant. There was some joking about setting up the deal because Fred, Jim, and Pete are quite good friends and obviously enjoy working together. A discussion ensued concerning where the deal ought to go down; a busy street in Metro City had been suggested. [I'm not sure if the idea was to grab the guy and take him to Suburban County and lock him up or what, or develop some ruse to say that they had to come back to Fred's house to pick up the money, etc.] They were still planning to develop a buy-bust for the following night.

The problematic aspects of narcotics enforcement are seen in these examples of the buy-bust scenario. The irregular behavior of dealers and users, from the agent's point of view, makes the phone calls often long-awaited, and their timing inconvenient. The inability to plan or make contingency plans for everything that might happen, and conversely the rationale that this belief gives someone time to act spontaneously and impetuously in contradiction to a plan, is obvious in many buy-busts. The limited personnel available for the coverage that officers wish to provide for each other often means that they are caught up in situations in which they would rather not be involved. They must act without adequate support. Because in the buy-bust situation large amounts of money are often on the scene, which is legally critical since it is evidence and personally important to drug dealers for obvious reasons, and guns to protect it if it is not small amounts of marijuana, much risk is involved. Further, such an arrest is almost certain to result in conviction because it involves a hand-to-hand transaction with money and drugs as evidence, as well as, ideally, eyewitness evidence of other officers. This is well known to dealers and makes them wary and jumpy.

A final element of the situation makes it tense for officers. The most common place for a meet for a buy-bust is a shopping mall or large parking lot with many people nearby. It is felt that this gives protection to participants, but if a fight or chase does ensue, it can be dangerous to citizens. The central metaphor in buy-bust is escalation, because one wants to make larger buys from a dealer larger than the person from whom the first buys are made, one hopes to involve larger and larger amounts of cash, and thus the risk to all parties increases. Agents are worried because the money might be ripped off, and drug dealers are worried about their drugs being ripped off as well. Both groups carry weapons into such scenes. Both distrust the other. Like the other kinds of enforcement, the higher the risk the higher the gain, but the greater the loss if something goes wrong. It very often does.

Warrants and Raids
The search warrant/raid combination is said to be less commonly used in Suburban than the buy-bust but is still an important part of the operation, partly because it is an alternative to buying up to the point of making a buy-bust work. If the case cannot be pushed further, either because a person refuses to divulge his source or is buying from someone at the same level as he himself deals, or because there is too little money (setting aside agent-expedient acts), then a raid may be said to close out the case. The following case, a raid in which I participated, was based on information provided by an informant who made a buy from a previous case on which Officer Fisher had made an arrest. The informant was working off the beef, making the buy on the raidee. The raid is described in some detail below because it contains a number of significant aspects of raids that come up empty; the frustration, the danger, the anger that is involved, as well as the human pathos, tragedy, and insensitivity that is revealed.

As I walked into the investigator's room at about two o'clock, I heard Don Gordon explaining a case to Fred Fisher. I later learned that Gordon had asked Fred to supervise serving a search warrant for him. Officer Fox later explained to me that Gordon did not want to appear at the raid because he had made the buys, or had done the control buys, and did not want to burn himself or his informant.

They were trying to mobilize more people to go on the raid. Sergeant Jones discovered that Lightenup had called in sick for the day and that

Jim and Collage were already on something else. Jones called Fox who was unavailable or was out, and then reached Paul Gun and asked him to meet us at Salem Station in approximately twenty to thirty minutes. He then called Herman and asked him to go to the Salem Station. That gave us four. The sergeant also called the day supervisor, EOC (Emergency Operations Center) and told him that a raid was going down in the Salem District and supplied the address and said it would be occurring in the next hour. Then he called the captain at the Salem District substation and informed him. Then he called the desk sergeant and asked that two uniformed men meet us at the substation. He then explained to Fisher that the guy lived in the basement apartment and his parents lived upstairs. He also said that he drove a grey van and it would probably be out in front. Gordon pointed out that there was a toilet in the basement so they might want to come in through the back door into the basement to keep Chakey from flushing the dope. Gordon explained to Jones that although he did not have a floor plan or a drawing, that the kid lived in the basement with his "chick," that the parents lived upstairs, and that he drove a van. If the van was out in the front he was probably at home. He also said that the dope was probably secreted in a shoebox or a cardboard box against the wall farthest from the door. It was later noted that when we called Gordon to verify this information that he said one probably could reach it from the bed. Someone said he would have to be a rubber man to reach the box from the bed, as it was from six to eight feet away.

Fred Fisher began to hunt for cameras, picking one camera, then another. He finally decided to take the big camera kit. The Sergeant found the hammer and the raid kit and readied it. When we were all ready to leave, I walked with Fred, carrying the sledgehammer while he carried the raid box and the camera. As we walked out he said that was one of the disadvantages of the present mall location: we had to walk out the front door carrying the sledgehammer and raid kit and get into his car in the main parking lot of the mall.

We drove for fifteen plus minutes to the Salem Station. Shortly after we got there, Gun and Herman arrived. We went inside and waited a few minutes for the two uniformed officers, who eventually appeared. I was not introduced, nor did the narcotics investigators introduce themselves to the uniform men[13]

While in the station, Fred laughingly described himself as a "raid-co-ordinator." Another corporal said that he wasn't using the proper word according to general orders: he was the "field coordinator"—they joked back and forth about what the proper term was without agreement upon it. Then Fred turned to describing the kid's apartment in the parent's home briefly, saying that the downstairs apartment was used by the kid. He owned a van, he lived with his chick, and the dope was supposed to be secreted against a wall. He instructed the uniformed officers that they would probably go to the basement and hit the door without knocking. While they entered and were down in the basement, they would ask a uniformed officer to go around front to make sure somebody didn't leave through the front door. They might try to lure him out the front door. It was never decided; Gun then suggested that perhaps we lure him outside by having uniformed officers drive up front and say that they were investigating a hit and run and they wanted to discuss the matter with him.

Gun, the senior man, who with his long hair, T-shirt and jeans looks rather young, looks his thirty-eight years when seen closely, suggested we "play it by ear." We then split up with the plain clothesmen, Gun, Herman, and Fred in the front seat and myself in the back. We rode in Fred's car to the raid site. The two uniformed policemen would meet us in the elementary school lot. We then discussed how to get there. Gun knew the way. We had been given very precise directions earlier by the desk corporal at headquarters. We drove down a street and turned right, sighting the house on our left (one house from the corner; where we turned). As we did, we saw the uniform car turning a block further on down and coming up the street toward us. They had turned a full two blocks away from the house so they would not come past it. It was a smart technique; probably the uniform men knew the area. We swung in the elementary school parking lot, turned around, and went back down toward the house, saw the van out front, went by it and ran into a three-way-dead-end: each of three streets that went off of it for a time were eventually dead-ends. We four men packed in a car went down past the house, turned right, had to make a U turn and come back past the house. This certainly would have "tipped him" had he been looking out his window. We went back down the road and into the elementary school parking lot where we met with the patrol car. As we were talking to the officers, Cohen, and Collage appeared in Cohen's car. I am not sure how they knew where we were. They asked if we needed help. We declined it, although eventually they returned after we unsuccessfully searched and had called the station for assistance. They were sent out, I think, by Sergeant Jones and spent the last hour and a half or so on the scene.

On our second trip past the house, we noted a large dog in the backyard. We discussed who would handle the dog. If we were to go around back and tried to hit the door, then the dog would raise a noise and might give Chakey time to flush the dope down the toilet. We decided that the hit-and-run story was the most viable. They wondered whether they should call another unit and have them bring their shotguns. It was decided that we didn't need the shotgun and that the uniformed men would go up to the house and would feign an investigation of the van, scrutinize it for apparent marks of an accident, and that then they would go up to the door and ask him to come out and have a look at the van. It worked beautifully. The uniformed men parked in front of the house behind the van, went up, took out their clipboards, carefully looked over the vehicle, then went to the front door. The young man answered the door and then walked out with them to the van. As the man came out to the van, they had been instructed to hold him. They did, and Fred served the warrant. Three officers tumbled out of the car and dashed in the front door of the house.

No account had been taken of the fact that a woman was in the house. She may have flushed or stashed the dope. Neither the existence of the dog nor the woman, nor the fact that according to her, she slept downstairs and he slept upstairs, was mentioned by Gordon. Whether or not his informant had informed him, whether or not he had scrutinized the scene himself, or whether or not this was simply inadequate information, I could not determine. However, in the absence of intelligence about the house, its layout inside and out, who would be there, particularly the young woman, the possibility of seizing any dope was very unlikely.

The three investigators who rushed into the house with the uniformed men secured the premises. Fred asked me in. I came in and stayed with the uniform men on the first floor. They handcuffed the suspect and sat the young woman down in the front room. The two uniformed men stayed on the main floor with the two suspects while we went downstairs where we had been told the dope would be found. At this point it was not clear who was the raid-evidence assembler and who was to take the pictures. Eventually Herman did the evidence and Fred took the pictures. The search of the downstairs was very unsystematic. One of the uniform men looked in the john upstairs, while the three of us downstairs were subsequently joined by Gun. Fred went upstairs and Gun and I searched downstairs. There was a kind of "randomness" about the search with people going upstairs and downstairs; the search was not done from left-to-right, top-to-bottom, front-to-back, etc. Nor was there any concern about it until much later when people had begun to ask if this and that area of the house had been searched.

It was then decided that they would have the suspect come down to the basement. We had been in the house for about 20–25 minutes. When he came down Fred told him, "You have one of two roads—you can either make it easy for yourself or you can make it hard for yourself. We have the authority with the search warrant to turn over the house. We can tear it apart. We can start to tear up the ceiling, we're going to take off the panelling, and we're going to keep looking until we find it. Or you can tell us where it is." The suspect asked, "Can I go back upstairs?" He said, "No, you're going to talk to us." He said, "No. You told me that if I didn't have anything to say I could go back upstairs." Then Fred said, "You're not talking then?" He said nothing, and turned and went back upstairs. This was said twice. Threat one and threat two, the second time somewhat more angrily. Fred, a young and rather gentle fellow in some ways, was trying to carry off an authoritative role with a person barely a few years younger than he. He obviously was not scared by Charlie and his calmness suggested that she either flushed it or secreted it, or that he had not had dope in the last few hours.

In the basement there were two storerooms, one stacked completely full of boxes and boxes of family items—canning goods, old shoes, clothing, the usual kinds of things that families accumulate — the other a work room with tools, screwdrivers, etc.. The workroom was searched by Herman. The main room in the basement contained a table which had a number of pottery materials on it, eight marijuana plants growing under a florescent light with Reynolds Wrap surrounding it to maintain the proper light, and other plants. There was also a hide-a-bed in the center of the room. There was an outdoor entrance. A huge dog was cavorting in the backyard. It was lucky we didn't have to come in the back door. Also in the room was a large three piece couch, a sofa in front of a gas-log fire, and a coffee table. Against the wall to the right of the bed was a bookcase and a number of boxes stacked one upon the other, each of which contained, as we subsequently discovered, a number of items relevant to the search. I looked around a bit, putting my hands up behind an open flue area, and didn't find anything. I was then cautioned by Fred that if I should find anything to call him. I said I would not disturb any evidence; I would let him handle it. He subsequently told me that if he wanted to tear apart a house like this for twenty grams of heroin, he would have to take out the air ducts, because that amount could be hidden virtually anywhere. Earlier, somebody had remarked that a guy who had been using dope this long (I think he has been a heroin user for four or five years), would know pretty well where to hide his stuff so that he could dispose of it quickly if need be.

On a small coffee table we found a small airtight vase which contained some marijuana seeds, a roach clip, and some spoons. In one box we found syringes, while in another we found two burned spoons that could have been used to heat heroin for injection. It was not clear who was sleeping where in the house. The dope subsequently found, the (alleged) one gram of heroin, was stuffed in one of the drawers in the parents' bedroom. A knife was found in the basement. Since it was never ascertained definitely who lived where, it would be very difficult to get a charge. There was no evidence found to establish possession of the dope and the implements. By this point, this evidence had been found: a bong, several marijuana plants, marijuana seeds, the spoons, some white powder (which didn't test out to be heroin), and the syringes.

At this point, we still had not found "anything." Since we had no heroin, people began to get somewhat frustrated. They began to slam around a little more and although things were not broken, they were thrown around and greatly disarranged. There is a tipping point in a search after which police begin to feel violent, when property is destroyed, and when people may be slapped around.[14]

It was repeatedly mentioned how small twenty grams of heroin was, how easy it was to conceal, and how difficult it would be to find it, particularly in this now very messy basement. A little bit of grass was found in a kleenex under her bed. They also discovered a bottom drawer full of methadone bottles. Throughout the house and in a room upstairs were twenty to thirty prescription bottles for valium. Downstairs were prescription bottles with his name on them for a K.E. County Methadone Clinic. Why was his methadone in her dresser downstairs? Herman tried to call K.E. County to ascertain whether one could take methadone home. The clinic was closed; they decided not to take the bottles as evidence.

I wandered upstairs. His bedroom and the parents' bedroom was being turned over. When the young man had been threatened earlier with an extensive search, it was said that they were going to turn over his parents' bedroom first, which was calculated to exite and worry him. They did it. He refused to talk. Then they found the gram of heroin and some money in an envelope.

About this time the young man's father came home. I saw a man through the front window walking up toward the house, and I wondered if it were he. I heard a commotion and went into the living room. The father was there. He asked what was going on; an officer explained to the father that they had a search warrant. He yelled that they had no right to be in the house, he didn't care who said they could be there. The uniformed man said, "Yes we do. We have the right by the search warrant." The uniformed man gave him the search warrant to read. The homeowner yelled, "No, you don't have the right. You can't come into my house this way. I'll sue the county over it." Then he asked, "Who's in charge?" Fred came upstairs and said, "Mr. Chakey, we've got a search warrant from the county judge." "No, you can't search my house," he yelled.

Fred then asked him if he knew that his son kept dope on the premises. The father said, "No, my son does not keep dope on the premises. There wasn't any dope here. Who claimed that? I'll sue him." At that point Fred asked him to come downstairs where he showed him the marijuana plants, pointed out to him that it was a felony to grow them in his basement, and then took out the syringes and said, "These are what you call syringes, you use them to shoot heroin into a person's arm." He then showed him the cooking spoons. The father denied knowing that the plants were marijuana. He said that his son told him they were "hops." He denied ever having seen the syringes and he denied ever having seen the cookers or the spoons. At this point he calmed down. Earlier, upstairs, he had been saying that he was going to throw them out and that nobody had a right to come into his house and he was going to call whoever it was who had given them permission. Fred told him that he was interfering with his functions and that if he didn't calm down they were going to arrest him. He then shouted out that they couldn't arrest him for drugs if he didn't have any drugs or keep any drugs. Fred explained: He was going to arrest him for being disorderly and for interfering with the police. He quieted down when he found that *he* wasn't going to be charged. He displayed another flurry of anger approximately fifteen to twenty minutes before we were going to leave the premises, threatening to throw us out, saying that we only had five to ten minutes to clean up everything before he threw us out. He had meanwhile gone in and out of the house several times. This made me nervous (he could have come in the backdoor with a shotgun) and I mentioned it to the uniformed man: "It makes me a little worried when somebody goes in and out of a 'secured premise' behind my back." Then he went back out. The same uniformed man later asked me in a very kindly way if I worked for the police department. I said no and smiled at him. But I didn't explain why I was there because we were in the living room in front of the two suspects. They could have asked me to leave, and legally I would have had to go.

I don't know who interviewed the woman. I found out later that they are both on welfare. About this time Fred sat them down and asked her if she had tracks on her arm by any chance. She said yes and showed them to him. She said she had been an addict for a couple of years, but that she had been on methadone for about two years now. It wasn't clear whether she or he or both were taking methadone. She also admitted to ownership of the prescription pads found in the room. She claimed that she had used them to take notes when she worked in the clinic in K.E. County. She had two notepads and probably had been forging scripts. She said that she lived downstairs and that he lived upstairs in the house with his parents.

While searching in the other upstairs bedroom Jim found ledgers, telephone books, and a listing of bags sold and obligated, as well as a wallet containing $350. However, he apparently owed people $400. They debated whether or not to take the book and money into the bedroom. It was decided that the ledger established that there was reason to bring the money in as evidence. It had been debated earlier whether to charge him on a felony for the marijuana growing and decided that they would (after he refused to reveal where the dope was hidden). Then it was discussed whether or not they had enough evidence at that time to charge him. It was agreed that the seeds and possession of the plants was enough. They were hoping to discover enough heroin to charge him with possession with intent to distribute. I don't know what he was subsequently charged with. At this point Jim and Collage were leaving. I decided to leave with them. Two others remained because they were going to take in the prisoners and charge them. Jim said on the way home, "Well, this is why we don't like this controlled buy shit and why we would rather have hand-to-hand transactions." As we drove home, I was half asleep in the heat, wondering about the general chaos produced and the rather haphazard way in which the affair had been undertaken, coordinated, and concluded. The entire process struck me as being incomplete in some unpleasant way. The absence of a "good seizure," when combined with the intrusive mess of the raid, the devastation of the house, and the pathetic personal situation of the man and his friend combined to leave me with a sense of ennui.

Surveillance and "Big Cases"

There are many uses of surveillance in narcotics work. One can use it to corroborate evidence received from an informant to check his reliability; one can establish the traffic patterns of a dealer and estimate the volume of his trade; one can obtain pictures or video tapes of these transactions using telephoto lenses; one can note changes in the vehicles used by dealers, their hours and coming and goings, and so on. Surveillance is a key or buzz word in an affidavit for a search warrant as it establishes that the information provided is based on police officer's observations and not exclusively on the word of a citizen or informant ("paid criminal in the employ of the police department" as defense attorneys have been known to say). It is also critical in establishing the extensiveness of an operation. In practice, it can sometimes be a general term for being on the street, as the term was used in Metro, or out of the office on undefined business. In neither office did officers sign in and out during the day, although they did sign in upon arrival at the beginning of a shift. They were required to call in hourly to the communications center in Suburban if they were out, but there was no such requirement in Metro. Officers would arrive at the beginning of a shift, talk to each other, make a few phone calls, read the newspaper, and then leave.

While I was observing in Suburban, two cases they viewed as important involved surveillance. One involved a person whose dealing almost accidently came to the attention of one of the officers and the other was surveillance mounted on a person previously known to members of Suburban Vice Intelligence Unit and DEA. It became a joint surveillance at the request of DEA.

The first case is the surveillance of the infamous Hampster Gerbil, explained to me initially as an ongoing investigation by a sergeant:

Jones: We have got a case now where we know that a guy is dealing because we know the people he is selling to are known users. We have information on it; we have been watching his apartment, we have been set up to watch him, and we may be able to put more surveillance on him. . . .

PKM: How did you find out how he was dealing?

Jones: We were able to watch him. People would come up, say, knock on the door, ring the bell, and sometimes there would be something slipped through the door mail chute, then they would reach in and get something back; sometimes people would go out in the parking lot and pick things up from the back seat or trunk of the car with a guy. Sometimes his wife would be selling—he wouldn't be there at all.

PKM: Do you have photos of these transactions?

Jones: No. We hope we can get a place to take pictures later on. We will have a position where we can do that. What we would like to do is get a pen register on his phone so we can get the numbers of his customers and then maybe try to work up or get his source . . . since we already have his customers.

PKM: How did you know that this guy was dealing?

Jones: He has about fifteen years backup time [remainder of sentence that must be served if parole is violated] under him already, his dealing came to our attention through an informant: We knew Gerbil was selling to him. He has been getting some of his stuff from another guy who is under investigation by us.

The same case was discussed in detail at a unit meeting held in Suburban. The day and evening crews were assembled at 3:30 and after several issues were discussed, the group as a whole took up the question of how to approach the Hampster case. The case came to the attention of the unit and became a working case through an officer's investigative work rather than through intelligence information or a system of major-violator targeting. It is an agent-targeting instance that illustrates the progressive influence of supervision as additional information was assembled.

Officer Gordon, who had initiated the Hampster case explained it to the assembled investigators. Through one of his informants he discovered that Hampster was dealing from an apartment house. Gordon explained that they had observations of hand-to-hand deals, of apparent transactions carried out by passing things through the mailbox and

in the parking lot, and they had seen money and brown bags exchanged. They had not yet made a buy from him. The fellow was very
"paranoid" and was very careful about who he dealt with. They were
hoping to take up a surveillance in an apartment across the way from
the dealer's apartment. The open apartment was going to be vacated
by a woman, who worked in the Suburban Communications Center.
They made a tentative arrangement with the real estate people to observe from the apartment for a period, set up a camera, and take photos of Gerbil's operation. Gordon explained that he was applying for a
pen register, was working heavily on the case, and that he might need
help from others. There were no immediate comments or recommen-
dations about it, but people were obviously interested. About a week
later, I sat with Officer Gordon in the parking lot of Hampster Gerbil's
apartment complex while we talked about the case:

The main purpose of the surveillance was to "set-up" on Hampster's
operation in an apartment house. We left the office about 10:00 P.M.
and drove to Hampster's apartment, where we sat for approximately
half an hour to forty-five minutes. Then we proceeded to check out a
couple of local investigations, simply driving by them to ascertain the
layout and the address, and so on. Then we came back to the apartment house complex and sat and watched for another fifteen or twenty
minutes. We came in at approximately 12:00.
   He sits up probably two or three times a week here and watches
Hampster's. When he's on day work, he watches him during the day for
an hour or so. When he's on evening work, he sits up in the evening
and watches him. He's tried to follow him but he's very difficult to follow
because he drives rapidly—fifty or sixty miles an hour. That means
that you either lose him or follow him at fifty or sixty, and very likely tip
him that you are following.
   Hampster keeps very little dope in his pad, probably for fear of being
busted. He probably gets it in, makes a few calls, and then deals it out
immediately, within a day or so. Gerbil has done time in another state
and is now out on parole. Dealers know that narcs don't work on Sunday and therefore are likely, in his view, to deal on Sunday.

   Another group discussion, a day later, involved formulating a strategy to further surveil Hampster and develop or locate an informant who
might be able to make a buy or get next to him, or even better, to introduce an undercover officer to him so that the officer could make a
hand-to-hand buy:

I went out, arriving about 3:00 P.M., and found the entire narcotics group there discussing approaches for getting into Hampster Gerbil. Jones suggested that with the five cars that they had available that they should set up at night and follow him wherever he goes. Gordon objected, saying it couldn't be done because there was no parking during the day on the street. But Jones counted on the fact that with five cars they could set up to pick him up in any direction he chose to go. The lieutenant had meanwhile read Gordon's request for a wire and had said that it needed to be fleshed out further concerning "the exhaustion of all police methods" and the "previous informants who had been used with no success." Then there was speculation concerning who among the informants they knew might be able to cop [buy heroin] from Hampster. Several of them suggested a name or names. Finally, the name Jimmie came up. He and his wife had been involved in a previous case. Sergeant Smith seemed well satisfied and left.

These developments in the Hampster case pointed out several of the important aspects of developing a scenario, or showing flair. The case originated from Gordon's interest and tenacity in digging up relevant facts, but then came to the attention of the Sergeant through discussions and because of the amount of time Gordon was spending surveilling the apartment. When Gordon decided that he wanted to develop a wire tap affidavit, the two sergeants and the lieutenant became involved in reviewing the affidavit, although an officer in Suburban County can develop and have a magistrate sign any affidavit, it is a courtesy to have a sergeant review it. Further, since Gordon had not previously written an affidavit for a wire intercept, he requested help from his sergeants. Jones reviewed and made suggestions to Gordon, although he showed no enthusiasm for the strategy; he had said earlier, "I am a firm believer in the hand-to-hand buy. It was apparent that Jones saw this as merely an exercise in writing an affadavit. In addition, the case, like all cases in narcotics, appears as an ambiguous and shifting matter, depending on how one defines the goals of the investigation; work up to a source, get an organization, make a lot of arrests, harrass a dealer, put the dealer back in prison, get experience in a variety of investigative strategies, make a big seizure. At times, Gordon's aim was to put this person back in jail, at times, to get experience, and at still other times, to "see the look in his eyes when I arrest him." Sergeant Jones wanted someone to "get next" to Hampster and make a buy and/or to get some arrest warrants. This would eventually raise the recorded number of arrests for the unit for the month, regardless of whether Hampster himself were arrested. At times, the strategy involved further surveillance to observe more drug traffic and perhaps to make more sales cases on Hampster. To this end they were hoping ro rent the apartment in the same complex mentioned above. Upon investigation it was discovered that one could not see Hampster's door from the other apartment. That idea was temporarily dropped.

The decision to use a wire intercept is the most complicated sort of decision because it ties up personnel, is very costly, and requires skills such as listening, typing and organizing inside, and checking leads, addresses, and tag numbers produced by the intercept, and surveillance of the suspects. An affidavit must be accompanied by political persuasion to have a judge approve it, and it puts the department out front symbolically. They have to present the evidence discovered in the form of a memo to the supervising judge every forty-eight hours. The investigation is closely monitored in this way, and errors in recording can lead to the entire case being lost through a defense motion to suppress irrelevant information that has been gathered. Sergeant Jones discussed these vicissitudes with me:

When I came into the office, Sergeant Jones was sitting at the desk talking with Sergeant Smith. The subject was wire taps. It was at first a kind of casual exchange, and I was politely listening, sitting across the room after he had invited me to come in.

Jones mentioned that he'd probably done about ten wires since he had been in narcotics [five and one-half years—he says the unit started around his dining room table]. Seven of them were used in gambling, three in narcotics, two of which worked. I asked how the permission for a wire is obtained. He explained that first one had to write up an affidavit, then this affidavit was taken to the state attorney's office. [They have a special liason man who goes to the state attorney's office with the affiant, then to the judge.] "As soon as the judge signs it, we're in business. That's the easy part."

Jones: It is difficult though because one little slip can throw the whole thing out, especially in narcotics where all kinds of calls will come through. We had one wire on a crash pad where they had calls all hours of the day and night. A girl would get on the phone at say 2:00 A.M. and talk until 4:00. In the course of the conversation she might say,

"Oh yeah, Bennie brought over some grass and we had a great time," or "Joe brought over some PCP," and it was pretty hard not to listen in on the whole thing because you were afraid you might miss an example like that, some information like that. In a narcotics wire you have to listen to everything, but there is a shut off point between the monitoring station and the recorder and you don't record or monitor any call that doesn't deal with drugs, or with the investigation, although you make a note of the time, date, etc. Then every forty-eight hours you send a memo to the judge. For example, the memo would be sent explaining how many calls; say there were ninety-six calls at such and such a number, and of those forty-two were drug related over the course of the previous forty-eight hours. This allows the judge to keep pretty close touch with any investigation involving a wire. Actually, all the background transcription is supposed to be done by a police officer, not by a secretary. Little errors can get the whole thing thrown out.

PKM: What kind of errors do you mean—that get narcotics wires thrown out?

Jones: Well, you remember what I said about having it signed by the state attorney? In the past there were cases that were not signed by the principal prosecuting attorney, which the law requires, and they threw out ten cases. Also, you have to prove in the affidavit that "all other means of investigation have been exhausted."

Working Informants

It can be seen from these vignettes-*cum*-cases that the dominant mode of strategy in Suburban or the combinations favored, namely the hand-to-hand buy, buy-bust, and the occasional big case using wire intercepts and/or surveillance, tends to reduce reliance on informants. Informants in this system are paid for their duties, especially in the form of rewards for seizures, and leads in big lab cases that result in seizures at the time of a raid. They are always paid after the results of the raid are known. Although the three most active investigators in the unit asserted that they preferred informants who were working off beefs, they worked them to make introductions to people so that the investigators could make hand-to-hand buys. This approach leads to solid court cases because they are based on the word of the officer and the evidence of the buy made by him. No informant, whose veracity, character, and past behavior can be questioned in court or doubted by a judge, is involved in the situation of the crime. Buy-bust cases can be of importance as judged by the size of the seizures. This means that the informant does not have to be coerced, threatened, or worked in the same fashion that one finds in Metro. In Metro, the case of a controlled buy and search warrant conclusion to an investigation depends on the informant's performances: whether he calls, whether he shows for an appointment, whether he shows on time, who he knows, where and how much he knows, how current the information is, who he is willing and/or can do (make a buy from) whether he will testify, how much demand he makes for miscellaneous expenses associated with his work (money for cigarettes, drinks, bus or taxi fare, bills, or drugs), how reliable he is in both the legal and personal sense, and whether he can remember details of a place from which he buys, addresses, numbers. In Metro, I heard stories about a color-blind informant who kept telling them people in green shirts were dealing on corners, and when they rushed out to arrest them, they found no green-shirted people. This continued until someone asked the snitch if he was color blind. He admitted he was. Another informant could not remember more than two digits at a time and could not remember addresses, phone numbers, nor the numbers of apartments from which he had bought dope even under the conditions of a controlled buy. He made up the last few digits.

But in Suburban there was little concern with these matters, and the officers' skills in working informants was far less developed. They did not tell as many detailed and complicated stories involving the deception and duplicity of their informants. They tended to be more direct about what they would do and had done when they had difficulties in working an informant. The interactive subtlety that is apparent in conversation with many investigators in Metro is absent in Suburban.

The person considered by his colleagues to be the best undercover man in the unit ("in the county"), described some of his approaches to informants. I asked Fred about the matter of protecting informants: I asked if he ever had a snitch arrested while he was working for him. He said, "yes."

PKM: Do you ever try to intervene? What do you do?
Fred: Nothing. They would be arrested and tried, period.
PKM: What are the consequences of that?

Fred: They just have to work a little harder on their charge.
PKM: Does it make a difference if it was a property or personal crime
they committed?
Fred: No.

I asked him if he ever had locked up his snitch, and he said, "Yes."
Another officer, Lightenup, was in the office while I was interviewing
Fred. He volunteered the following plan he had devised to "lock up his
snitch" that very night:

He was going to lock up a fellow named Charlie who had been working
as a snitch for him. He was to serve some time in prison on a burglar
charge in Southern State, but meanwhile it had been discovered that
he was dealing. I asked Lightenup if he often knew that his informants
were dealing, and he said it happened very often, and he was aware of
it. I asked him then how he became aware of the fact that his snitch
was dealing. He said that a Southern County officer had called and
said a snitch of his was going to buy from a Charlie who lived in Suburban County. He asked if there was any information in the files about
him. Lightenup was then informed, since it was his snitch, and talked
with the man. They decided subsequently that the Southern County
man would try to set up a buy with his snitch because his snitch was
going to buy from Lightenup's snitch. Charlie, according to Lightenup,
was under a charge in Suburban County, had been convicted, and
was awaiting sentencing. The buy had been successfully done once
before from Southern's snitch to Lightenup's snitch. Now they were
going to try again, and set up a joint buy-bust operation involving the
two counties. Sergeant Smith would presumably assist if it occurred.

However, after a couple hours of waiting, around seven o'clock, the
Southern County officer called, said he couldn't find his snitch and was
taking off for the night. Lightenup had been off duty and was simply
waiting to see if it would go down. Fred asked Lightenup if he knew
where his snitch was, and he said, "Yes," he could find his snitch, "It
was the southern state man who couldn't find his." This incident raises
questions about how well organized the other investigator is, and reminds me of comments made in Metro about how you find out if the
other investigator is "worth a damn" by these kinds of experiences.

I asked if there was any policy on working people who were to be
charged with assaults or murder, and Charlie said, "You can work off
just about anything."[15] Apparently, no pay is provided for informants

who are working off a beef. In 1973, they started to pay informants. Previously they had not paid. I asked if informants were primarily persons working off beefs, and if you didn't pay informants who were working off beefs, then to whom were payments made? Implicit in this question was my knowledge that large seizures had been made and that in order to provide intelligence such that large seizures can be made, one has to be involved in the drug world. Fred explained that one of his SEs (special employee: the term used in this department to refer to informants), who was given a large payment, had previously been under a charge, had worked it off, and then began to work for money. He had originally worked for Smith and then worked with Fred.

I asked if it was common for investigators to inherit a snitch from another officer or if this was done in order to help young officers get cases.

Fred: Now, if you've got a dynamite snitch, you're not going to turn him on to anybody else. It might occur, as a result of taking along a new investigator when you lock somebody up, that he or she will meet people who in the future will become SEs for them. Thus, the way a new officer gets his informants is primarily through arrests in which he/she participates.

PKM: Had you ever arrested your snitch to protect him?

Fred: Yes.

PKM: Under what conditions?

Fred: Well, if you have a dealer who won't deal except to people he knows or at home, you take along an SE, he makes the buy, you're there, and you lock them both up. Then you take them both to the station and you fingerprint and go through the whole works with both of them. But for the SE it's just for the show. He's never charged with the crime. It all comes out in court, anyway.

PKM: You mean you burn the SE?

Fred: Yeah, but it keeps him cool for awhile anyway. That is, in court the situation is explained, and the participation of the informant in the arrangement is revealed, and he's burned. Since the transaction was made from the dealer to the SE and not to the officer, you have to burn him.

Earlier, Fred and Jim Cohen had explained to me that they had once arranged to have themselves arrested and had even been allowed to escape.

Several aspects of legal control altered the pattern of working informants in Suburban County. The first is that the county attorney's office has no policy on what will be worked, and this in effect allows the arresting officer to set the conditions of working off a charge. A second and complementary matter is that the officer makes the charge in Suburban County, not the prosecuting attorney's office. This means that bargaining is over which, if any, of the charges will be dropped. Sergeant Jones explained:

PKM: I guess relationships with the courts are crucial. When you are working an informant, how do you come to an arrangement concerning his working for you?

Jones: We will usually make a recommendation to the state attorney about what ought to be done in a case, and they will generally follow it up. They will take our recommendation on working a guy and how we want to handle it. We have two guys in the state attorney's office who just do screening of various cases. The one limit is that on heroin sale there is no bargaining. He has to plead to distribution of heroin; if he is a major violator selling ounces or say a quarter-pieces, he may only take a plea to distribution. Usually by the time this kind of case comes to court, to the attorney's office, we have already made, say, seven or eight buys from him. We will let him cop a plea to a quarter-ounce sale. You can get as much as twenty years for sale.

Fox also interjected that you can often use the threat of dropping a charge against someone even when you don't have a case. They don't know your case is weak, and they'll often work. According to Herman and others, the state attorney will follow their instructions. For example, Herman had first arrested the fellow on whom a raid went down the previous week and didn't have a strong case against him. But he had been charged, and then Herman asked the state attorney to drop the charge against him. The doper didn't know this and told Herman that when he had arrested him before, "I got out of that charge. I went to court and got out of it." There is often a good bit of misunderstanding among users about what the nature of the charge is, whether the case will go to court, and what the processes are that lie between arrest, charge, indictment, and trial.

Third, the relationships between the attorney's office and the unit were close socially and officially. The county attorney had recently received about $1,000 a month for several months to improve relations with the police department. This was announced by a county attorney, at dinner with another county attorney, two officers from vice/intelligence, and myself. He offered to take Fred and Jim out to dinner when the program began. Previously, the county attorney had assigned one attorney a week as a liasion person with the department to establish communication between the department and the attorney's office. This attorney had rode on several occasions with Fred and had come to know him socially during this time. Fourth, in June, as the study began in Suburban, the county attorney in Suburban County announced that he would no longer prosecute personal possession cases in the county.[16] This decision did not change the behavior of the Suburban unit, since most cases of this kind were being brought to the attorney by the Patrol Division, and since the policy, frequently articulated in the unit at both the command and the officer level, was that they were not interested in bringing up cases involving small amounts of marijuana for prosecution. Of course, since the citizen demand for attention to such cases continues, considerable energy was given to investigating these types of cases.

Comment

Ecological conditions would seem to pattern the choices of investigators in the two units in the sense that there is no street scene in Suburban and therefore no opportunity to cruise, to carry out street rip-offs, or to headhunt. This means that short-term investigations must have formal approval if a search warrant is to be served. It should be emphasized, however, that a constant problem in Suburban during this period was that the officers would not draw up arrest warrants for hand-to-hand buys they had made, since they fully expected to mount a raid or to set up a buy-bust situation on the basis of the information gathered. In a sense, invisible controls are created by these social conditions, for the extent of unsupervised case-making in Metro was greater precisely because there were unlimited opportunities to make cases without approval, review, or departmental money. The elements required to make a case are fewer, the place of the organization less salient; the power and freedom of the investigator (the pharmacies and schools squads excepted), was greater in Metro than in Suburban.

Within the two units, the dynamics of actual cases are similar in the sense that the unpredictable aspects increase as one moves from cruising-hassling or the equivalent to more complex cases. The more complex the case, the greater the formal controls exercised by the organization, but the more that elements other than those controlled by the organization bear on the outcomes sought. The complexity is both relative and absolute. Even if the organization were to have no controls, if the agents were essentially vigilantes, they would still face the greater volatility of a buy-bust case when compared with a street bust, the constraints involved in working up the market system, and the greater deception and control exercised by larger dealers (compare Moore, 1977; chapter 1). The dealing pyramid in the heroin market as one moves from bottom to top, contains decreasing numbers of persons dealing larger and larger quantities of drugs. Dealers exercise greater control over their sales personnel, their marketing and distribution system, and their own sources of drugs (see Redlinger, 1969). Thus on a probability basis (there are fewer large dealers), on the basis of their degree of control of information, and the limitations on drug enforcement agencies, the constraints on more complex cases are multiple. They arise from the capacities of the organization, the skills and training of the investigators, and the structure of the drug market itself. Legal controls and inter-organizational constraints also enter into many cases.

As was shown in table 7.1 on targeting and the effect on the market, the more control the organization can exercise as one moves toward the major violator or intelligence mode, the less control the agent has. The outcomes that result because of these constraints and the examples in this chapter are not correlated with the intended complexity of the case or the degree of organizational control. The outcomes remain, in large part, unpredictable.

Three officers are sitting around with their feet up on their grey metal desks discussing race relations in the department, telling stories involving blacks and whites in various compromising situations. The phone rings. No one moves to answer it. One officer swivels around in his chair to see if the semi-competent clerk is at her desk. She is not. The phone continues to ring and then stops. The conversation flows on. Later the phone rings again. One of the officers picks it up (the receiver is upside down on the cradle) and tells the caller that the officer wanted is on the street. The clerk returns and bustles through the office to place yellow call slips in several officers' boxes. They may check these later in the day. Since they sometimes contain only a nickname, sometimes only a number, or at other times a name and a number, they must be attended to by the officer to whom they are addressed. To others, they remain inactionable mysteries. These scenes took place in Metro. In Suburban, clerks take calls, answering, "Hello, may I help you?" or just "Hello." During the day phone messages are placed on call-back or "while you were out" slips. After 5:00 P.M., if an officer is in the office, he will answer the phone.

Organizational procedures stating how these calls from citizens should be handled are rather different. Analysis of the handling of calls opens up the everyday operations of the units. What happens to such calls is described more precisely below.

Citizen-generated cases are very revealing of the operations of the two organizations. They arise from volunteered information coming into the organization. Organizationally generated clues, information, and cases that arise from the agents and major-violator modes contrast with these externally generated clues. In both types of cases the investigators' perspective, more in Metro than in Suburban, patterns whether received clues will be written down or noted, used, followed, how they will be followed, for how long, in what intensity, and to what end. Neither cases arising from citizen tips nor those created by the organization through means other than investigators' actions are accepted without question. The information received is encoded and shaped by investigators to their purposes. A citizen generated case is: When a case does not come to the attention of an agent from a previously known informant or from one who stands in a formal relationship with the organization as a source of information, nor from systematic intelligence passed on to the drug unit by another unit in the department (intelligence, patrol, internal affairs, detective), and in Metro is not defined as a case involving a major violator, then it will be considered to be a citizen-generated case.

Citizens' calls are received and processed in both units. In Suburban, clerks receive the calls during the day. The calls are handled with some concern and frequently entered as "locals," which require an investigation and report. In Metro, where there is one operator, calls are not assigned to officers. If there is no officer to answer the call the clerk asks them to call back and does not take a message unless an officer is asked for by name. Calls are problematic to varying degrees.

In both units there is some concern for public service and for dealing with and responding to citizens' concerns and anxieties about the drug problem. It is felt that the police department has legitimate service function to perform in this regard. This view was more frequently asserted to me in Suburban, where there were more mechanisms for insuring that calls were in fact dealt with in some fashion. Citizen tips are viewed by administrators as an important source of information in drug law enforcement, and they are viewed as such for both symbolic and instrumental reasons.[1] Some of the reasons are: they involve the citizenry in law enforcement and crime prevention; they broaden the base of citizen support of the police, and the realms in which the police can offer service, assuming that the citizen experience is a positive one; they often unexpectedly turn up a good lead and yield a good case; they can occasionally lead to a useful special informant in the employ of the unit; and they can expand the deterrent capacity of the unit if users-dealers are aware of the willingness of citizens to report violators. On the other hand, they are viewed by officers at the investigative level as a "waste of time," rarely producing a quality case. One investigator told me:

You see, narcotics cases are not like other kinds of cases, like in homicide, where you've got the body and the crime and you try to go out— to use the evidence to go out and find a person. You've got to. We know, for example, that there's something like, say, over 250 dealing pads in the city, but we need probable cause to go in there. That means—and you get a lot of calls. We get a lot of complaint calls, but what can you do? You can't investigate all of them. Somebody will call up and say, well, somebody's dealing out of such and such an address. You can go up and try to make a case out of it, for example, by visual observations or use of cameras or video tape, but one little mistake and one little point can sink the case in court. The whole question of credibility is important. If you've got a search warrant, of course, your case is better. But you can get a search warrant, get a buy, and even talk your way in, but a dealer still might—he might even say it's my dope. But in court he might claim that it was a threat, that he was confused, that he was asleep or something—"I didn't know they were officers"—or something. And that can get it thrown out of court. We have so many, such a large case load in narcotics that we won't devote a lot of time to a dealer who's, say, dealing in $10 bags just to get a search warrant when we can maybe get an SE to buy off some man— make a $50 buy somewhere else.

Oh, we'll go after marijuana if we see it, or we'll take it in just to take it off the street, but we aren't going to investigate it. Or we might go after some marijuana if we've got a real good informant.

In addition, officers did believe that one can never tell about a call: it could yield a major case, seizure, or lead relevant to a current investigation.

In both organizations there were internal and external pressures to respond to citizen calls in some fashion. These pressures are weighed against self-interest by the officers. From the officers' point of view, control of the work had to be balanced against demands and pressures from both external and/or internal sources. The officer has to be open to receive new information, be flexible enough to alter priorities and interests in order to pursue something that shows promise; evaluate the information and use of it, if possible, under the circumstances. On the other hand, the officer attempts to control the level and pacing of work, given a perceived time frame, in order to reduce if possible uneven demands on time and effort. An officer realizes and lives with the fact that a host of uncontrollable forces pattern the work but he seeks to limit and control choices about the allocation of time and effort. The officer's choices cannot be predetermined, for when a tip comes in, one must be able to prospectively guess at its promise, weigh it against other options, and anticipate the demands and the pay-offs that it might yield. These choices are worked out in practice.

It has been argued here that officers tend to take the most expedient route unless the organization constrains them. Unless there is organizational influence of some kind, choices will be worked out at the immediate and proximal level rather than in advance on the basis of some predetermined criteria concerning the worth of cases. The more choices are made at the proximal level, the more short-term investigations of investigator-defined cases will predominate. In this chapter it is shown how officers work with externally generated pressures for attention and time. These external demands stand in opposition to the militaristic or major-violator types of targeting, which are in a sense highly internally or organizationally defined. The investigator's perspective shapes, controls, delimits, makes sensible and possible the actions associated with these cases. When other organizations provide tips, they are acting analogously to citizens. They possess fairly weak authority and resources with respect to determining or even altering the practices of officers. Decisions made tacitly generally result in advantages for the organizations that requested the service.

There are three subtypes of targeting in the citizen modality: the big issue form of targeting, usually set by the chief or higher-level personnel; citizen targeting, and quasi-citizen targeting, in which organizational relationships are important in bringing issues to the attention of the unit. The first subtype, the big issue form of targeting, was not observed in the course of my research.[2] The irregularity of its appearance does not diminish its impact on police organizations, which tend to be crisis oriented. The second subtype, in which organizational relations become the basis for a case, can be seen in Metro in the pharmacy and school squads' investigations. However, the pharmacy squad rarely receives organizational tips, and so also can be considered as marginally acting within the agent-informant mode. Neither mode of targeting clearly predominates. Both Metro and Suburban had recently launched school busts. The most important sort of interorganizational relations that lead to targeting are those with other organizations in the criminal justice system.

Organizationally based cases are included in the citizen-generated modality because, from the officers' point of view, the information that comes in from another organization such as the DEA, a state police organization, or a school, is externally generated; the officers do not know the informant, do not know the past history of the person(s) being investigated, and so do not have a moral stake in the outcome. This means that the element of trust is often missing, and the level of information is viewed as being fairly low. Although it seems likely that the apparent power or prestige of the requesting organization would operate here, it generally does not. The rational network of organizational action does not bind the officer, organizations, and enforcement strategies, and thus interorganizational relationships are basically power-centered, ad hoc competitions worked out on a case-by-case basis (see appendix 8A).[3]

The citizen-provided subtype is a continuing problem in both units because it occupies considerable phone time in Metro and because, in Suburban, assignment of locals means that calls will occupy at least some investigator's time. There are more calls of this type than can be fully checked, yet they do represent citizens' concerns and do pay off in some instances.

Most of the following material from both departments concerns citizens' tips when the investigator had to decide if he would answer the phone, what to say and how to say it, and what, if anything, to do about the information received. All these decisions are made in the absence of even the vaguest guidelines for handling the general category of citizen call. There are no guidelines at all in Metro, and there are none in either unit for how to deal with the specific problem at hand. A conversation between a citizen-caller and a narc is virtually always a little bit like a dance between two equals: it is not clear who is leading whom where, for what purpose, by what means. The citizen tip magnifies the information-trust problem of the drug investigator because while it is received without prior knowledge about the caller, it is also frequent.

Tips are often not useful because the citizen refuses to give a name or will not divulge his phone number, address, or states he will not appear in court. This is often done immediately. Their information is often intentionally vague in order to protect themselves, their relatives, or their friends. Frequently information arises from the classic revenge motive (compare Harney and Cross, 1960). They may state that a person living at XXXX Fifth Street is dealing in heroin and that the police should come out and arrest him but will refuse to provide any further information. People fear retaliation if they "snitch." In addition, investigators feel that persons often lie when providing details of a possible investigation. Thus when officers do get past some basic facts, and the person is willing to give some details over the phone, such as the name and address of the dealer, or his license tags, or something about his operation, there remains the issues of trust and of time to give to such an investigation.

Trust is critical because the conversation is out of context. No background facts are available on the person talking; no facts may be given that the officer on the phone can personally corroborate; files available at the time, if any, may not yield information on the person; and the drugs involved may not be of interest because of the types or sizes involved, their form, or the drug. But both units did investigate marijuana, did make mostly marijuana arrests, and most investigators were happy to have the arrests on their record. So, if the call was viewed as having potential, or being valuable, then the phone interaction between narcs and tipsters was interesting to observe. There are a great many more phone calls received in Metro than in Suburban, and since the officers usually answer the calls themselves, the decisions made there are perhaps a richer source of data than those made in Suburban. In the following section on Metro, I have tried to outline a kind of "decision-tree" officers followed (tacitly or "unconsciously") in analyzing calls.

Metro

The interaction between the caller and the answerer can be diagrammed to show a series of decision points (figure 8.1) The first and most important split is between a known and unknown caller (1). If the caller is known to the officer answering (1A), then the series of interactions described in chapters 7 and 8 will take place. It is no different than other agent-informant interactions (2). If on the other hand, the caller is unknown (1B), as was suggested by the nature of the anonymous tip, then a series of questions are raised. These have to do with

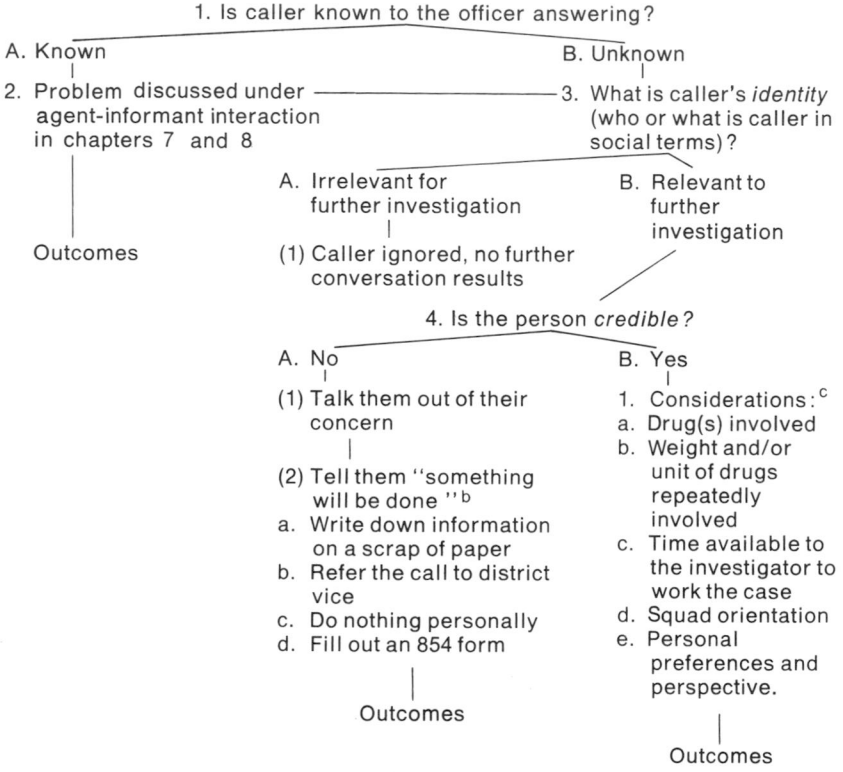

1. Is caller known to the officer answering?

A. Known   B. Unknown

2. Problem discussed under ——————————— 3. What is caller's *identity*
   agent-informant interaction   (who or what is caller in
   in chapters 7 and 8   social terms)?

                       A. Irrelevant for   B. Relevant to
                          further investigation   further
                                                         investigation
Outcomes   (1) Caller ignored, no further
                         conversation results

4. Is the person *credible*?

                       A. No   B. Yes

                       (1) Talk them out of their   1. Considerations:[c]
                          concern   a. Drug(s) involved
                                                   b. Weight and/or
                     (2) Tell them "something   unit of drugs
                         will be done "[b]   repeatedly
                     a. Write down information   involved
                         on a scrap of paper   c. Time available to
                     b. Refer the call to district   the investigator to
                         vice   work the case
                     c. Do nothing personally   d. Squad orientation
                     d. Fill out an 854 form   e. Personal
                                                preferences and
                                              perspective.
                          Outcomes

                                                            Outcomes

a. When the call is not related to the target set by intelligence, is not in reference to a major violator, and is not an assignment.

b. Not all of these choices are mutually exclusive. An officer can investigate and do an 854 (before or after investigation), can refer and do nothing or fill out an 854 and do nothing.

c. This list is meant to indicate the kinds of variables that might be taken into account by the officer as he tries to decide what, if anything, to do about a call when an unknown caller with a relevant identity and credible information is on the line. The variables are not listed in order of importance or weighting. They do not indicate the sorts of social values that come into play at these decision points and that subsequently pattern the outcomes produced by a unit.

Figure 8.1 Some contingencies in the flow of information when the citizen targeting modality is operating* in Metro.[a]

identity and credibility of the caller and pay-off of an investigation as assessed by the officer in light of his perspective.

For the purposes of discussion, assume that a caller is not known and pursue the series of options the officer faces in Metro. After the first message was given by the caller, and it was decided whether the caller was known or unknown (1), answerers attempted to either establish the identity (3) of the person named in the complaint or specifically what he or she does. If it is decided that this information is irrelevant or that the police can do nothing, the caller is ignored (3A). If the person does continue, and is able to give information of potentially actionable interest (3B), then the question is whether this information is credible (4), that is whether the person is credible. This is usually established by asking whether they will testify in court, whether they will talk to an officer who comes out to meet them either in their home or elsewhere, and what the context of the complaint is. Context means what the person wants the police to do and why. Sometimes these interactions are very frustrating:

Investigator Lyman answered the phone while talking to me. The caller gave him some information, an address, and he asked her to tell him some more about this person. "Where does he deal this stuff?" "What size, what does he do—pieces, quarter-pieces, ounces?" "How do you know this, Miss?" He listened. "When is this going down?" "How many people are going to be involved?" "Where are they coming from?" Each of the questions was followed by a period where he listened to the caller. "How do you know this?" She apparently told him, from what Lyman told me later, that she had been the dude's mistress, that he had beaten her and thrown her out of the house that afternoon. The man, her lover, was dealing in heroin and was expecting to meet and pay for a shipment of dope from Baltimore or New York that night around 11:30 or so, but she would not say where this exchange was taking place. The conversation was a dance. He would ask more detailed questions, such as the address where she was, her name, and then she would refuse, and he would emphasize to her that he could not do anything unless she could give him more details or agree to testify. Then she would refuse and hesitate to tell more, saying she feared retaliation for telling him this much. He repeatedly asked her if she would call him from a pay phone somewhere and then meet him or allow him to pick her up so that they could discuss more details of the incident. She refused. He asked for more details about the shipment —how much was involved, are there guns involved? How many men?

She was vague, saying that she was not sure when they would be arriving, how many men would be coming and exactly what weight they would be transporting. He listened attentively, periodically making faces. Finally, she promised she would call back in an hour or so, but would not give him her phone number or address so that he could contact her. I asked what he thought would happen after he hung up, and he said, she'll never call. We waited for an hour or so, during which the investigators discussed various alternatives; go out to the area she had described and look around; set up a surveillance in the area, and hope that they could identify the car (she had said that it was a "big white car"); try to get an informant who knows the area or another officer who knows the dealers in the area. None of the ideas were well received, and when she didn't call after two hours, we left.

Sometimes you get guys coming in telling you they're going to have a —they've got a big tip for you. I had a guy come in yesterday, had a badge, flashed it around, just about hit me on the head with it. Tells me that he was working for Sergeant Bull. The dude told me I should call him. He said that Sergeant Bull said he should call him whenever he had a big deal coming down. Well, we don't give out any phone numbers to anybody, have anybody call at home, so I figured I'd call [Bull] and if he wanted to do something about it, that was his business. But this guy was a real Looney Tune. He said, he said he'd seen seven bags of heroin in attache cases in a pool room. I asked him if he'd actually seen it: He said, "Yeah. Got pictures of it. Been taking pictures of it."

When Sergeant Roy called Bull and told him he had a man here who had a tip, who had seen twelve attache cases full of heroin, the guy said, "Hey, you don't have to build it up!"

Well, that was a real Looney Tune. If he'd said an ounce or a half-ounce, well, maybe I'd believe him, said we could do something about it, but he said they were going to try to get rid of it or cut it. Man, they'd need, they'd need twelve cases of cutting material. They'd need a quarter of a million dollars just to cut it. He ought to use sand, it's cheaper.

I reasoned at the time that the point of this story is that it is so absurd. The guy was probably only interested in impressing a police officer, in getting back at someone, maybe the owner of the pool hall, but it was obviously such an incredible story and highly unlikely. Therefore, it was not even worth pursuing. Even at that Roy called Bull and let him deal with the question of whether to investigate the tip further.

If, at this point, the information/person is considered worthless, then one of two options is open to the investigator (4A and 4B). He can either say that something will be done (4A, 2), or will attempt to talk the person out of the belief that the police can do anything (4A, 1). If an agent says he will do something, there are four options available in Metro (4A, 2a, b, c, or d) (also figure 4.1). (4A, 2a) One can write down some information on the nearest piece of paper. These facts are usually the phone number and/or the address of the caller, some aspects of the case such as, Jerry Y. deals out of his car on the corner of X and Y, mornings from 10:00–12:00, and the caller's name. What follows is discussed below (4A, 2b). One can refer the call to district vice for the area from which the call originated, if one has that information. It may die because the person refuses to provide an exact area, but will only give a name. This occurred frequently while I observed in Metro:

Acumen answered the phone. The caller talked at some length; a minute or two. He said, "These are marijuana plants, Ma'am? I know you're concerned, and we try to deal with all the information that we receive, but there is a lot of marijuana being grown in the city, you know?" He looked at me and smiled. He wrote her phone number and address on a handy piece of paper. He told her that someone would look into it and thanked her for calling. He then tried to call the district vice unit in the district where the caller lived, but could not reach them. He made a note on the edge of the paper. He then explained that there were so many calls like that, that they (the central or headquarters division) could not handle them all. I was told that marijuana cases were generally referred to the district vice officers. Central officers did not tell citizens to call districts, but officers would call the district vice and give them the information. Although I was told that they referred these calls, I never heard an officer do so.

This option is usually taken in marijuana cases.

(4A, 2c) One can do nothing personally. One can do nothing even though a "promise" has been made to the person that someone will look into it. The "looking into it" has occurred during the phone conversation. In Suburban, on the other hand, the process is somewhat more complicated. One can, after promising to do something, write up the case on a form and give it to the day sergeant for assignment and investigation. One can look into it oneself. One can do nothing.

(4A, 2d) One can make up an 854 on the information, including the names, if any, and give it to the desk clerk in the office to take out the names that are mentioned and put them in the files along with any information on license tags, automobiles, nicknames, and addresses.

He will then file this information in the appropriately cross-indexed files for use by other officers. This process was described to me by the clerical officer in charge of this filing.

He is basically a clerk for the investigative reports. These intelligence files are sent in on an haphazard basis. There are no deadlines concerning how soon officers must file these kinds of reports. The clerk stated, "There's an unpredictable flow of these by day and by month." He said you couldn't estimate the number, and although he said they average "from three to five a day," he was working with approximately fifteen or twenty that day [Friday].

PKM: How many copies do you make, are made, of the investigative reports?

Clerk: Well, there are five copies.

PKM: To whom do these go—how are they distributed?

Clerk: Well, they come in and kind of go around the desks, you know, from me to Sergeant Long to the lieutenant. There could be as many as five copies, but you know, if someone needs an extra copy, I'll go and xerox it for them.

PKM: Why would they need an extra copy?

Clerk: Well, say they want to take it with them for investigation or something from a few months back, something like that. We've got an intelligence file that's monthly from back to front, that is, the first of the month is at the back, and these are filed in daily order. Then you've got an investigative file which is basically the major violators file. That's determined by investigation, by the sergeants, by the lieutenants, you know. There's this copy that circulates around the office. The captain comes to me and then to Sergeant Long, then to the lieutenant, and maybe something important might go up to the captain and to the inspector. There's one copy for me, that's the fourth, and then maybe there'll be an extra one. After I finish filing and indexing them, I destroy any that are left.

PKM: Oh, I see. How do you check these files with your other files?

Clerk: Well, there's a cross file up here on related cases. [I noted that a category of related files could be checked in the upper right hand corner and numbers filled. It might be, for example, a PD-68.]

PKM: What's a PD-68?

Clerk: Oh, that's a vice complaint. It might come in on the phone—you know, one of these things where there's a black, a Negro male dealing drugs on the corner of A and B—you know, one of those things.

PKM: Well, about how many of these 854's do you get? I mean, is it fifteen to twenty a day, I mean, how does it work out?

Clerk: Well, I don't know. Could be three to five, or so a day.

PKM: Let's see, if it's three to five a day, that'd be, say fifteen to twenty, say you've got maybe fifteen to thirty-five coming in a day.

At this point, Sergeant Long interjected, "Well, I don't think it'd be quite that many, that'd be on the high side. But we do get files sometimes as big as this" He showed me some about an inch or so thick.

PKM: Well, how many would you estimate you get in a month? Ninety, a hundred?

Clerk: (He paused to think and scratched his head.) . . . There wouldn't be any reason to know that . . . well, I did do a report on that.

If a person is to be talked into accepting the position that the police can do nothing about a reported drug problem, it will take some time and effort on the part of the officer. For example, if the police receive information that a child of the caller has a baggie of grass in their underwear drawer, the main task of the police is to point out that this cannot be the basis of legal action unless the parents want to have the person arrested. Often this option is not even mentioned because the police do not want to arrest young children under those circumstances on a possession charge. It would most likely be thrown out of court or refused for prosecution. The police suggest that they can destroy it for the parents, but suggest that the parents ought to handle it themselves. Or the case can be referred to the juvenile bureau, where the citizen will be given the same story, and where they will also try to persuade the parents to talk to their children.

I once spent some forty-five minutes on the phone in Metro with a young "speed freak" who had once been an informant of one of the officers I knew. He had called because he was frightened that he would be killed by the persons on whom he had informed, because his door had no lock on it, and because he felt (implied) that the police may try to "force" him to inform again. He wanted police protection. The officer who had worked with him was present when I was given the phone. I was introduced as an expert in the field working with police, but refused to talk to him, indicating my refusal in mime: shaking my head, and waving my hands as if to push the person and the phone away. Eventually I listened, feeling incompetent to speak to him, lacking any means of helping him, fascinated by his tale nevertheless, and wondering how to ease him off the phone. It was as much a joke on me as it was on him, and was unsatisfying for both of us. I was told that he was a "nut" and that he called in spurts, asking to talk with someone about his problem.

In general, control of the caller when one does not intend to do anything is accomplished by misrepresentation, lies, deceit, and duplicity.

Whether one decides to investigate a tip in Metro depends on the "investigator's style" or personal choice (4B, 1). One officer put it:

But nobody really asks the question, "What is the best approach for a local police department for the control of junk, drugs, thought of as a prime objective?" And then asks, "What's the method we need to enforce that?" No one says, "Don't do major violators. Get somebody on the book to make it look good." To make it look good to who? Well, the captain, sergeant, the inspectors. But that's the way it appears.

Thus, resolutions are left to squad and/or personal decisions (4B, 1a, b, c, and d). Why do the officers in Metro continue to investigate such tips? First, they must on occasion; second, they may when responding to an occasional assignment made by their sergeant, by the day administrative sergeant, or by a higher supervisor; third, there is the element of uncertainty that plagues and haunts them. What if I don't investigate and as a result miss out on a big case or a big seizure? I was told several stories by officers in Metro about these kinds of unexpected good tips:

We once got a call from someone who said that a major dealer that they had been trying to arrest for several months would be driving down Seventh at a certain time and that his license tag would be loose or off [thus giving probable cause to stop and investigate the car and driver]. The car was stopped. It was being driven by the dealer they had sought, and a search yielded an ounce of cocaine from under the seat.
    A caller said that a dude was dealing heroin at a particular corner and was out there now. She described the person's clothing, the place on the corner where he was standing, and claimed that he had secreted his dope under a garbage can on another nearby street corner. They went out, turned over the can and seized the dope.

The teller did not reveal whether they arrested the dealer who was alleged to have control over this dope. These are typically very difficult cases to make, because establishing his control over that material without a witness was impossible unless he admitted it. These kinds of "constitutive possession" cases are similar to the "dropsey" cases studied in New York where officers alleged that they saw a person drop a heroin bag to the ground when they saw the police coming and that, therefore, they were in legal possession even though it was at their feet at the time of an arrest. These cases are routinely thrown out of court. (compare Whitebread and Stevens, 1972).

This problem is an important source of logical dilemmas for officers. That is, there are a number of contradictory views of phone calls and tips that are received, and neither written nor operational policy in the sense we have discussed provides irreducible answers or guidelines. Consider the following rules that one can derive from conversations I overheard about how one should handle these calls and ascertain their promise:

We can't investigate everything; it takes too much time, the drugs are not of interest to higher-ups (supervisors in the P.D.) and may not be prosecutable.

There are no rewards for spending a lot of time checking out these allegations, that is, they rarely yield arrests, good seizures, or quality cases.

We are supposed to be investigating major violators, and they will not be turned in by phone callers. They're too careful and smart. But:

• Sometimes a tip can lead to a good arrest and/or seizure right away — one can go out and get a street rip-off;

• You can never tell when something good will come from a careful investigation, even though the original facts are skimpy;

• You've got to keep busy, keep "meat on the table" and "lines in the book" [arrests];

• You've got to "cover your ass" in case the complaint comes back on you in some way, and it is charged that you did nothing. This could be a minor irritation if a caller calls the sergeant or lieutenant directly after getting no satisfaction from an officer who answers;

• Accidents do happen, as they do frequently on patrol.[4]

One can never tell in narcotics. That is, even if one's own experience is not consistent with the view that such calls have promise, others talk about their experiences. There are stories about good things coming from calls told by others.

As a result of these logical binds, officers must build up their own resolutions in practice, and certain praxeological resolutions are made to these binds. These rationales and practices are discussed in chapter 10. The essential point about these resolutions is that they are actor-based to a considerable degree, and they persist in viability precisely because the organization has no capacity, until very late in a fairly well-developed process of a particular type of case, to effect the pattern that results. Praxis rules because the organization has no rewards that might tip the balance in the direction of a more collectively oriented resolution nor a means to insure more consistent monitoring by supervisors. This individualistic approach is especially characteristic of the ways in which citizen calls are handled in Metro. It is combined with a middle-management level philosophy that sees one of three options available to control or supervise the actions of officers: transfer in new people, transfer out present people (or some combination of these two approaches), or altering present partner combinations. Thus the resources at the command of the organization for modifying modes of handling citizens calls are few. In the Suburban unit there are somewhat more controls because of the rules regarding how incoming calls should be handled initially.

Suburban

To discuss the process of case assignment in Suburban, one must refer to figure 4.2 depicting the organization-centered or administrative model of narcotics investigation. Note that in the figure any call can be handled by an officer at his or her discretion without filling out any official paper (the dotted line between phone call and local investigation or "lead sheet"). If a lead sheet is filled in by the officer who answers the phone (the model of assessing information parallels that described on page 200), then there are two options that are exercised by the shift commander. The lead sheet can be filed in the "information only" file, or it can be assigned by the shift commander to an investigator. Each of the nine officers is assigned to an area; these are mostly located in the largest cities in the county, while "out county" investigations are assigned by the shift commanders to any available investigator. There are two officers assigned to Center City itself, headquarters of the Suburban Police Department; two to Salem, two to Churchville, and three to Vista. Although there are no official partners, officers do work together on a regular basis, and these working partnerships are not based on areas to which they are assigned. At the time the case is assigned it is given a number and written down under an officer's name in the sergeant's book. When it is closed, it is marked off in yellow. Thus at a glance, the supervisors can see how many cases given officers have outstanding, how many they have worked in recent months, and the disposition of the cases.

Officers are given two weeks to investigate and close their cases. On August 25, for example, the following open cases were assigned to officers: Jim Cohen, 8; Fred Fisher, 14; Norman Fox, 6; Paul Gun, 3; Herman Williams, 2; Pete Collage, 6; Bill Peak, 4; Sergeant Smith, 1; Sergeant Jones, 2; Don Gordon, 5; and Tim Lightenup, 11.

This list is merely an example of the case load that is officially carried by the investigators. There is another dimension to these assignments. They indicate not only what has been officially assigned, but other aspects of the social structure of the unit. First, if an officer dutifully fills out a lead sheet and does not investigate it, he may make a note on the sheet or mention to the sergeant that he wants to follow through on the case. This request is usually honored. Second, there is more crime in some areas of the county than in others, as in Vista, around the Metro line, and the investigators assigned to this area are sometimes assisted by others who take cases in the Vista area. Third, if there is currently a big case in the unit, everyone is involved and takes part in the investigations. At that point deadlines for locals are allowed to slide and no one works on his locals. Fourth, the assignment of cases and their disposition reflects the status of the officer. The two officers considered to be the best undercover men (Fisher and Lightenup) had the two highest totals of outstanding uninvestigated assignments.[5] Fifth, as has been implied, these locals are not considered very important sources of good cases. Officer Fox said, "You have to understand that locals rarely result in anything. They are just a name and an address, and there wasn't very much you could do with them. We get much better results out of those we instigate [initiate] ourselves." He also felt that some officers were not clearing them and should, and that they would soon start assigning them in order as they are supposed to; then the numbers of open cases will be more even across investigators. While noting that the work load was not even across investigators, he complained that he had too much free time.

Taking this in context, locals are viewed as having little value for individual officers, and the case flow depicted in figure 4.2, where the case yields an opening and closing at the same time when an arrest is made and is given a radio dispatch number assigned to the vice intelligence unit, is both more satisfying and more important in terms of the control of drugs in the county. On the other hand, locals serve as a mode of control over investigators, a way of checking on the pattern of dealing with citizen complaints. Their investigation is based on certain rules and sanctions by which supervisors can control investigators. A few examples of such citizen targeting will give the flavor of the investigations of locals in Suburban.

Sergeant Jones has a "favorite lady" who calls him frequently:

A woman had been calling him almost nightly and reporting tag numbers of cars of suspicious people driving around or parking in the area. He suggested after awhile, since he was spending an hour or so just about everyday on the phone, that she bring him a list of tag numbers every week or so. She did this: and beside each tag number she had written little notes like, "acts suspicious" or "foa." He found a lot of "foa's" on the lists and asked her what it meant. She said, "Fear of apprehension." He went along with this for quite a long time and finally decided that he should tell her that he was referring the case, because it was very important and contained a lot of leads—more than he could work on—to Corporal Gun. In the future he suggested she should provide her evidence directly to Corporal Gun. According to Jones, she still calls Gun with information and brings in the tag lists.

Since he is frequently in the office and is more an administrative than a working sergeant, Jones receives a number of these calls himself. Many are truncated in the same fashion as they are in Metro:

Jones took a telephone call. It was a girl who wanted to know if Jones could set up a buy or buy-bust from a Spanish male. In the course of the conversation, she said that her interest was only in getting a newspaper story. She wanted to know if he could set it up. He told her to call him back later if she determined that she could make a buy, and that she could then "walk him in" and he would make a buy. They would set up a buy-bust. After she hung up, Jones discussed with Smith why she might be calling. Smith said that she had previously called DEA and two nearby state police units, asking them what sort of information they had on people in a particular area. They suspected that she was trying to pump them to see what sort of information they had. They both suspected either she, or her boyfriend, or the fellow she lived with, is a dealer and that they were trying to find out who and what they knew about him or her and their friends and also, perhaps to try to get them to do away with some of their competition. It turned out that they had a file on both her and her boyfriend and miscellaneous information. They further suspected that she probably would not call back.

The following day, Jones received another phone call from her. At first the call was cut off. Then she called back. This gave him an opportunity to set up a tape recorder on the phone; he recorded the conversation. She claimed that the suspect would not deal to her and that obviously she couldn't cut in Jones. He asked her further whether she knew anything more about him. She said no, providing only incidental information, like he liked to play soccer in Creek Park and so on. Jones suggested that he was paranoid and she agreed, yes he was very suspicious. Then she mentioned a couple of other people saying that they knew Jones. He said yes, he knew the people she named. He jokingly said to her, "You seem to know a lot of our friends around here . . ." She said, "Oh, I used to hang around with those people, but I don't anymore. I just called you because I wanted a story. I'm a newspaperwoman now.' He chuckled and told her to call again when she had such "hot information" to give him.

I spent two periods with officers investigating locals and found the process rather frustrating and futile.

I came into the office one morning and found Officer Fox doing some paperwork in the investigator's office. He was the youngest person in the unit, the last one to be transferred in, and was generally being treated as a "gofer". He was preparing to take the marijuana plant he had seized in a raid over to the judge at the county court with the search warrant since the plant was evidence and had to be turned in with the served warrant. I asked if I could come along. We walked, the plant wobbling between us, green and healthy. I was embarrassed; he was proud. He gave it to the clerk at the County Court House and turned in the warrant. Then he took a broken radio to be fixed at the radio shop about five miles away. We spent about forty-five minutes there, talking about radios, about the high cost of parts, the fact that this was the third time that the radio had been in for repair in the last month. We left the radio to be repaired and went over to the lab and turned in the drug evidence for analysis. (This included drugs bought and seized in raids.) We talked for a while with the lab man. Fox then told me that he had to go and check out a few locals. We then drove by four addresses, first one way and then the other slowly past the doors of the houses. All the officers had micro-cassette tape recorders, and they used them in their local investigations to dictate case notes. These are subsequently typed by secretaries and filed under the case number. He did not get out of the car, ask any questions, walk around, or take any pictures. Each house had a number of vehicles parked around it and he noted them to run checks on the tag numbers later. It was about eleven o'clock in the morning and there were few signs of life in the neighborhood. "Dopers," he said, "sleep during the day and come out at night. They're all asleep." He said he recalled that some "bad guy" lived around here but could not recall his name. He dictated the description of the houses, the cars, and his impression that there was nothing further to investigate.

We then drove to the northern edge of the county to investigate a call that reported marijuana plants in the window of a second story apartment at a certain address in the city. I asked where these calls came from and from whom, and he said he didn't know, that the previous houses we had looked at had been named as having a lot of activity in and out of them at various times of the day and night, presumably reported by the neighbors. We drove into the parking lot and looked at the windows of the building. We could see no marijuana plants. It was by now about 95°, and neither of us wanted to get out. We drove around to another side of the building and again looked up at the second, third, and fourth floors. There was nothing remarkable to be seen there. We did not get out. We asked no questions and gathered no further information. He thought that one of the bad guys they had arrested earlier in the summer lived around here as he remembered, but he could not recall the address. We then drove back into Vista to have a hamburger, and he called in to say we were stopping at a hamburger place. After lunch, we drove around the city while he pointed out highlights of the city based on his work there as a traffic ticket officer. There were places where arguments had occurred, where one could watch "suspicious colored people," where big traffic tie-ups take place during rush hour and so on.

We then stopped at the doctor's office where he had an appointment. I walked down to the shopping mall and looked at towels and sheets, bought a pastry, and then strolled back to meet him. He said that these appointments and so on were on work time, but that he had given the sergeant the number of the doctor's office and had called in just before he went into the office telling the sergeant where he was if he was needed. He said that this time was sort of owed him, given all the time they spent working overtime. Since there was no comp time in the unit, there was a very informal way of keeping track of non-paid overtime which was worked out between the sergeants and the particular investigators. We walked back to the car sweating all the way, got in, and went to a drugstore to pick up a couple of items. I wandered around, looked at a few magazines and met him at the cash register. By this time it was mid-afternoon, and we drove out to the maintenance department at the other side of Center City to pick up a sign for Gordon. The sign, which read "No Parking, Suburban County," was going to be placed on a side street so that Gordon could park under it unobtrusively and observe the goings and coming of Hampster Gerbil. We looked at several signs and decided on one. We drove over to the county gas pumps and filled the car. It was nearing the end of the shift and with the locals successfully disposed of, we drove back to headquarters.

The second period I spent investigating locals was briefer, although no more satisfying.

After we sat on [surveilled] Hampster's apartment, we went out to check on a few locals. Gordon, like all the officers in the unit, prided himself on knowing all 256 square miles of the county, all the streets and addresses, and being able to "run on a call" and find the place without a map. This sometimes lead to embarrassment both for uniformed officers and for narcotics officers if they are going somewhere or are following verbal instructions on the radio from other investigators. On this night he had great trouble finding an address in Vista on the Vista/Salem line, and he circled around for about half an hour. The area is a middle-class suburban one, and there is no grid system; most of the streets wind around, changing their names, and are cross-cut by short roads, cul-de-sacs, and developers' cute innovations. He was not lost, but neither could he find the address. He gave up. We went to look at another house and found cars parked out front. He drove back into the station since it was about 11:00 o'clock and near the end of the shift.

These furtive nights and unsatisfying forays into the county are not found in Metro, where there are no assignments of this kind. In a way, because they are generally so fruitless from the investigator's perspective and a response to what they feel are political or administrative pressures, these investigations are viewed as time fillers. However, they also serve to keep new and inexperienced officers busy, acquaint them with the area and the "drug scene," and give them some semblance of an investigative task. For the most part, locals are exercises in administrative control and supervision, and although they do not yield many arrests, they do tend from time to time to symbolize the organization's interest in the everyday activities of the officers. That would appear to be a worthwhile aim.

Comment

The extent to which the organization affects targeting decreases as one proceeds from the militaristic mode to the major-violator mode to the agent-informant mode, and finally to the citizen mode.The control of the investigator increases as one proceeds from the episodes discussed in chapter 5 through those discussed in chapters 6, 7, and 8. Although different proportions of types of cases are found in the two years of arrest statistics studied for the two units, all modes of investigation are found in both. Suburban uses the buy-bust mode, it is smaller, and controls the flow of cases into the unit through the mechanism of the local, it has closer supervision and more enforced formal rules. Suburban is a more organizationally centered unit than is Metro.

Targeting is a very significant word for it implies a great deal of forethought, planning, rationality, and close linkage between the environment and the plans of the investigators. The events described are on the whole not very dramatic, not very orderly, often were abortively planned and executed, and undertaken in ignorance. Thus even within the confines of planned and constrained execution, drug policing is largely based on the individual's vision of the possible and social structure or social organization only outlines the edges of the possible. It cannot reduce dreams, hopes, visions, and fears to hard realities.

Appendix 8A

Transactions between organizations are not well understood, and much research is required. (See, for example, work in Hasenfeld and English, 1974, on interorganizational relationships, especially Levine and White, 1961, papers in Rosengren and Lefton, 1970, and Turk, 1973.) My data on them are intriguing, in part because they are so incomplete, and primarily "war stories" of events I did not observe but was told about by officers who had either heard about the events or told me about them. It is only possible to outline a frame of reference within which to consider these transactions rather than to consider them in detail. There are no formal rules stipulating how these calls should be handled. There is always a problem when a call comes into the unit and is recieved by an officer rather than a supervisor because a discretionary decision may be made at that point based entirely on the investigator's interests. But given that it is officially noted or received, a personalistic and situational dimension remains. Any call for assistance, joint investigation, or information is embedded in a historical context of relations between the units and can involve personal relations between the officer and other officers in the requesting unit, personal relationships between the commanders of the two units involved, and between the units as wholes that are seen in personal terms. Thus, although some general points are made about such calls, the fuzziness of the distinctions reflects the diverse ways in which they are processed. The rules governing the processing of these calls are subtle, tacit, and are only occasionally visible to the outside observer.

Two basic types of calls are received from other organizations. The first is when an organization, generally outside the criminal justice system such as a pharmacy, physician, chemical supply house, or school, calls for assistance. Such calls for assistance involving organizations outside the criminal justice system are different in the two units because Metro has a schools squad while Suburban does not. Metro aslo has a pharmacies and doctors squad, while such calls are investigated on an ad hoc basis or referred to the state police by Suburban officers.

From a strategic point of view, then, Metro was better able and more likely to respond systematically to requests coming from either of these sources and was better able to routinize both the receipt of information and organizational response to it. The second sort of call, to be considered in more detail here, is one from another organization within the criminal justice system. They may call to report an activity, to ask for information or assistance, or request (or imply the need for) a joint operation. These calls may be received from local, state, or federal agencies, and can be classified in terms of a two-variable table (see table A8.1).

Table A8.1 Rates of exchange of information, degrees of cooperation, and salience of personal contacts between agencies in the criminal justice system in the Metro-Suburban area, spring and summer 1975, by whether the cooperation was legally required and the valence of the image of the organizations involved

Relationship Legally Required?	Valence of Image	
	Positive	Negative
Yes	A High rates of information exchange and cooperation. Medium salience of personal contacts in initiating and sustaining communication.	B Medium rates of information exchange. Little cooperation. High salience of personal contacts in initiating and sustaining communication.
No	C Medium rates of information exchange and cooperation. Medium to high salience of personal contacts for communication.	D Low rates of exchange of information. Little to no cooperation. Highly personalized basis for contacts and communication.

Table A8.1 shows some aspects of the exchange of information and working relationship among and between the units in the criminal justice system. We can briefly examine these exchanges in terms of their basis in legal requirement and the kind of image of each other the organizations maintain. Some interchanges are legally required (see rows of table A8.1). The courts and the district vice units in Metro are examples, as are drug treatment agencies in both areas. There are a number of interorganizational transactions that are not mandated by law, and these are very frequent in both units. The majority of these are between the various police drug control units in the area. The most important of these are the five counties in the Metro region as well as in Metro itself and its district vice units, which have their own informant files, monies, tacit policies, and division of emphasis between the various vice crimes that they are expected to enforce.

A second dimension along which interorganizational relations can be classified is the degree to which a positive or negative imagery is shared by the two units. Looking at other units from the perspective of the unit that initiates the call, or first has the information, the other organization either has a positive or a negative valence. The most positive the image of another organization, the more it is trusted. Where there are not formal rules prescribing or proscribing exchange of information, then trust becomes important. In the police context, as many observers have argued, exchange of information is based on a personalistic view of authority and has a rather restricted code of relevance (Peabody, 1962; Bittner, 1974; Manning, 1977a.) If exchange is legally required and there is a positive imagery shared between the two units (A), one finds high rates of information exchanged, cooperation on investigation including the sharing of publicity, credit, and perhaps arrests. Personal issues such as the personalities of the commanders of the respective units are not salient. This was true for the relationships between Suburban and the county prosecutor's office and between Suburban and the drug control commission of the county.

When there is a negative imagery of each other and legal mandating of exchange (B), medium rates of information exchange will be obtained, there will be little cooperation (it could be characterized as foot dragging), and personal relationships will be critical in making something work. This was the situation between Metro and both court systems in which they worked; and the relationships between central and district vice in Metro.

Where exchange is not required and the relationships are based on a positive image (C), then there will be medium rates of information exchange, cooperation will flow, and there will be fairly great dependence on personal contacts and knowledge of investigators and personnel in other units. This was the pattern between DEA and Suburban County. In general, Suburban officers were much more positive about their relationship with DEA than were the Metro people.

Where exchange is not legally required and there is a negative general image of the other organization (D), then there will be low rates of information exchange, little or no cooperation, and the relationships will be highly personallized and individualistic. This was the case between the two units studied, between DEA and Metro, and between Suburban County and King Edward County. Suburban abutted King Edward County on the eastern boundary. King Edward also bounded Metro across almost the entire northern boundary of the city.

It is a contradiction to evaluate or assess conduct by formal criteria that are not valid from the perspective of those evaluated (at any level within the organization), irrelevant to their everyday work, or inconsistent with the tacit, or real means and aims of the organization. There are serious impediments, structural and social-psychological, which obviate evaluation and mitigate the impact of formal evaluation within police drug units. Evaluation is neither systematically utilized nor taken seriously by participants in either unit. It is viewed quite generally as an object of disdain and mockery by virtually all involved in the process. Those who support evaluation, those of lieutenant rank and above, are so dependent upon their subordinates' reports and assessments that their concern is an empty one that lacks substantive detail.

The frame of reference adopted here does not negate evaluation, nor reject its value, but it does impy that any evaluation must be contextual, taking into account the particular meanings of the types of events that are repeatedly encountered; the lack of concensus within the organizations concerning the proper means and ends of their work, the perhaps necessary discretion allowed to agents, and the systematic eschewal of general policies and carefully enforced and sanctioned procedures.

Evaluation in People-Processing Organizations

There are profound but not insurmountable problems in evaluating people-processing organizations. The researcher investigating people-processing organizations lacks a paradigm and there is no agreement about the units and measures that should be employed in studying outputs. In the absence of a clearly formulated unit, interpretation of measures of production is problematic. However, this interpretative problem remains regardless of one's choice of performance and output measures. The product, trained persons, human services, treated persons, is not easily isolated for measurement. What constitutes an "educated woman"? How is mental "health" to be measured? What is a "crime-free" environment? The complexity of human action virtually guarantees that a variety of aspects of human conduct will be altered by any prolonged treatment, rehabilitative, or corrective process, but what changes are specifically and exclusively attributable to the socialization or resocialization process? Further, the value of the product is likely to be debated among the recipients, even if there is consensus among the producers about product values. In this context, organizations have tended either to seize on convenient measures of means to the end (for example, how many students have been graduated rather than the quality of the education they have received; number of arrests rather than the prevention of crime); redefined their goals to make them more proximal (reducing the crime rate from last year or decreasing the rate of increase); or have avoided the problem by obscuring their functions in the rhetoric of sacredness (as in churches, education in general, and private mental health organizations). This pattern of obscuring the relation between ends and means, and the very real problems associated with evaluation of people-processing, means that it is difficult to engage in comparative organizational research that attempts to assess such organizations by output measures.

The field of police research is no different; the same measurement problems occur with respect to productivity.[1] One of the most common modes of adjustment to the evaluation/productivity problem has been to use efficiency measures or the allocation of resources, the costs of engaging in a particular line of action given budgetary limits or obligations. The relative costs of police patrol can be judged by comparing the cost of operating cars in different sized districts, or the cost of patrol on foot can be compared to the costs of automobile patrol, or response time can be used as a measure of efficiency.

In the drug field, measures of arrests serve this function of measuring efficiency: the cost of each arrest can be determined by dividing arrests into salaries, operating costs, and other expenses, such as buy money, rewards, and salaries paid to informants. None of these measures permits one to measure effectiveness such as the impact of the activities of the police upon crime, or their impact upon drug use or dealing. It is impossible to measure something for which you have neither concept nor data. How many users of opiates are there? There are no accurate and reliable figures for any given city or for the nation as a whole. What does their habit cost them either in dollars or dollar equivalents such as stolen property, goods, or services? What kinds of drugs in what amounts (both legal and illegal) are in use? Where do the drugs originate? No one knows the answers to these questions. Furthermore, in the absence of figures, control organizations will construct, manipulate, fabricate, and make "best guesses." This is so because all organizations are in a competitive environment and must justify their existence through quantitative figures if possible, and because for a variety of reasons the control of crime, and especially the crimes that are associated with drugs, is seen as something akin to a moral crusade. Moral crusades are sacred enterprises, cloaked in mystery, carried out in secret, fraught with ambiguity, and suffused with emotion.

Certain features of the nature of policing amplify the problem of evaluation at the organizational level. The first is the negative view of paperwork, the second is the informal basis of evaluation, and the third is the absence of carefully kept case files.

Paperwork as Dirty Work

Dirty work is viewed by E. C. Hughes as something considered, within one's own occupation, as beneath one's dignity or as potentially disgusting (1958:49–53). Police officers view paperwork as a kind of "dirty work." The police define their "real work" as clinical, tactical, face-to-face interaction with people in need of help or control. They see the work as being bounded by and limited to the street, concretely defined in terms of persons and events, and seen as human conduct only converted by administrative fiat into paper after the social significance has been drained off by officer decisions (Manning, 1977a: chapter 6). Paperwork in the two units studied was significant because it was defined as something other than action. It is not red tape in the sense that Gouldner (1952) has used the term (paper that is excessive or when definitions of real and ritualized action are in conflict), because all paper is viewed as irrelevant to accomplishing the officer's work as defined by the officer. The concept used here directs attention not only to those administrative actions that are seen as relevant and necessary, but to the fact that administrative decision-making, responsibility, and evaluation are discredited as non-police functions. When the reality of police work is on the street, then all other forms of reality assume a lesser significance. Further, this means that the primary code into which all other events will be transformed, and in a way retained as reality, will be the code of the street.

Several of the consequences of such a view of paper are significant, for the lack of relevance of control based on written records means that other modes of control, planning, evaluation, assessment of unit effectiveness, and quality control are salient in drug units. Paper is the defining characteristic of formal operations; but is rejected as irrelevant. In this way paper becomes the negative, or contrasting conception, against which real work is measured.

The negative view of paperwork means that complaints received by phone will remain inactionable if they do not become paper after the investigator receives the information. They may become nonofficial paper, such as notes in an officer's file or in his personal notebook, but no official forms are used to record the incoming data. In other words, they disappear as leads, clues, or cases and cannot be traced, retrieved, reinvestigated, or tracked to discover their disposition.

Paper, because it is viewed as negative and "unreal," cannot serve as a meaningful locus of planning. More specifically, long-range planning is systematically eschewed because it involves written ideas, intent, shared conceptions of action and priorities, and a set of limitations on individual discretion that would be both anticlinical and tactical. Because it would involve paper, sharing ideas, which might give some officers advantage over others and would implicitly relinquish control of street action to others (at least logically if not in fact), planning, and paper assessments of future options are viewed suspciously, with some hostility, and considered irrelevant to the job.

If paperwork is viewed negatively and as ex post facto reconstruction of previously meaningful events, then action that is represented for the officer only in terms of paper will be viewed as suspicious and only obliquely related to the reality of the events captured and described on paper. A microcosmic example of this is the arrest and charge situation (Manning, 1977a: 188–192). The conditions under which the charge is made are different from those under which the arrest is made. For example, charges are discussed with other officers in order to frighten the arrestee into confession, that is, officers lie to them about what they will be charged with, thus making the relationships between the arrest, evidence, and charge tenuous. Because large numbers of people may be arrested when officers have no intention of charging them, arrest and the paper are not isomorphic. Evidence thought to be narcotic after laboratory analysis may be found to be harmless and non-narcotic: face powder, dextrose, strichnine, aspirin, cocoa. Thus the case as written, based on the presumption of having legally admissible narcotic evidence, is only tentative since chemical tests on the scene may be inconclusive or the wrong test may have been used. Arrests may be made and charges brought in order to harrass a person regardless of the anticipated evidence available to assemble against him; they may be thrown out at any level above the investigator; sergeant, lieutenant, the prosecutor's office, etc.

Built into the processing of police paper is the fact that the decisions made on the street by the officer are reviewed, discussed, recast, argued about, and reformulated in the office. The arresting officer may or may not have a part in this negotiation, either with a partner or a sergeant. Thus the paper reality seems to stand apart from the street reality. The issue is precisely how the rules and procedures of the orgnization can be recast, describe, or rationalize decisions taken in complex, chaotic, sometimes rapidly occurring events. Consistency between reports and events is bought at a cost and does not favor behavioral events more than reported formalized accounts.

Statistics, case files (unless they are one's own informal records), and evaluations are a special instance of the above point. They are created quite literally from the stuff of experience in the investigator's offices. They are talked about, talked out, and shaped. Quantitative records, as a result, stand in ambiguous relationship to officers' versions. The written record has a variable relationship to any reason offered as an account for the production of that paper. Papering, or filing a case, was controlled by agencies other than the police and therefore was viewed as a marginal police function.

Paper is a synecdoche for the place in which it was found. Paper centers, or offices in drug units, are defined as places where one does trivial things, personal business, and makes short-term arrangements:

Trivia: Complaints must be processed; evidence must be wrapped and shipped to the drug analysis labs; incident forms must be filled in (expense reports, incidental vouchers for money for payment); arrest forms must be typed; search warrants and affidavits must be processed. The latter is perhaps the most important of the work done other than the typing of the arrest form done when prisoners are sitting waiting to be processed.

Personal business: Calling wives, friends, and lovers; dealing in real estate; doing favors in the department for non-police friends (checking on the disposition of cars that had been impounded, licenses revoked); calls to family on the long-distance phone used for checking leads that involved surrounding counties and more distant locales, eating, reading newspapers, and gossiping (some of which is case-related).

Short-term deals: Calls are made to investigators concerning deals that are to go down, surveillances in progress, and arrangements are made to meet informants and/or other officers by phone.

The office is defined by what is done there and is viewed as a place for accomplishing non-serious and/or minor paperwork related to the job. The serious business that is transacted in the office, limited in amount, may well be serious personal business. As a result, in both units people habituate the office only when they have "nothing else to do," with the following exceptions: typing up arrest papers, search warrants, raid plans and reports, affidavits, requests for money needed immediately, which is only the case if their sergeant does not have money in his kitty for immediate use, or awaiting a phone call from an informant. These are usually fairly brief tasks, limited to around fifteen to twenty minutes a piece except in the case of "waiting," an arrest, and the processing of relevant evidence.[2] If a person hangs around the office excessively, he will be questioned by his sergeant, usually jokingly. As a result, from around 8:30 or 9:00 A.M. until 2:30 P.M. or so during the morning shift, only one or two people other than clerks will be in the office. The units were quiet and deserted during the day and for most of the evening shift (4:00 P.M.–12:00 A.M.) as well.

Paper is neither kept, kept up to date, nor kept in a form that would

permit sharing across units within the department unless the case resulted in an arrest, charge, or other formal action, and then the records
would be found in the central records department, not in the unit. Once
these formal records are made out, the likelihood that the information
contained therein will be available for supervisory scrutiny increases.
But the fact that the supervisors can look over such records may mean
that they will mistake what is written for what has been done or could
be done. In the two units, this assumption was not made by supervisors, and they generally tried to chat casually with investigators from
time to time to "see how things were going."

The two organizations do differ in their capacity to monitor, guide,
and control the officer, and part of this capacity results from different
paperwork systems. The ways in which cases are opened, "investigated, and closed is variable in the two units. Both organizations must
attempt to order the behavior of their investigators with an understanding of the problem of drugs crimes in general. However, the capacity of
the two organizations to track the flow of information received, located
in cases, and the number, kind, potential, and possible outcomes of
these cases are different.

These conceptions of paperwork introduce a patterned complexity
in the operations of both units. To the uncertainty seen in the enacted
environment are added the uncertainties that result because virtually
all the significant enforcement decisions are made informally and are
rarely formalized in writing. Those segments of the organization that do
not believe in paperwork, namely but not exclusively the lower participants, believe that planning and the like is not expected of the police
by the public, nor do they themselves view their work as one of executing paper plans articulated in detail a priori.[3]

The Informal Basis of Evaluation

Other aspects of police work in general and drug work in particular
make evaluation of agent performance and unit performance as a
whole quite difficult. In general there is an abiding and readily apparent conflict between the investigators' rationality and administrators'
rationality. Officers deny the legitimacy of formal authority as a basis

for evaluating their work (see Freidson, 1975:183), supervisors claim that they are aware of what each officer is doing and why and that they trust them. They subscribe to a personalistic, individualistic, and context-bound view of the work and of the evaluation process itself. They prefer informal means of assessment and are most comfortable with it in their own dealings with each other and with drug users and dealers. They have confidence in sources they personally view as trustworthy and in informal means of gathering information on their colleagues. If a narcotics officer were to adopt fully the formal means of evaluation, he or she would be denying the centrality of trust. This position would obviate the basic rules of the work that revolve around the assessment and maintenance of personal trust relationships. Further, then, the adoption of formal methods means a rejection of the informal bases of the work. It is apparent that in both units the officers maintained a profound attachment to informal means of evaluation and trust assessment. Instead of viewing the administrative measures as realistic, they continued to see them as another foreign form of rationality that was largely irrelevant to their day-to-day work. The measures, they felt, were somewhat arbitrary and were perhaps chosen more for their utility as supervisory tools than for their validity as indices of real work or good police work. They felt there was obvious wisdom contained in this observation and were quite mystified by the persistence of some paper pushers who sought complete, or at least, written records of cases. The tension this perpetuates is considerable and lasting and is a source of contradiction between the public statements of goals, objectives, and measures of effect and the assessment of officers of the quality of their work and that of their colleagues.

In both units there is considerable unease about stipulating the overall purposes or goals of drug enforcement. Although general and rather abstract goals can be elicited in interviews, there is no consensus about what the overall aim is and what relationships there are, if any, between these goals and the indices of success, such as seizures, arrests, charges, search warrants served, drugs bought, etc. Even among agreed upon measures, there was disagreement within the administrative component.

The measures of success vary. One could choose from among the several indicators asked for on the activity sheet; in Metro, search warrants applied for and served, assisted on, and arrests; and in Suburban, value of seized drugs or arrests.

The measures are not applied in the same fashion in the two units as Metro tends to evaluate individual officers, while Suburban gathers data only for the unit according to the administrators.

Official reports vary in what is reported. Reports for Suburban contain data on arrests, search warrants served, monies expended, and seizures, as well as a brief description of major cases with successful outcomes undertaken in the year. Metro only publishes arrests made and charges lodged in their public reports.

In addition to this absent agreement, there is a cloak of cynicism that surrounds and embeds formal written reports of all kinds, whether by the unit, the department, by other agencies, or businesses. There is a sense in which the organization discounts and dismisses its own records as accurate portrayals of its work. When they are required, they are done grudgingly, are not trusted, and are set aside as beside the point when discussing what has been done, what will be done, and how well it has been done. Activity reports of individual officers, which contain information on their arrests, assists on arrests, warrants served, court appearances, and so forth, are called "scandal sheets," or "lie sheets," and it is implied that they are mannered misrepresentations of the actual activities of officers.

Knowledge is defined as knowledge possessed by individual officers, as personal knowledge. Although this is readily admitted at every level on an informal, face-to-face basis, it is officially viewed by officials as undesirable. It is denied as being against policy. All information, according to the official postition in both units, is organizational information. This is true for both informants, who are meant to be the unit's informants not an indivdal officer's informants, and case-relevant information. Since knowledge is of this personal and context-bound sort, it cannot very well be simultaneously universal, trans-situational, and formalized knowledge. It cannot be reproduced, passed on to other units or officers, stored for future reference, tied in with other ongoing investigations unless this results from face-to-face contacts, and cannot be reproduced accurately at some future date for use by others. Personal knowledge, as Crozier has suggested (1964), is a source of power and independence. On the other hand, it creates dependence by the supervisors and administrators upon the lower participants. The more the lower participants know about their cases, the less is known by their supervisors, and the more power accrues to the lower participants. As a result, the less case information, the less control the administrators can exercise over the accumulated knowledge base of the unit. The power of the lower participants to choose their cases, to work and drop them at will, gives them autonomy from further supervision. The information is cast in an invisible code because it is not formulated in a way that can be independently verified by supervisors. This control, discretion, and source of power gives the drug officer a great deal of power and shapes his role in an important fashion.

Cases are viewed in the context of making cases. Since other things besides the actions of the officer can affect the outcomes of a case, he is only held accountable for getting some cases and informants to work; working, keeping busy, being a self-starter, and being self-motivated; and imagining outcomes that might occur if other things do not intrude, or anticipating some of the things that might intrude. Thus there is a double-bind in the evaluation process because although the paper may show one thing, what people are actually doing or did do are considered as quite another thing. Depending on the aspects of performance that are seized upon as the basis for evaluation in a situation, either the visible (arrests, seizures, buys) or the invisible (making cases) dimensions, are salient. This contradiction, that either one or the other is used, but both are from time to time most valued, and that they lead to different conclusions about the quality of the work done, is mediated, as shown below in the two units, but it blurs the rational tie between output and input since these are joined in the minds of supervisors in complex ways not given in the reports produced by the investigators.

The most significant audience for the officer is other officers. Officers defer to each other's judgment in investigations when they ask for advice but otherwise try to pick up tips and styles of investigation from officers they admire. In both the units there were a handful of officers who were universally thought to be good policemen. Although their preferred work styles were slightly different, several liked to work undercover; they were thought to be shrewd, intelligent, hardworking, always able to anticipate what a bad guy would do, always controlling their informants and not being controlled by them. These were the persons others pointed to when they were asked for examples of good police work. I was referred to them to interview because they were thought to be the best in the unit. The two sergeants in Suburban were viewed as skilled and were deferred to, but only one of the ten sergeants in Metro was generally respected; there were strong differences of opinion about all of them except this officer. None of the higher administrators was mentioned in this context.

Not only are informal evaluations preferred to formal evaluations, the most important source of evaluation is other officers. Many of the stories told by officers had a braggadocian quality that seemed intended to impress, much like the bullshitting stories of hitchhikers (Mukerji, 1977). They were ego-boosting tall tales to punctuate or make less dreary the otherwise rather boring and mundane aspects of the work. "War stories" are not just an accidental product of police work, for they strike me as the primary mechanism by which the dreary is made dramatic, the tedious made traumatic, and the boring made bold.[4] Officers are oriented to each other's evaluations not only because it is self-protective in the short run and minimizes the intrusion of outside supervision and the imposition of external criteria of success but also because it is consistent with their long-term interests in the department.

Case Files as Personal Knowledge

The key organizational record, the most salient item from the point of view of formal rationality, is the file. According to Weberian thinking, the file is the focal point of all office work because it maintains a comparable, historical, non-context-embedded record of decisions taken in the past and of anticipations of the future. Around the file hinges formal rationality. However, in an important and consistent manner, files are not only not kept, they are not kept for carefully considered and quite principled reasons. There is a fair amount of evidence from other studies that investigators are very hesistant to maintain full and complete case files (Greenwood, Chaiken, and Petersilia, 1977; Wilson, 1978; Williams, Redlinger, and Manning, 1978). The reasons listed below are not idiosyncratic to these organizations or to drug investigators but tend to reflect social organizational and social-psychological features of police work.[5] Many files are not created for cases, clues do not become formalized as cases, and even if certain leads are followed but do not produce, they are not filed in case jackets. Obviously, as a result, cases cannot be tracked and the time spent on them measured. The ratio of time or effort to yield cannot be measured, and cost benefits cannot be calculated.

Why Case Files Are Not Written Up and/or Not Filed

Competition between individual officers and/or squads means that "open files" would give others a chance to have access to same information, and then they could make the arrest first. Cases can be closed with arrest at almost any time, and there are no clear constraints as in other crimes of particular felon(s) being sought. As a result, there is a general fear of others having this information, which is defined as personal property, gained through skill, persistence or luck, available to others. This availability would act as a symbolic transformation of the data from one code (private, personal) to another (public).

If squads differentially specialize, as they do in Metro, other officers could change or alter the nature of the investigation from a street case to a conspiracy case.

Written files could make filed information available to other units within the department or other agencies, which may be perceived as being in competition with the agency.

Files could be used to check the quality of an investigation, key decision points, evidence available/gathered, witnesses or the like. Investigators may resist making files for this reason.

Private files protect informants from being subpoenaed to court by defense attorneys, thus exposing other ongoing investigations or informants.

Relevant information is defined as that needed to make a case accept-able for prosecution. Some aspects of this definition may obscure or make invisible certain legally relevant facts; informants and their reli-ability, strength of facts documenting the choice of the target, other methods or strategies utilized. These facts are also those needed by other investigators to "branch-off," follow up clues, and pursue related cases.

If there are no organizational controls on opening or closing a case, a practical "closing out" attitude operates. In a sense, all cases are opened and closed by means of the creation of the file at the time of arrest, that is, cases have or take an official life or status at that point.

Each case in the file is seen as a closed or dead item, not closely con-nected to other cases. If it were "alive," it would not have been written up in this fashion. From this view, the drug system is not seen as a sys-tem or network of transactions but as a discrete set of persons vulnera-ble to arrest.

Making up a file containing full details of all actions taken in connec-tion with an investigation is an exception in the two units studied. The rule is that officers keep their cases in the form of scrawled notes on the backs of napkins, bits of paper torn from notebooks, telephone message forms, and other handy kinds of paper. They tend to keep the working conception of the case and what it's about in their heads or in their desks, and rarely keep completed files in their desks to be used as an ongoing repository of information categorized and placed in some meaningful order that is understandable by others. A case may be limited to a few telephone numbers, a name or two, and an address. Sometimes a few descriptors such as "deals from his apartment," or "Slick's sister," or "worked for J. before" may accompany the names and numbers, but they are idiosyncratic marks, standing outside a clearly shared paradigm or format that is universally understood by other investigators and supervisors.

The desire to conceal what has been done and might be done is based upon a realistic desire to maintain some secrecy about opera-tions and reduce the probability that information will be leaked to tar-gets of investigations. But there are two other reasons why statistics and assessments based on reports and files are viewed with little regard. When officers in Suburban were asked to put down the distribution of their hours spent in particular functions, they felt it was a totally unrealistic exercise because the implication of such a scheme is that there is a reasonable expectation of consistency among time, effort, and outcome. This equation is considered by all involved in drug enforcement to be spurious and misleading. There is an element of uncertainty that officers perceive in the constellation of events that might lead to a big case. On the one hand, they recognize the possibility that any tip, call, or informant's comment might lead to a good case, and there is virtually no certain way to predict outcomes from initial information. On the other hand, even good tips, well investigated, and well planned, can yield nothing because of events that lie out of the control of the investigator, such as when the person does not show at a meeting set for a buy-bust because a friend comes in from out of town and they go out rather than do business. Simple traffic stops based on broken taillights can yield substantial seizures, although well-planned and executed wire intercept cases yielding enormous data and knowledge of dealing activities can be thrown out of court on technicalities having nothing to do with the work of the officers.

This reservation implied another: even the most routine case, other than street rips and their equivalent, can involve enormous waiting time. This waiting time is unavoidable but somehow not real work. It was not "real work" because it was done in the office, and because it was not on-the-street investigation. The things for which officers wait are different in content, but the result is the same. One sergeant demonstrated the characteristic pose of the narc. He swung his feet up on the desk, crossed one leg over the other, and tipped back in his chair with his hands clasped behind his neck.

Metro

In Metro, there are two types of evaluative contexts: the major violator context and the other contexts including agent-informant and citizen targeting. Each is the reciprocal of the other because one or the other must be the context if it is evaluative. (Some of the problems of the appearance of this context have been detailed in chapter 6 and are not repeated here.) Since the rotor, major violator, does not enter the context when other types of investigations are being considered, the arrest focus tends to close off the more obvious difficulties seen in most investigations undertaken in Metro.

Mobilization, Evaluation, and Goal Attainment in the Major-Violator Mode

Narcotics law enforcement is in many respects open-ended and punctuated by uncertainties. The attainment of an organizational goal, the control of major violators, is embedded in a number of situational contexts.* Since there is no written policy in either setting and no guiding procedures concerning the precise where, when, and how of narcotics work, and only 5 percent of the officers have training other than on-the-job training, the ways in which axial terms are situationally defined guides enforcement. If there is to be guided action to control major violators, then there must not only be prospective definitions of the target term (major violators) and its features, but also day-to-day control monitoring and evaluation of critical activities. These critical activities are those that surround the purchasing of narcotics by agents or informants. With the evidence of a purchase, an officer can apply for a search warrant and make a raid on a house allegedly containing drugs, possibly make an arrest and seize drugs. The internal control system is crucial as an interactive arena in which meanings are negotiated and from which sanctionable violations emerge.

Agents in Metro Department must have prior approval from an official for any narcotics purchase. The purpose of this rule is to maintain control over the types of cases being made, to elicit an explanation of the purpose of the purchase, and to maintain some balance between amounts spent on purchases and informant payments, arrests, and drug seizures. The vouchers submitted by investigators for repayment once an advance has been drawn and paid out to buy drugs, information, or miscellaneous services are simple. They require only a one-

*The following section appeared in a slightly different form in P.K. Manning, "Rules in Organizational Context: Narcotics Law Enforcement in Two Settings," *Sociological Quarterly* 18(Winter, 1977):44–61.

sentence summary of the purpose of the payment: "For information received in narcotics investigation, Metro P.D. to SE ——— , ——— dollars" and are signed by the investigator and supervising sergeant.

Officials review these payments monthly, at least, as does the financial division of the Metro Department. The review aims to monitor the effectiveness of purchases of drugs and information although no specific rules are laid down to guide this process. Rough rules of thumb are used. One lieutenant said, "I call in the sergeants and speak to 'em if they're not getting results; they know what's a reasonable payment and that we have to keep the costs down here." The definition of a "reasonable payment" is shifting, however, and is only known in light of ex post facto knowledge received by the official who approves the payment. The success of an investigation that involves payment is based on the number of arrests, size of seizure, significance of the dealer arrested, etc. In any case, once results are known, they rationalize expenditures.

It is not necessary for investigators to seek prior approval for buys or payments made. This is true for the following reasons:

Buys or payments can be made by investigators from their own miscellaneous expense monies or from reimbursements recently received from prior vouchers;

Payments can be made from the investigator's own money for which he plans to be reimbursed after a buy or raid has occurred;

Payments can be made from money allocated for a previously approved deal that fell through and from which the officer has retained the money;

Some sergeants, in addition to the $200 kitty assigned to them for payments to their squad members, retain additional money, which they obtain by writing IOU's to the sergeant in charge of the funds in the main office of the unit. This money can be allotted to investigators for needed buys on short notice;

Some investigators do not submit vouchers immediately but let them accumulate, thus masking the actual use of the money, especially if it is expended in small amounts or taken in the form of an advance.

Since investigators do not require prior approval for buys (or investigations), they can determine in large part not only what cases they will work in what fashion, but the payments they will make to their informants. Judgments concerning prospective worth, potential, or even the cost of an investigation cannot be made by supervisors as a result, and they tend to affirm decisions already made. Thus a judgment about whether a case involves a major violator cannot be determined from the amount of payments made to an informant unless they include very large payments. Guidance and direction to a level of the market can only be accomplished when a very large payment (above $150) is involved. Such large buys will always require approval. There is no guarantee, conversely, that a series of small buys and payments will not result in a large seizure of drugs and an important case being developed. Paperwork does not provide control necessary for evaluation, for it is seen in precisely the same prospective-retrospective set of situationally defined controls. Payments and records of payments can be seen as a means to provide ongoing monitoring of the level and direction of agents' activities.

It is assumed by investigators and officials that a single voucher request covers a variety of phenomena. The one exception is money for a drug buy that must be accounted for after a buy is made. However, the amount bought, the price paid, and the money given the informant can be manipulated by the investigator; a person makes a $10 buy of heroin, is shown to have bought a $15 bag and been given a $10 fee for doing the job. A voucher is written for $25. The investigator can pocket all but the $10 for the buy. More commonly, the investigator wants to "lay a little extra cash on" an informant to keep him loyal or interested, so he simply makes out a slip stating "paid to X for information received." This is possible if the investigator also tells his sergeant in conversation what the general rationale for the payment is. Such verbal explanations or accounts expand or redefine the nature of what is stated on the written voucher. Vouchers require little explanation to be provided. Once the officer has made such payments or prepayments to informants, he has few sanctions to force the informant to work on the next occasion they meet. Thus the feeling is always that informants are getting more out of you than they should. They are always in arrears to the investigator if the investigator has had good luck with them in the past and if the investigator keeps mental notes on the relationship between work done and payments. Certainly, some of these payments take the form of gifts that cannot technically be calculated along the same lines as payments for services rendered. Vouchers can cover a bonus for doing a good job after making several buys or for information provided by an SE that led to a large seizure (ranging from $15 to $300); gifts to dealers; small personal needs (phone bills, transportation to meet the officers); straight payment for work done at the rate of $10–$15 a controlled buy and occasionally a weekly salary.

However, payments are not understood by investigators in the above-described logically partitioned fashion. Because of the oblique relationship between payment and action and because administrators so infrequently have independent knowledge of the activities of the SEs, except through the verbal descriptions of an officer and the paper he generates, the investigators' definition of proper payment determines what is actually paid. The understandings or implicit norms held by the investigator embed each request and each amount submitted for ex post facto approval by officials. These shown facts, amounts paid, indicate roughly the investigator's prospective decisions. When I asked what tasks would be paid for by $10, or what a $10 fee would mean if it had been paid an informant, one investigator told me:

Well, it is very difficult to answer this because you have to ask yourself several questions. O.K., the first is what do I owe him previously? The source he is buying from—is he a major dealer? Is he dealing in quarters, eighth pieces or ounces, or is he dealing in $10 bags? What class of informant is he? Is he a guy who is working on a major class of informants, bigger things, or is he a guy who is only working $10 bag people?

Payments are never context-free: Any task is embedded in a set of ongoing relationships between the informant and the investigator. A "$10 buy" is virtually always embedded in the investigator's expectations: What is the nature of the investigation? What risk is involved for the informant? Where is it going? At what level of the market are you hoping to intervene? What arrests and seizures do you expect? What have you expected from this informant in the past? What is his potential in that particular investigation, and what has he done in the past? Therefore, one cannot elicit an answer that would generate conditions of a $10 buy because the $10 is always linked to a set of other activities and other payments that constitute it as one event in a sequence or series of events. In other words the payment reflects both the nature of the personalized moral bond between the investigator and his informant and the instrumental aims that the investigator hopes to obtain from this particular investigation.

Also taken into consideration in setting payments, but not placed in writing, is the constraint of the past relationship that the informant has established with persons with whom he is transacting drug business. For example, if an informant is a heroin user, he can make buys from particular individuals at very little risk to himself by acting in a fashion that is consistent with his past behavior and requires few new introductions or ingratiation. His previous social ties in the dealing-using network enable him to work successfully as an informant. However, it is possible for a $10 buy or a few $10 buys to lead to something important if one is buying in order to get next to a higher level dealer, or if one hopes through that strategy to enable an informant to introduce an undercover man to the dealer or to broaden the investigation by subsequently making larger buys. On the other hand, if the informant is expected to work in a larger investigation, and if the informant becomes involved in making bigger buys, the informant takes greater risks. He must have been involved previously in a network that would permit him to make those buys, and therefore must run a greater social and personal risk because of the limited numbers of people with whom a major violator will deal. A dealer of an ounce or more will deal carefully to only a few selected and trusted persons. Therefore, a limited number of people can be identified as possible betrayers or snitches if the dealer or one of his lieutenants is arrested or caught in a raid. If a person who was previously a $10-bag buyer wants to make a $50 buy from a dealer, questions are raised by the dealer. It is very unlikely that a small-time user will have money for such a purchase: If he has previously bought at a particular level then his income is such that he will continue to buy at that level. It is assumed that "a strung-out junkie is a strung-out junkie." If he begins to buy opiates in larger amounts, such as half or quarter pieces, then it is likely that he will switch dealers.

These structural/economic constraints are the source of important interconnections such as those between the class of informant, the level of the dealing structure, the amount of money involved, and the personal risk entailed. Consequently, it is assumed that money compensates or motivates the informant to provide information necessary to lead to the arrest of a given dealer. The more risk and the higher the level, the higher the fee. All the phenomena are interconnected. While a $10 buy is viewed in the context of the implications and consequences that can be foreseen at the time, its meaning and worth change both prospectively and retrospectively.

Prospective meanings of what information is worth are contextually evaluated by the officer in terms of the variables outlined. Of course, the precise implications of the social relations change as new information comes into play. For example, if it is found that a person is no longer dealing but that his brother is dealing, then the former relationship between the informant and the dealer may no longer be relevant to the case. Indeed, it becomes another case at that time. The promised information may not be produced by the informant, the raid may not produce the promised drugs or persons, or it may never be mounted. The practice among virtually all officers is to avoid setting a price and certainly to avoid payment until after the named task is completed. If possible, the money may not be tied to a specifically named task, but to a number of cases. If the informant is not a paid informant, but is working off a charge, then he will be expected to work it off at the rate of two or three for one (two cases for their own reduced charge). The definition of a case is left to the officer. He will not name a price in advance, and the worth of the case in social and monetary terms continues to vary until the officer decides that it is "closed" and decides to pay off the informant. In general, however, officers prefer not to owe informants for several jobs because informants forget, try to get more money, will exaggerate what they have done, and try to pressure the officer into giving them petty gifts (cigarettes, drinks, a six-pack of beer). The larger the unpaid balance, officers feel, the greater the social debt that they can be construed to owe the informant by the informant. All this results in pressure toward fast working, opening and closing cases, and paying small amounts on a regular basis to informants as they produce. In effect, though, the prospective meaning of a case is viewed as an unrealistic guess by officers, and they prefer to review rather than to preview the worth of informants.

Retrospective understandings are also important. In Metro, unlike Suburban, no fixed bonus is paid; a percent of the value of the seized drugs or payment for guns seized, and good seizures are defined by investigators in line with what they have initially expected. If a raid yields a larger quantity of drugs and more arrests than had been anticipated, then a bonus of up to $300 will be paid to the SE. Retrospective determination is also made if information that might clear another crime, such as a homicide, is provided by an informant to a narcotics officer. If the arrest warrant is served and the person is charged, then a bonus will be paid, but not otherwise.

The amount shown on a voucher reveals or indexes the monetary amount paid (assuming one trusts the investigator to have paid the SE the stated amount), but conceals how the previously discussed socially meaningful determinations are situated and practical decisions made by the investigator out of the sight and supervision of an official. This paper figure is also reflexive. It establishes a fact, the payment, and thus outlines the obligations of the organization to the informant but excludes that which is not seen as "organizationally relevant" (the moral relationships between informant and investigator), while standing as a characteristic of the organization as a formal entity. Although the reflexivity of the payment as standing for and "folding back upon" the formal organization reveals meanings, it also conceals the quite different investigator understandings about "how one works informants." The reflexivity is thus of a special and limited sort that maintains simultaneously the particular ties among officer, organization, and informant and denies them as organizationally relevant matters.

Organizational control of strategic enforcement actions is negotiated and situational. One must keep in mind not only the retrospective-prospective nature of the assessment of effective usage of monies, that is, the importance of the visible results in determining whether the money was well spent and in the proper amount, but also the ambiguity in defining success given the uncertainty of the investigation of drug crimes. Investigators with variable amounts of supervision make the determination of a good case and make subsequent decisions concerning the length of investigation, the techniques used, the level at which the case will be terminated, and the amount of money to be spent on various facets of the case. Thus adequate payment is not only retrospectively determined in practice, but specifying conditions for enforcing the rule or prior approval for all payments would reduce investigator's discretion and flexibility, two of the most important facets of being a good narc. Inherent in the successful investigation of this type of crime is a variable need for cash and uncertain outcomes.

Failure, as administratively defined, makes expenditures a visible target for criticism and/or invoking the sense of the prior approval rule. If success in an investigation results, it is very difficult to negatively sanction it by invoking or attempting to enforce the "prior approval for buy" rule. It is these features of organizational practice and the organizational milieu and mandate that produce patterned ambiguity in procedural rules. The "prior approval for buy" rule is but one instance. In order to sanction an officer for violation of this rule, one would have to bracket previously understood practices within the unit and to turn a blind eye to the expediency necessary for enforcement. This has been done by sergeants whose police experience was not in investigative work but in the patrol division, or whose previous experience as supervisor was not in narcotics. However, when experienced sergeants or the lieutenant evoke the "prior approval for buy" rule in order to sanction an errant sergeant or investigator, they are signaling that the officer has lost favor, is under suspicion, or is thought to be incompetent, as the example of the dynamite informant suggests (chapter 6). When the criticism was made, it was not explicitly in terms of violation of the prior approval rule since the sergeant makes such approvals himself, but rather in terms of retrospective knowledge of outcomes unforeseen by the sergeant; he had expected his work with this SE to yield important and impressive results. It also suggests that given the uncertainty in narcotics enforcement, the lieutenant was selecting a special case. The lieutenant told me that he didn't have to talk to every sergeant or directly to the investigators about such things because he knew that the fact that he had spoken to the sergeant would "get back to the men."

The rules are resources by which higher officials can control lower participants. The holistic quality of organizational activities made the instance, even though it was not a violation of the prior approval rule but of the sense of that rule, indicative or suggestive of personal, racial, and relational attributes as determinant of the sanctioning. The general and more ambiguous nature of sanctioning is made less problematic when there is an immediate and visible closure of an investigation and when it has not yet involved much money. Thus, the arrest focus is a product of the dominance of agent-informant and citizen targeting. They complement and are mutually supportive of each other.

Agent and Citizen Targeting: The Arrest Focus

Metro does not have a quota for arrests as a matter of policy, and there is a realization that arrests may be a misleading indicator of success in narcotics enforcement.* However, a number of pressures within the organization tend to reward arrests and behaviors that produce arrests. Although making cases and showing a flair for investigation were mentioned by command personnel, the most visible means of displaying activity is by arrests. Arrests are the focal point for a majority of Metro agents for several complex reasons:

Because of the size of the unit and the secrecy that prevails, the only time persons see what others are doing is when investigators "bring in a body" and fill out the statement of facts for court forms in the investigator's room. This is a dramatic moment, which piques everybody's interest and curiosity, and is accompanied by questions about how much dope was seized, how many people are arrested, what the charges are, etc.

Arrests, because they concretely and psychologically terminate and bring closure to a case, are satisfying.

*The following section appeared originally in P.K. Manning, "Organizational Problematics: Resolving Uncertainty," *Quaderni di Criminologia Clinica* XIX (April–June, 1977): 137–196.

Arrests put "meat on the table"; they keep "something on the book" (the arrest book).

Arrests and the associated court time are the only way in which a Metro policeman can receive overtime pay. (Compensatory time off can be earned in other ways.)

Conversely, activities or investigations that do not produce arrests and associated self-esteem rewards represent a set of opportunity costs for investigators. To the extent that they undertake or invest in longer-term investigations, they lose the rewards produced by court appearances, visible activity, and termination and closure.

Because of the low skill level and the apprenticeship-type training, undertaking a long-term investigation may require learning new skills, finding a new partner, and changing or adding to one's set of informants. Thus the conservative consequences of the reward system are made more enduring by the complementary effects of the socialization/training system.

This phenomenological focus on arrests does not imply that a large number of arrests and charges are actually made. Data from Metro from the period 1968–1974 show that approximately 80 percent of all drug charges are made by the patrol division and that since the "heroin epidemic" in 1971–1972, the percentage of charges for hard drugs (opiates, cocaine, amphetamines, barbiturates, and hallucinogens) has continued to drop from 57.6 percent of all charges in 1970 to 28.6 percent of the charges in 1975. Thus, the slight and uneven increase in charges shown in table 9.1 can be accounted for by the rise in drug related charges and, more importantly, by a steady increase in the number of marijuana charges made.

Further indication of the level of the department's concern is that a mere 13 percent of hard drug charges are made for intent to distribute or distribution, and only five percent of all charges are made for intent or distribution. The relative focus of the narcotics branch on drugs other than marijuana can be seen in 1975 by noting that nearly 96 percent of all marijuana charges and relatively fewer, 75 percent of hard drug cases, are brought by patrol. The production of charges by narcotics branch officers is highly variable and low. Metro officers in 1975

Table 9.1 Drug charges made by the Metro Department, Patrol and Narcotics Branches, 1968–1975

Drug Charges	1968	1969	1970	1971	1972	1973	1974	1975
Marijuana	31.8	10.2	5.6	10.3	31.4	53.9	59.8	55.4
Hard drugs	44.5	68.6	61.7	57.6	48.0	34.8	29.6	28.6
Drug related	23.7	21.2	32.6	32.0	20.6	11.3	10.6	15.9
Percent	100	100	99.9	99.9	100	100	100	99.9
(N)	1,077	2,224	4,729	6,204	5,304	4,177	4,479	5,261

From files of MPD. Data for the last quarter of 1975 were extrapolated from January–August figures.

averaged slightly over eleven charges apiece, six hard drug charges and slightly over two marijuana charges in the year; the remainder are drug related charges. The officer in central narcotics in Metro makes on an average about one charge a month and about one hard drug charge in six months. This low level of activity can be seen also in the search and arrest warrant activity for 1969, 1970, and 1971 (table 9.2). Although the percentage of search warrants applied for against those executed rose, the average number executed per officer fluctuated from about 1.5 to 3.4 and was down to 2.2 by 1971. Most arrests are not made with warrants, which in turn means that they do not involve lengthy investigations since establishing grounds for a search warrant usually requires a reliable informant and some surveillance.

There are some cases made at a higher level (felonious drug possession or distribution), and these are justified by officers in a quite different fashion. Investigators who focus on longer-term investigations shift the meaning of success away from this baseline of arrests, which the lieutenant and the inspector also attempted to do informally. They did this in three ways. Success was redefined in terms of cases made, that is, on the basis of assembled evidence on the activities of a target network that is convincing to the investigators involved. This belief stands apart from subsequent arrests, charges, prosecutor's decisions, or court actions. The belief is that the dealing network was too insulated from the street to permit street buys to reach it and that money was not approved by supervisors so that it could be fronted to make buys from the principal figures. Denial of an affidavit for a wire intercept and mysterious court actions (convictions, acquittals, re-

Table 9.2 Search warrants issued and executed for Metro and Suburban Narcotics Units for selected years[a]

Search	Metro			Suburban	
Warrants	1969	1970	1971	1974	1975
Issued	131	194	127	47	25
Executed	73	169	107	42	25
Unknown disposition	0	0	0	0	0
Percent executed	56	87	84	89	100
Number of investigators	49	49	49	11	11
Executed search warrants per year per officer	1.49	3.45	2.18	3.82	2.72

a. Data available only for the first six months of 1975.

scheduled hearings), are situations seen as being beyond the control of the investigators. The facts, in the minds of the investigators, were adequate to support the belief that a good case had been made. Second, they derogated the activities of those who made arrests, calling them "door kickers," "street hustlers," and headhunters. Third, they considered arrests to be misleading indicators of effectiveness. They pointed out that one large dealer can supply fifty to a hundred users, and thus one such major arrest is equivalent to fifty street addrests. They also pointed out that the headhunters bring in the same strung-out junkies again and again. So even though their arrest figures are relatively higher, they have no impact on the dealing structure or the demand conditions on the street. It is argued further that street rip-offs are the easiest sort of arrest to make—anyone can make a street arrest, it is said, but most of them will be thrown out (no papered).

The rationales thus substitute another criteria in one instance, derogate the practices of the others in the second, and redefine the meaning of the conventional criteria in the third. All such resolutions maintain self-esteem in the informal system, and since these criteria of success are supported by supervisors, at least on occasion, the minority segment maintains its integrity and autonomy in the face of organizational pressures to accept and operate with the conventional arrest criteria. However, in Suburban Department, no segments in the organization define their roles and aims as different from other segments and further, ironically, their arrest and search warrant figures are higher than those of the Metro officers on the average. Perhaps this production figure is a result of the higher degree of interaction, ethnic homogeneity within the unit, and the closer quality and quantity of supervision in Suburban. The perspective of the officers is complemented by the formal structure.

Suburban

Suburban Department has no policy concerning arrests. Arrests are considered by supervisors to be of less significance than closed investigations and the value of drug seizures. Expenditures by month and year are assessed against the street value of the drugs seized and presented in tabular form in *Semi-Annual* and *Annual Reports* (see table 9.3). A series of undercover buys without result, a series of controlled buys in which the investigator does not make a buy himself, or a search warrant raid that does not produce drugs are visible evidence that may be cause for informal or public criticism at a unit meeting between shifts.

For several reasons arrests are not the dramatic focal point of agent activity in the Suburban Department. As in the Metro Department, practice departs from stated emphasis. Suburban officers averaged 13.8 arrests in 1975; brought 22.5 charges, 14.0 of which were hard drug charges and 8.5 of which were for marijuana. In 1974, officers served, on the average, 3.8 search warrants apiece, 89 percent of those applied for, and in 1975 served 2.7, 100 percent of those applied for. Although search warrants and arrests are featured in *Annual Reports*, major emphasis is placed on the relationship between expenditures, seizures of drugs and money and comparisons with the previous year. Local investigations and their disposition are presented rather than arrests resulting from this activity. In presenting the data in this way, the organizational-centered model is underscored, for these assignments and their disposition are controlled by sergeants and the corporal of the unit, while arrests come from the initiative of investigators. The miscellaneous expenditures and controlled drug substances

Table 9.3 Expenses, controlled dangerous substances purchased, and total expenditures for Suburban Department by the month for 1974

Month	Misc. Expenses	CDS Purchases	Total Expenditures
January	$ 615.95	$ 960.00	$ 1,575.95
February	161.16	1,867.00	2,028.16
March	200.21	3,255.00	3,455.21
April	360.00	2,930.00	3,290.00
May	221.41	840.00	1,061.41
June	159.89	1,879.00	2,038.89
July	151.35	2,885.00	3,026.35
August	111.38	1,914.00	2,025.38
September	208.06	3,065.00	3,273.06
October	441.45	1,770.00	2,211.45
November	261.69	1,492.00	1,754.19
December	125.12	915.00	1,040.12
Totals	$3,017.67	$23,772.50	$26,790.17
1973 Totals	$2,154.16	$ 9,611.00	$11,765.16
1973–1974 Comparison	+$ 863.51	+$14,161.50	+$15,025.01

From *Annual Report* of the unit to the chief, January 28, 1975.
Note: A total of $1,198.00 was paid to informants for information leading to the arrest of persons involved in controlled dangerous substance (CDS) violations as well as the seizure of controlled dangerous substances. The largest payment to an informant was $500.00 for information leading to the seizure of one pound of Cocaine and the arrest of one adult male. In the comparison of expenditures between 1973 and 1974, there was an increase over 1973 in both miscellaneous expenses and monies expended purchasing controlled dangerous substances. Significantly, there was a direct relationship between miscellaneous expenses expended and controlled dangerous substances purchased for both years. In 1974, there was approximately two times as much money expended as was in 1973. However, there was two times the amount of street value of controlled dangerous substances seized; 1973, $96,867.50 and 1974, $200,921.00.

(CDS) purchases shown in table 9.4 can be added to the general operating costs of the unit to see why pressures in all narcotics units are brought to keep costs down. The average cost of a hard-drugs charge or arrest, when the costs of buys and informants fees were added and divided by the number of arrests made in 1975, was $96.55, while the added costs for a marijuana arrest was $32.24. It is costly to make opiate arrests if they involve purchases, and the more purchased, the higher one can go in the dealing chain. Thus a low-level focus is in large part patterned by the absolute amount of money available for buys regardless of willingness of supervisors to approve requests for large amounts. Consequently, the $25,000 fund from LEAA Law Enforcement Assistance Administration used in Suburban permits greater operational flexibility. Metro has a fund of some $120,000 for purchases and information. The largest amount expended was for purchase of heroin and cocaine, making the average added cost per narcotics unit arrest over $132.00 in Metro.[6] Opiate-focused enforcement is expensive.

The high rates of informal squad interaction and the numerous joint projects are sources of integration. For example, it is usually necessary to ask someone from another shift to assist on search warrant raids because four or five persons are needed. If members of a shift are on other duty, assistance will be required. Informal discussions of case strategy and tactics on all major cases held at shift meetings reduce the importance of producing visible results. Additionally, the small size of the unit means that individual competition is reduced. Conversely, informal sanctions are brought to bear on "rate-busters." (The one "hustler" in the group who "always has something going" is a focus of constant joking.) Few of the assigned cases or locals result in an arrest. At the same time they do serve to close cases and to reduce uncertainty. Overtime pay is granted for any work for which the sergeant has given prior approval. Practically speaking, however, sometimes this approval is after-the-fact.[7] It is significant that the operating norm is that even if overtime is approved a priori by a supervisor for a buy-bust attempt that falls through, no overtime pay will be requested by the officers involved. This means that investigators need not make arrests to obtain overtime pay, but informal norms have developed to

Table 9.4 Added costs of arrests resulting from buys, informants' fees, and miscellaneous expenses, Suburban Department, for six months in 1975[a]

Drugs purchased and number of buys	Cost of purchase	Number of arrests	Percent of arrests involving this drug	Percent of buy money spent	Cost per arrest
Opiates 2	$5,310	13	5	38.5	$408.50
Cocaine 4	2,820	23	9	20.5	122.60
Amphetamines 3	396	20	8	2.8	19.80
Barbiturates 2	65	13	5	>1	5.00
Hallucinogens 8	2,396	71	28.6	17.4	33.70
Other 2	110	14	5.6	>1	7.90
Marijuana 6	2,150	80	32.2	15.6	26.90
Hashish 4	510	14	5.6	3.7	36.40
Total	$13,757	248	99.0	100.5	$55.47[b]
Miscellaneous expenses	967				
Informant fees	515				
Total	$15,239			$15,239 ——— 248	$61.45[b]

a. Omits court time, fixed overhead, salaries, and overtime, etc.
b. Average. Assumes expenses and information fees are equally distributed among drug arrest categories.

constrain excess. Court time is paid at the same rate for other overtime work. Given the preference of narcotics policemen for working out of the office, court is not regarded as desirable duty without additional rewards. Working the streets and appearing in court are not mutually exclusive activities. Investigative work does not mean loss of income. On the contrary, it can be more rewarding if lengthy surveillances are required. In sum, these pressures mean that officers are not oriented to arrests, that is, to shorter investigations, and the organizational milieu encourages buying up (given the money available, undercover strategy, and working for buy-bust closures on cases). The seizures listed in table 9.4 support this conclusion.

In the two units, officers orient themselves both to the formal and informal rules, and to implicit standards and tacit assumptions about working narcotics. The pattern of outcomes associated with these perspectives and rules are somewhat different in the two units.

Rules and the Sense of Rules

In the discussion of major violators, it was argued that certain features of the person, the relationship between the person and the case or supervisor, or the kind of case involved were determinant of the kinds of sanctions that were used if an account was called for. There are several important features of evaluation that occur when the major violator mode of targeting is not dominant, and these issues are generic in the evaluation of drug units. Rules and rule breaking have only been discussed briefly: It was argued that the social organization of drug enforcement is outlined by modes of targeting but that the relevant rules are tacit and assumed. This has a set of implications for organizational analysis as well as for the evaluation of drug policing.

Rules and rule-guided behavior must be examined in context and with reference to the subjective definitions that actors attribute to contextual conduct (compare Winch, 1958). Like the rules of games, they constitute and make visible not only acts or moves but acts viewed as mistakes and violations of rules. The context in which rules are seen, not the rules themselves, nor rules about rules that are so characteristic of formal organizations, determines the meanings of acts (in the sense of consequences). Therefore, situated interactions, accounts, and shared understandings must be examined in any sociological analysis of organizations. The sense of order that emerges from and is displayed in organizationally bounded encounters is partly dependent. upon the rules that are called upon or invoked by participants to order the interaction. Rules, although tacitly understood, make salient the set of assigned features of events that participants take into account as members-in-role. Rules are thus resources to be used tactically by participants, and by so doing participants, in an important way, negotiate the limits upon organizationally sanctionable activities. But all participants are not equal in such negotiations.

An analysis of organizations that sees rules as being purely ideational matters or as external constraints is misleading, as Douglas (1971) has shown. Resources, which are not equally distributed between organizational segments and which are sources of potential power (money, knowledge, skills, and administrative experience), are brought to bear on participants in situations such as those discussed in the above examples. Organizational knowledge, for example, is not simply filed for general use but is differentially distributed. The power to conceal and differentially reveal information relevant to investigations lies in the administration after the fact and prospectively in the hands of investigators, since they keep much of their information either in files locked in their desks or in their heads. Other bases of authority maintain the control of the higher segments, but information control and the power to conceal are tokens of the power system of the organization.

These brief comments on the existential bases of rules and rule enforcement only suggest a set of issues, the most important of which is that the formal bases for organizational guidance, evaluation, and sanctioning, both positive and negative, will consistently conflict with informal and nonspecific bases for informal assessment. The narcs' game is dominant at this level of the evaluation of conduct, regardless of the formal rules and procedures for guidance. And the sense of conflict is not passing or occasional but an abiding one that creates and maintains tension at several levels of the organization. The conflict can be seen between the public claims and stances of the organization and its accomplishments, between the formal procedures and aims and the actual practice and goal-setting, between the individual sense of accomplishment and the unit's or squad's level, and between the various meanings of key terms, such as success, and the range of dimensions against which an individual can assess his or her behavior. Such conflicts and tensions stand as internal sources of change, and are thus a kind of primitive organizational dialectic. Increasing the capacity of organizations to punish or to monitor and surveil officers can only create a facade of complicity with rules as long as the informal under-life of the organization is not only tacitly deferred to in action, but is seen by participants as the most valid or "real" basis on which the work proceeds. Evaluation is a strategic means for uncovering what is covered but not a very valid way to assess that invisible or assumed world that underlies social life in general as well as drug enforcement units.

Conclusion

Evaluation in people-processing organizations is accomplished only within a context. In the field of police research, there is no consensus about the standard units in which evaluation should be cast, there is conflict about the standards that should be invoked, the ways to measure impact, whether to measure effectiveness or efficiency, and what the overall aims and goals, as well as the means to be employed, ought to be. I have not attempted to show what should be evaluated, only the inadequacies of the present approaches. There are three characteristics of police organizations that amplify the general problem of evaluation in people-processing organizations: the negative view of paperwork, the commitment to an informal basis for evaluation of agent performance, and the absence of standardized case files that contain full information on the ongoing investigations undertaken by agents. It is argued that the problem of guidance and targeting is "solved" in practice by the arrest focus in Metro and the focus on buy-bust arrangements in Suburban. In effect, though, since information control by agents at the lowest level covers their delicts, and supervisors have only post facto knowledge of most of what is done, the ways in which officers rationalize their actions take the form of accounts or verbal rationalizations for previously taken actions. The encounter between officers and supervisors, no matter what the mode of targeting, tends to take the form of a ritualistic assertion of the dominance of the higher echelons in the organization. What are the implications of this kind of evaluation for the constraining effects of targeting modes in the two organizations?

With respect to targeting by militaristic means, officers do not give formal intelligence much credence unless they know the officers who provide the information. It tends to be circulated in the form of memos or general advisos posted in the unit and to take on a somewhat abstract character rather than to be rooted in specific cases. It is not seen as having relevance unless it has a bearing on a case on which they are working.

When the targeting is agent-informant targeting, there is more concensus among agents who work with informants that arrests (maybe with seizures) are the primary indicator of success. There is thus some agreement between agents and sergeants about what is a successful case after it has gone down.

In the case of the patrol mode, the evaluation of what uniformed officers do and its relevance to narcotics enforcement is made totally irrelevant by two structural characteristics of both units: The arrests made by patrol are credited to patrol division, and/or kept separately actuarially, and they appear in the unit only in the form of paper (arrest reports that are posted). The only practical relevance of patrol activities occurs when a patrol officer calls for assistance in an arrest, when he asks for assistance in assessing the evidence in such an arrest, or when the arrested persons are brought to the unit for processing and/or when patrol officers seek advice about the charges.

Finally, the citizen-generated mode of targeting is considered of interest when the praxeological rules operate in selection of cases worked and their outcomes. Once an investigator has judged that this mode provides a lead worth working, then the outcomes produced are considered to be the result of the choice.

It is fairly clear that in both units, for the general reasons cited and because of their own traditions and operations, there is little or no interest in systematic evaluation. What evaluation there is, is informal and takes the form of gossip, innuendo, complaining, and an occasional "talking to." Field work is a needed independent source of data, for without it, it is not possible to substantiate any claim made by these units about success except in their own terms and on the basis of their own data. Neither is it possible to sort out the relative sources of cases, the effects of modes of targeting, or the consequences of agent choices at various points in the investigation of the cases. Common-sense knowledge and the wisdom imparted by belief in the enacted environment serves very well the need to justify that is being done in the name of enforcement.

Dramaturgical communication, by selectively presenting and concealing messages, maintains our sense of what is significant and important about our selves and identities and, more important with regard to the problem addressed in this book, it produces these effects for organizations as symbolic entities. Most persons have learned, as a result of socialization to the conventional meanings attached to government, policing, and the law, to view policing and especially drug policing as a series of dramatic confrontations between good and evil, in which the police possess the preponderance of resources, skill, and virtue. We expect that they will emerge victorious, given adequate resources, if they display sufficient courage and determination. We focus attention, therefore, upon successes, are given little information on failures, and naively view police action as exclusively creating solutions to the drug problem. When the organizations that produce these meanings are closely examined backstage or by actual workings, as well as public fronts and rhetorics, it is quite clear that they rarely achieve success, even defined in their own terms, that they often produce unanticipated negative effects, and much of what is done is determined by individual agents' practically determined decisions.

For a variety of reasons we expect too much of the police and of drug police and understand too few of their limitations. The constraints on a police attempt to eradicate drug markets have been simplistically cast, and the public has been credulous; willing to assume that these problems are easily surmountable if more resources are provided and to believe in the ultimate efficacy of the effort. As a result of the legal, organizational, social-psychological, occupational, and at a less abstract level, informational and budgetary constraints, as well as the fundamentally overdetermined and highly gratifying nature of drug use itself, policing is a marginal activity with a limited impact on drug markets. It is, on the one hand, a game that occupies some police officers who by and large enjoy the challenge, and on the other hand, from a social point of view, a ceremony that celebrates what the powerful segments of the society consider appropriate levels and kinds of drug use, proper styles of life and occupations, the correct place to live, and moral commitment. Drug police, like priests, are more important for what they symbolize and stand for than for what they do.

Constraints

Two kinds of legal constraints are in effect in American society. The first is our use of the prohibition model of drug control, which brings with it corruption, illicit profits, and the protection of licit markets in similar substances. This model intends to punish and deprive the user of the substance and eradicate the market. But it is in conflict with other segments of the criminal justice and social control system that try to treat, cure, educate, or otherwise reform the user and especially with the courts that aim to circumscribe the legal tools available used to suppress these markets. This structure of control produces a contradiction between a crime control-eradication model and a justice model emphasizing procedural guarantees. The police mediate some legal constraints by arrogating certain decisions to themselves (Skolnick, 1966; McDonald, 1973a). They thereby judge guilt or innocence, avoid legal review, and create their own forms of justice. Important examples of discretion are their decisions to work a case, to arrest, to charge, or to spin or turn a person and thus make an informant. Only the shadowy indications of these consequences are touched on here, but they are both a product of the attempt to control markets by the law and the decision made by lawmakers to use the police to control styles of life and taste preferences as expressed in substance use. The second legal constraint is that exercised by attorneys and judges whenever the process requires a priori sanctioning in seeking affidavits, charging with crimes, or making deals to alter, reduce, or drop charges in exchange for working for the police as an informant. These procedural protections are limited but important when they are exercised.

The perception of the environment shapes enforcement practices. The environment in which drug enforcement takes place is an enacted environment. It is problematic because it is politically volatile and easily shaped by readings of public opinion. It is not monitored with reliable and systematic valid information. The tasks involved are ambiguously defined by unclear standards, in part reflecting the structure of the drug trade. Without information of a systematic kind, officers continue to define their tasks as being information-based. The information that is possessed, however, is personal knowledge, patterned organizationally as tacit knowledge and rarely collectively available for general use. There is no binding policy to guide organizational action, little close supervision or prospective guidance, and little negative feedback. It has been argued that negative feedback is one of the characteristics of bureaucratic organizations, but this capacity, hardly developed in police drug units, is obviously differentially characteristic of formal organizations of all kinds. Informal and formal rewards, seen in the context of the investigator's perspective, are conducive to quick closures of cases by arrests, finessing of public demands for service of other kinds, and eschewal of long-term investigations. Complex, larger cases, as important as they might be for the attempt to control market movements and structures, are risky, expensive for the organization and individual, and require skills and patience not possessed by most members of these two units.

Their skills are limited, even where their aims and intentions are appropriately visionary. Since these agents have little or no formal training for the positions they hold, and their skills are those they have learned through apprenticeships, they are inclined to do the work as it has been done before and largely in terms of their sense of what is valued by their colleagues. What is salient in maintaining self-esteem is how other officers evaluate what one is doing (even though they may not know precisely what one is doing), and this sense of doing well is more important than any formal written evaluation of the work. The freedom to open, work, close, and otherwise make a case is, within the limits outlined previously, largely unlimited. The organization, seen as a set of controls or constraints on agent discretion when acting in organizational role, exercises little control, no matter what mode of targeting or control is attempted by the supervisory levels of the police departments. Evaluation is informal, paperwork avoided, and case files erratically kept. Success, a rare event even in the narcs' terms, is often aleatory and ironic. These constraints operate, from the broadest legal and social ones through to those of the individual attributes and training of the agents, *no matter what the legal resources, personnel, money, and equipment made available to the organization.* Police work, so constrained, is an important ritual nevertheless.

Police Drug Work as Ritual

People are inclined to believe that police action has an impact on drug use or on the drug market and that this impact has the sole effect of reducing consumption and/or demand. There are enormous costs in money, personnel, time, and effort at all levels in the criminal justice system. The public and legal focus on outlawed drugs encourages the public to view them as the most dangerous substances rather than to see the dangers associated with and caused by the use of tobacco, alcohol, and prescription drugs. This belief or set of beliefs is perpetuated by the mass media working largely on information provided to them by the agencies themselves. The drug problem should be seen in the same way as the various other sources of fear, threat, and disorder: witches, heretics, communists, subversives, hippies, and the like. These figures dance along the edges of our society, telling us we are not them and are therefore something else and symbolizing the edges of the moral order. But to mistake them for the real threats, distrust, fear, intolerance, hate, and violence is to mistake the sign for the referent. And the fact that we do mistake the sign for the referent means that we may continue to mount counterproductive operations, wars, and other militaristic entities (compare King, 1978), which do not contr ol the feared, but reify it and produce the unanticipated negative consequences outlined in the previous chapters. Apologists do little to clarify issues, as the work of many experts shows (DuPont, 1978).

Policing is shaped by and celebrates fundamental values and beliefs and is thus a ritual of affirmation. Our beliefs in the efficacy of the police are mythological, that is to say that they are not based on factual knowledge. They arise from our commitment to the moral and political order, and our attribution to the police of a semisacred status. It also suggests or points to our commitment to the political state. The structure of the drug police "cops and robbers drama" arises directly from our devotion to the sacred. Much of the governmental action, as writers as diverse as Bagehot (1963), Arnold (1935), and Edelman (1964) have written, is ritual designed to assure more than to accomplish, to celebrate rather than to solve, to remark upon rather than to realize.

While crime control serves many functions, as does drug law enforcement, such as information, deterrence and punishment, it has more to do with hopes, dreams and fears, myths and ideologies than with producing any impact on, or evidence of any impact on, crime of any kind. It is a public affirmation privately shaped and molded to quite diverse agendas. Individual careers, security, and rewards, organizational expansion, survival, and maintenance, and in general, autonomy, on a day-to-day basis supersede concerns for achieving the publicly designated mandate.

The crimes that we have called transactional crimes are ritualistically enforced with inadequate resources (by any definition of the problem). Hence, they are also selectively enforced, are the basis for corruption and widely used discretion, and for the maintenance of wide gaps between public rhetoric and action. They are costly to enforce in whatever fashion one wishes to define cost: socially, politically, or economically (see Kaplan, 1970; Hellman, 1975). Enforcing laws against transactional crimes is futile, and enforcement activities do little but inflate police power, suggest to an ignorant public that something is being done, and perpetuate aspects of the police myth.

The drug laws and drug law enforcement have a number of consequences, most of which are negative and therefore unanticipated by the architects of such laws. The most important consequences of these laws and the resultant structure of pseudo-enforcement are several. The major drug problems of this country are the excessive use of over-the-counter drugs, tranquilizers, and antibiotics (Illich, 1976), and the everyday demons of tobacco and liquor. Until there are production controls on the legitimate drug industry, there will be little real progress in dealing with the drug problem in this country. The fact is that there are no accurate figures on the production of amphetamines, barbiturates, and tranquilizers, so we have no idea how many are being produced, sold, and consumed even in the legitimate market (Pekkanen, 1973; Silverman, 1974). We have not seen through the smoke screen of concern about recreational drugs and have not dealt with the problem of controlling the powerful, addictive and destructive, massively ingested everyday drugs.

Alternatives

These implications could lead to the conclusion that a tighter and more efficient organizational structure should be evolved (compare Williams, Redlinger, and Manning, 1978). It is my view that the externalities, or the costs that are encumbered by the very attempt to prohibit and punish the use of drugs through the criminal law, are too high to warrant this kind of technocratic tinkering. Even if the organizational structure were to be developed that would efficiently enforce these and subsequent laws, would the costs of loss of liberty and personal privacy, and the corruption of the police be worth it? I do not think so. What other alternatives are possible? Three suggested reforms follow.

Decriminalization   Decriminalization has a number of meanings, including retaining but reducing criminal penalties for possession, especially for the possession of small amounts of marijuana, making the possession of drugs a ticketable offense something like a parking ticket, and repealing all drug laws. Most of the arguments about decriminalization refer to the reduction of penalties for personal possession of marijuana. Decriminalization of the opiates and other dangerous drugs has also been discussed, usually in the context of making them available more generally under specific conditions for the treatment of illness and disease This is already a legal option for physicians.

If some combination of reducing the penalties for possession of all dangerous drugs and making marijuana a ticketing offense were to be enacted at the federal level and the states followed this trend (there are some fifteen states with minimal penalties for marijuana possession), the same fundamental problems that are associated with the present pattern of enforcement would remain. Changing the penalty structure alone will do little to change the routine practices of agents who will continue to make short-term, easy, and fast busts on the street. Police organizations do not closely control the actions of their drug agents, and agents will continue to arrest people for marijuana possession. The high arrest rate will maintain a similar level of costs for court processing, enforcement efforts, and to other agencies in the system. The proportion of marijuana arrests may even rise since the lowered pen-

alty structure will make charges more likely to be accepted by prosecutors.

As long as an enforcement structure is heavily financed, it will retain
a vested interest in self-perpetuation, maintenance, and expansion.
Organizations will find new targets, redefine their goals and means,
and go to great lengths to survive (Epstein, 1977). They will produce
new demons, they will raise new spectors, they will obfuscate public
opinion and generate new public threats. This has been done, for example, in the last ten years for cocaine, PCP, and LSD. In each case
the public is led to believe that it is addictive, either physiologically or
psychologically, which means dependence on something someone
else does not approve of; that it leads to bizzare, self-destructive acts;
that it creates a penchant for crime or other immoralties; and that the
very least it releases you to enjoy sex. All of these are presented with
fabricated stories, usually later proved to be false, and accompanied
by a media barrage orchestrated by NIADA, HEW, or DEA itself (see
Musto, 1973; Epstein, 1977; LEAA Newsletter, September, 1978).

Although it is needed, decriminalization is only a partial reform. It
does not alter the political and organizational problems associated
with the attempt to prohibit drug use by criminal law and police agencies. In the absence of other legal and organizational reforms, it will be
ineffective.

Limit the federal enforcement structure   Recent hearings on drug enforcement by the House Select Committee on narcotics and the Senate
Subcommittee on governmental operations have clearly and unequiv-
ocally shown that drug law enforcement is decentralized, focuses
mostly on lower-level users, is avoided by some agencies with a legal
charter to cooperate in the enforcement of these laws, is characterized by chaotic self-serving operations and an utter lack of cooperation among federal agencies, rivalries, and political backbiting (see Interim Report, 1977). Whatever useful information available on drug use
and consumption (with the exception of DEA's monitoring of emergency room and hospital mentions of certain drugs), is known by the
agents. Lack of control over their choices and cases means in effect
lack of close information on drug use and dealing. The federal struc-

ture is so decentralized that regional and local offices have great autonomy from central office policies. Informal structures and rewards far outweigh formal statements of intended goals and targets in the absence of any alternative means to reward, punish, or otherwise guide lower-level participants.

There is need for some regulation of the importation of drugs, in part as a matter of control of quality and price, and in part as a matter of reducing the potential that is inherent in criminal organizations becoming involved in importation of drugs for large tax-free profits. Practically and politically, it seems unlikely that DEA will be disbanded. Controls over the actions of the agents may be attained by reduced budgets for informational and drug purchase money. Political pressure by Congress may means that the agency will cooperate with Customs and work more intelligence or conspiracy cases in cooperation with local agencies. Many intelligent observers, such as Congressman Wolff and Chief Counsel Joseph Nellis of the Select House Committee on Narcotics Abuse and Control and his staff, conclude that the wish to control the drug trade should lead us to focus our activities on control of the production and distribution of the drugs of interest (mainly cocaine, opiates, and marijuana), rather than to perpetuate an ineffectual domestic police enforcement effort. This is an important and meritorous suggestion, providing that this strategy does not include the use of U.S. federal agents acting in an enforcement-undercover capacity abroad, as is being done by DEA. The United States has no moral, political, or economic interest and no legal right to enforce its laws on the sovereign soil of other nations. This aspect of federal enforcement should by summarily terminated and all assistance in drug cases to other nations left to ad hoc agreements made at their request. It is apparent that strengthening the capacity of Customs will do far more to produce seizures than will vigilante efforts of American agents abroad. Many urge disbanding the entire federal structure (King, 1978; Lindesmith, 1978), and the suggestion merits serious consideration.

Reorganize police drug units   Even if no major changes in the laws and in our general prohibition model of control are made, profound and important reorganization can be effected in local police departments. These changes will reduce costs, improve morale, increase public service, and reduce corruption.

Three changes should be undertaken. The first is to disband all specialized drug units within local departments. This experiment has been undertaken by the Baltimore Police Department, and they have reported great success (Baltimore Police *Newsletter*, 1976). The budget for drug enforcement (the informant and buy monies) should be exorcised, personnel transferred, and any case files and intelligence information given over to intelligence or crime prevention units. The drug law enforcement function should thereafter be carried out routinely only by patrol, and by detectives on a referral basis, as it comes to their attention via informant information, citizen calls, or internally generated information passed on by intelligence, internal affairs, or patrol. Proactive or agent-initiated cases should be limited, selectively worked only on a closely supervised basis, and done in cooperation with other units, especially the federal, state, or local district attorney's or state attorney's office.

A second needed change is to train patrol officers in drug law enforcement, (laws, evidence handling, intelligence-gathering), and to routinely send them to schools to learn skills and new knowledge.

The third reorganization recommendation is less major than the other two. It involves creating a very small pharmacy unit to investigate the leakage of licit drugs into illicit markets. This unit could be housed with other vice units, intelligence, or with the detective division. They should in addition, take the responsibility to assist physicians and pharmacies in the area to be on the alert for fraudulent prescriptions, stolen prescription blanks, over-prescribing, and pharmaceutical dispensations for a profit, either of stolen goods or by changing the names of drugs. The aim of this group would not be to punish the user, but to police or regulate the dispensation of drugs by physicians and pharmacies and be alert for corrupt and illegal business practices. This work depends highly on the cooperation of local medical societies, physicians, pharmacies, and their employees and should not, conversely, rely on clandestine undercover operations.

These changes, made in concert, would clear the air for more innovative approaches to the regulation of drug use and perhaps move toward a less interventionist stance by governments in general with respect to the drug problem.

Concluding Comment

Police organizations act out their own visions and must live with and within them. The lack of organizationally-based constraint on agents' choices is sustained because of several interconnected external constraints that cannot be controlled by the agencies themselves. These include information, cooperation, the dynamics of the markets themselves, legal constraints and international politics that influence the flow of drugs around the world. Internally the constraints emphasized here are those of information and informational sharing, evaluation, targeting, and supervision (lack thereof), skills, training, personnel, and monetary resources, as well as equipment. The most obvious constraints are not at all obvious. More money, resources, and personnel cannot have an appreciable effect, given the organizational structure of local policing and the external constraints outlined above. Whatever the rhetoric used to formulate intent, the actuality of the day-to-day work is that it is boring, unsystematic, catch-as-catch-can, and focused on obtaining immediate rewards and arresting low-level users. Targeting is an ironic metaphor used only to highlight how little targeting of any kind there is that is controlled by supervisory level persons within the organizations studied. Although the organizations respond in some way to what they sense the community might want or expect them to do, they have no rational means of gathering that sense, interpreting it consistently, and determining the extent to which their actions have fulfilled or failed to fulfill community expectations. Since organizations do not act, persons in roles do, and these actions in turn are very indirectly, if at all, linked to expectations of given segments of divided communities, there is a loose coupling maintained between the environment and the organizations studied. Further, these actions are not determined by the policies, pronouncements, or general orders issued by command personnel. The aggregated actions that constitute local drug law enforcement are only loosely coordinated, loosely ordered and controlled, and largely stand on their own. The organizational context of these actions is vaguely perceived, and the narcs' game proceeds apace.

Notes

Notes to Chapter 1

1. I have drawn these several conclusions from the work of Becker, 1963; Brecher, et al., 1972; Ball, 1965; King, 1972; Lindesmith, 1940a, 1940b, 1965; Goode, 1969a, 1970; Dickson, 1968; Musto, 1973; Reasons, 1974; Helmer, 1975. The precise reasons why such dynamics took place remains an empirical question requiring further research, but the role played by the attempt to prohibit use and eradicate the markets in drugs is well established.

2. Although the precise effects of pumping money in this fashion into drug markets has not been empirically measured (since the volume of trade of which such money represents a proportion is unknown), it is clear that the overall effect of making buys, paying informants with money and/or drugs, and "investing" or fronting money that is not returned (either allowed to ride in order to buy up to a larger dealer, "ripped off" or stolen from agents in attempted buy-bust situations) is considerable. One author estimates that federal monies produce a stimulus effect of increasing demand some four or five times above what it would be without the infusion of federal enforcement dollars (Browning, 1976; see also Manning and Redlinger, forthcoming a).

3. It would appear that the extent to which drugs become either the necessary or sufficient conditions for the formation of a moral-political-economic system ("subculture") is variable (compare Schur, 1965), but studies of opiates (Dai, 1937; Chein, et al., 1964; Finestone, 1957; Lindesmith, 1947; Fiddle, 1967; Agar, 1973; Gould, et al., 1974; McAuliffe and Gordon, 1974; Waldorf, 1973; Ray, 1964; Hughes, 1977; Weppner, 1977), amphetamines (Davis and Munoz, 1968; Carey and Mandel, 1968; Grinspoon and Hedblom, 1975), cocaine (Sabbag, 1976; Woodley, 1971; Ashley, 1976), psychedelics (Blum, 1972; Aaronson and Osmond, 1970; Carey, 1968), and marijuana (Solomon, 1966; Goode, 1969b, 1970; Becker, 1963; Goldman, 1975; Kamistra, 1975; Grinspoon, 1977) show that complex and nuanced meanings of drugs support a status system, that a network or networks are generated for the distribution of the substance, and that the activities of social control (although only vaguely discussed in these works) have a differential impact upon use, costs, and consequences of using or dealing. (See Hughes, 1977 for a study sensitive to the impact of treatment and punishment on heroin copping areas.)

4. In this review I have avoided discussion of the numerous biographies and autobiographies of drug users (among the better are Hughes, 1961; Larner and Tefferteller, 1964; Trocchi, 1960; Burroughs, 1963) and fictional treatments of drug experience such as Rudolph Wurlitzer's *Nog*, Nelsen Algren's *The Man with the Golden Arm*, Aldous Huxley's *Brave New World,* James Mills's *Panic in Needle Park,* and others. There are a number of the same genre that glorify the exploits of drug police. These are more revealing for what they do not reveal than what they do. They are occasionally informative (R. Moore, 1971; Whittemore, 1973; Eszterhas, 1974; Maas, 1973). The personalities of

users have been studied extensively and fruitlessly (Dai, 1937; Chein, et al., 1964).

5. See Josephson and Carroll, (eds.), 1974, works of DuPont, Greene, and associates (see references) O'Donnell, et al., 1976; Hughes, 1977, and Johnson, Peterson, and Wells, 1977.

6. However, see the works of Lindesmith, especially his *The Addict and the Law,* 1965; Dickson, 1968; Becker, 1963; Moore, 1977, and Wilson, 1978.

7. See the works of Kaplan, 1970; Schur, 1962; Packer, 1968; Becker and Stigler, 1974; Becker, 1976; Hellman, 1975; Bonnie and Whitebread, 1974; Eldridge, 1967; Heller, 1973; Stigler, 1973; and Schneyer, 1971. These studies overlap in their themes with the studies of the violations of procedural guarantees that reportedly occur routinely in enforcing narcotics laws, and the economic studies cited below in note 8. Since concerns with violations of the procedural law are enduring and very little is said about them here (but see Manning and Redlinger, 1977, 1978), it should be noted that the effects of the law, both substantive and procedural, on drug enforcement are considerable. The primary concern of legal thinkers has been the ways in which police procedures mitigate procedural guarantees (Oaks, 1970; Hellman, 1975; and Dix, 1975) to create the conditions under which the law itself is undermined or made less effective (Packer, 1968; Kaplan, 1970; Hellman, 1975), or to produce negative or unanticipated consequences (Heller, 1973; Dash, Schwartz, and Knowlton, 1959). Other social critics have echoed these concerns (Schur, 1965; Skolnick, 1966; Goode, 1970; and Gooberman, 1974). In what follows I proceed on a legal-realism model, patterned after the ideas of Ross (1958) and Bittner (1970) as these ideas apply to drug law enforcement. What this means is that from the perspective of the officers in the units studied, the law intersected with their personal job concerns only under certain conditions, and they did not see the law as universally constraining, but rather as an occasional unpredictable obstacle to the achievement of what otherwise appeared to be a "good case."

8. See Preble and Casey, 1969; Carey, 1968; Redlinger, 1969; Koch and Grupp, 1971, 1973; Moore, 1970; Levin, Roberts, and Hirsch, 1975; Brown and Silverman, 1974; Erickson, 1969; Ianni, 1974; Holahan, 1972; Rottenberg, 1968; Soref, 1975.

9. In particular, see Banton, 1964; Preiss and Ehrlich, 1966; Skolnick, 1966; Niederhoffer, 1967; Bordua, 1967; Wilson, 1968; Reiss, 1971; Laurie, 1972; Larson, 1972; Rubinstein, 1973; Cain, 1973; Clark and Sykes, 1974; Kelling, et al., 1974; and Muir, 1977. Westley's dissertation was published in 1970 by The MIT Press.

10. See Skolnick, 1966; DeFleur, 1975; McDonald, 1973a, 1973b; Johnson, 1973; Johnson and Bogomolny, 1973; Webster, 1975; Johnson, Peterson, and Wells, 1977; and Williams, Manning, and Redlinger, 1978; Manning and Red-

linger, 1977, forthcoming a, 1978; and Manning, 1977b, 1977c, forthcoming a.

11. Burns has succinctly paraphrased Weber (1947) to distinguish organizations from other institutions: they transact with the environment in terms of rationally conceived means to expressly announced goals (paraphrase of Gouldner, 1959); they attempt specific definitions of the tasks and division of labor located within the formal system; there is an enduring authority structure based on rational compliance; and there are sets of formal systems of rewards and punishments, responsibility (career or "office") is emphasized, as are organizational identities salient within the setting (Burns, 1967:131 ff.). I have expanded upon the general categories suggested. It is apparent if one reads the organizational literature and the most intelligent summaries of this literature Blau and Scott, 1962; Heydebrand, 1973; M. Meyer, 1977; Haas and Drabek, 1973) that these definitions are only reasonable within some accepted context of discussion and do not serve well except as indices or as clusters forming an ideal type. The definitional problem becomes more acute when comparative, cross-cultural, or historical analyses are undertaken. It is perhaps most reasonable to define formal organizations as systems where the norm of rationality is emphasized, where goals are formally stated and means associated with them, and where there is some ongoing basis for collective action binding participants. It is the latter that is of most interest here, and the former that has been most frequently studied.

12. For examples of frozen decision making, which are typically studies of attitudes toward decision-making situations and kinds of managerial decisions (Nebeker, 1975), see any recent issue of the *Administrative Science Quarterly*. For an exception to this generalization about decision-making studies, see March and Olsen, 1976.

13. The classic studies of this genre, such as the work of Hughes (1971). Becker, et al., (1961); Westley (1951, 1953, 1956); Hall (1946, 1948), Roy (1954, 1960), Strauss et al., (1964); Dalton (1959); Roth (1963); and other important work and organization ethnographies by Ditton (1977), Lupton (1963), Becker, Geer, and Hughes (1968), and Glaser and Strauss (1967) have few peers in their detailed treatment of the work situation.

14. Limitations of the Chicago perspective have been noted by recent critics, who have argued for increased attention to issues of power and authority, and the dialectic that occurs within the organization, between the organization and the environment, and between the members of an interorganizational network (see especially Benson, 1975, 1977a; Denzin, 1977; Maines, 1977). The Chicago approach to organizations has restricted attention to descriptions of given organizations in a particular time and place, with their own peculiar sort of micrologics, ideologies, and internal morphologies. In particular, close ethnographic work has not developed theories and therefore does not clarify many emergent theoretic issues in the field of organizations (and has been further ignored as a result); has often been ad hoc and insufficiently grounded

in data that is comparable, reliable as well as valid, and comparative; ignores questions of power and authority, and seems to describe a world dominated almost entirely by ideas and meanings. If the technological rational fallacy is committed by most organizational studies, then many ethnographic studies commit the idealist fallacy.

15. The limits introduced by studies that derive all their data from questionnaires given to top management have been noted but the underdog bias of the Chicago School is equally a liability.

16. Foucault's brilliant series of studies is perhaps the most useful kind of example. The discourse through which organizations are made visible and the indexes, marks, and symbols by which they are known, shape them and their impacts: Changing conceptions of madness during the Renaissance period in Western Europe were instrumental in changing the organization, personnel, authority, clientele, and operations of asylums in France (1965; see also his work on language, 1972; the clinic, 1973; and the prison, 1977). It is useful to remind ourselves of the phenomenological bases of organizations, Collins (1975:315 ff.) writes, because ". . . there is no organization except in the actual behavior of real people in some moment in time; the organization is whatever they do and think and say. . . . The 'organization' is only people attempting to get certain things for themselves and using others as a means; . . . 'organizational structure' is only a way of referring to how people behave repetitively toward each other. . . ." Rather than seeing organizations as being in a position of interchange with a complex environment composed of objective forces, pressures, demands, and the like, the existential view argues that the perceptions and conduct of key organizational actors must be elicted and serve as the primary data of organizational analysis.

17. Even the most committed positivists, such as M. Meyer (1977), Steers (1977), and Aldrich and Pfeffer (1976), in respective systematic reviews of organization environment interchanges, have found that the concept of environment as used in organizational studies is "slippery." (See note 1, chapter 3.)

Notes to Chapter 2

1. A "juggler" or street peddler buys heroin at street quality in small bags, extracts some for his own use, adds another "cut" of an extending agent, and sells the bags at the price he paid. He supports his own habit as a "dealer" in this fashion.

2. The Metro Department increased personnel some 64 percent between 1968 and 1976, even though it has declined approximately 2 percent over the last five years. In Suburban Department, on the other hand, a steady growth has occurred. The rapid growth in narcotics personnel in Metro was in part accounted for by the policy of employing undercover agents, young unexperienced officers from the Police Academy who were unknown to "street people." From 1971 through 1973, some fifty additional officers were employed under-

cover. The numbers in district vice work have also fluctuated between forty-nine, the present total, and more than seventy-seven, in the period between 1970 and 1973. In Metro Department, the narcotics personnel expanded some 92 percent between 1968 and 1972; while declining 44 percent over the next five years. The net increase is 14 percent. On the other hand, Suburban Department increased at a somewhat slower pace and in a later time period. From 1970 (when the narcotics unit was established) to 1972, the unit increased 29 percent, increased 46 percent in the next five years, and has increased nearly 62 percent since its inception. In 1974–1975, the narcotics unit in Suburban Department stabilized at 1.61 percent of the total force. During 1969, the percent of the force in narcotics law enforcement in central narcotics in Metro was approximately one-half of a percent. During the 1971–1973 period of rapid growth, central narcotics, counting undercover agents, accounted for 2.2, percent, and with the district vice people, numbered around 160 officers, or around 3.2 percent of the force.

3. A local newspaper article (July 14, 1975) reported, "The use and availability of illegal drugs is on the increase in Suburban (sic) County following a long period of abatement, officials said yesterday. . . ." The article noted, however, that the director of the residential facility for young adult drug users had no statistics to demonstrate this increase: "Although the officials had no figures available, they said the increase is shown in a higher number of persons seeking help, from police records and drug confiscation and the drug users themselves." The county does not sponsor a methadone treatment center, although at least two of the adjoining political jurisdictions do.

Notes to Chapter 3

1. See, for the general position, Terreberry, 1968; Thompson, 1967; Lawrence and Lorsch, 1969; and the summaries in Haas and Drabek, 1973 and Aldrich and Pfeffer, 1976. Some of the more important research carried out in this tradition includes Burns and Stalker, 1961; Trist, et al., 1963; Katz and Kahn, 1966; and Lawrence and Lorsch, 1969.

2. This position can certainly be inferred from the residual and undefined status of the concept in most of the recent research on organization within the positivist tradition (Blau, 1977; M. Meyer, 1977). Consistent with the implied position of open systems theory itself, a boundary between the organization and the environment, or conversely the boundaries of organizations, cannot be easily marked. They are viewed as a nested set of interrelated, hierarchically governed systems in constant process and interchange. If the boundaries of organizations cannot be easily located and measured, then they may be at least in part a function of the ways in which actors define their organizational roles, commitments, loyalties, and organizationally relevant encumbrances. Conversely, if the organization cannot be neatly separated out neither can the a1environment. Alternatively, the term environment and the associated rational

organizational adjustment may be a function of the institutionalization of certain rules and premises about formal organizations in a rationalized society rather than their technical behavior. Referring to the open-systems theory claim that internal structure reflects the complexity of the environment, Meyer and Rowan demur, aruging that the myth of rationality is more legitimating than the exchange system:

Quite beyond the environmental interrelations suggested in open systems theories, institutionalized theories in ther extreme forms define organizations as dramatic enactments of the rationalized myths pervading modern societies rather than as units involved in exchange — no matter how complex their environments (Meyer and Rowan, 1977:346).

There remain a number of unclarified conceptual issues associated with the open systems view.

3. The term informant is broadly used in narcotics units. It can refer to some or specifically one of the following: (a) anyone who calls in information to the unit; (b) anyone who has in the past called in information to the unit; (c) someone who has worked in another unit, or the district vice units in Metro, for an officer. There are funds to pay informants in burglary and robbery as well as in district vice units around Metro City. Suburban detectives also have some funds to pay informants, but they are thought to be more limited than those of the vice unit. (d) A person working off a charge, either a drug charge or another type of charge; (e) a person who is working for payment, for information received, either by task or on salary; (f) a person who has worked for pay in the past; (g) a person who is working for pay, and (g1) has been approved by the sergeant, and (g2) has been written up and placed in the department's informant files, and (g3) has had his activities written up in these files some or all of the times that he has worked for an officer in the unit; (h) a person who is reliable in legal terms, which is variable on the two units. It can be broadly defined as a person having given information that was corroborated by other independent sources and shown to be correct, has proven through deeds that his information is valid, for example, has claimed to have seen drugs in a place where they were in fact found upon the serving of a search warrant. Often in drug units, having made a controlled buy (where the informant is stripped-searched, found to have no drugs or money [or the serial numbers of the money given him as recorded precisely to identify his money], and instructed to make a buy of drugs of a certain amount from a certain person if possible, and in a designated location) is crucial for establishing reliability.

The term "informant" is not a restrictive one, and covers a variety of meanings. When combined with such adjectives as "good," "my," or "reliable," the range of possible meanings increases. I have purposively avoided citing or detailing the elaborate, legalistic debates about informants, their control and protection, and issues of fourth amendment freedoms that the use of informants raises. From the officers' point of view they are ex post facto legalisms of only marginal interest. Summaries of this literature are found in Rebell (1972) and Dix (1975), but they are for the most part written by and for lawyers. It has been fairly convincingly argued by Oaks (1970) that the exclusionary rule has minimal impact on everyday police practices. This position is consistent with my observations.

4. Even in patrol there is a certain irony in employing these measures. For example, the convention is that a vehicle is "out of service" when it is in fact "in service" attending a call or involved in an investigation). Therefore, availability, or rapid handling of calls, cannot uniformly indicate efficiency but may indicate sloughing off of calls or failure to accept one's obligations. These are adjustments to demand that do not happen in precisely comparable fashion in vice work. However, I do not want to overdraw the distinctions between patrol and narcotics and fail to emphasize the considerable differences that also exist between vice work and other forms of investigative work such as that done in burglary, robbery, homicide, checks units. Patrol officers do exercise control over their calls, as does the organization itself in the form of the filtration provided by police operators, dispatchers, and radio codes. What is received by the patrol officer, as Van Maanen writes (personal communication), are "citizen complaints, . . . but these are virtually always filtered through the organization's coding system and are replete with errors, misinformation, and distortion of the sort that occurs between the citizen to police operator, police operator to dispatcher, and dispatcher to patrolman communication links." Any complaint is imperfectly known until after the officer arrives on the scene and assembles information on his own. Further, the legally actionable status of a citizen complaint should not be overemphasized because officers generally deal with calls as something to be handled, if at all possible, in a non-legal (and non-informal and therefore non-paper-creating fashion) and the citizen complaint per se rarely in and of itself brings about legal action. I agree with Van Maanen, who argues that one of the most important distinctions is that between traditional post facto detective work and narcotics work. He argues that the patrol officers' concern with order and maintenance, requests for service, heavy reliance on the misdemeanor and municipal ordinance codes, disinterest in any investigative problems beyond their field of vision, and their mediation between citizens and investigative units, set them apart from the proactive investigative units (vice in general) and the reactive investigative units. Both comparisons are being made here, with the most explicit one being that between vice-proactive work and reactive work of various kinds taking place at different stages in the legal process.

5. Variations of a few persons (two or three), when used to estimate a year from an initial six-month period, can give an inflation factor of over 1,800 additional addicts, (for example, three persons for a six-month estimate who are defined as dying from overdose by error, doubled, equals 6 times 200, yields 1,800 additional addicts.). The Baden formula, based as it is on a small number, can yield wildly varying swings due to random fluctuations in the numbers of overdoses in a given period.

6. Mark Moore's virtuoso summary of various methods of estimating the addict population in New York City (1977:70–92) shows that findings of different levels

of use and cost of habit characterize surveys of actual usage. The fiction of a single kind of addict, using some fictious average habit is very misleading. Among other things, the size of habit varies with the cash available to buy drugs, connections accessible to the user at the time, and his or her relationship to the dealing structure itself (Redlinger, 1969). This problem is not solved by self-report studies, but is, of course, compounded (Billington, et al., 1969; Stephens, 1972; Ball, 1967; O'Donnell, et al., 1976). These reports of type of use, date of first use, costs of habit, etc., tend not to be very accurate, not only for the obvious reasons that memory may fail, that people may distort or telescope events, but they may misrepresent in order to either gain or maintain their patient status. The admission of such information can make one legally culpable or at least at risk for investigation.

7. Under conditions of contagious spread of heroin use, as DuPont claims was the case in the late sixties and early seventies in Washington (DuPont, 1971, 1973; DuPont and Greene, 1973), social characteristics of users change rapidly, and this both inflates the number of potential overdose cases in using population (compare Becker, 1967) and changes the character of the population to which one is trying to generalize (Hughes, 1977: chapters 5 and 6).

8. If one uses different methods of estimation, even given the same data, different answers will be produced (compare Hunt, 1974, and Redlinger, 1975b). For example, Rockefeller, while mounting his own war on drugs in New York, used highly exaggerated numbers of addicts based on pure hyperbole (Epstein, 1977:42). At other times he used a daily habit figure to estimate the number of crimes committed by addicts, and the property values of items they needed to steal to support their habits, given the hypothetical daily habit cost. These methods produced an estimate of the rate and cost of addict crime that exceeded the actual figures for all crime in New York City at the time, and a rate of stolen property far beyond what the property crime rate could be shown to involve. (See also Singer, 1971.) A similar pattern of lying and deception was used by Nixon's domestic planners according to Epstein, who had access to the files of presidential assistant Egil Krogh (who was in charge of this facet of the President's domestic program). The entire enterprise was based on dubious assumptions, such as the BNDD's artifactual estimate of the number of unknown addicts and projection of 559,000 addicts; that each addict required $16,750 worth of heroin every year to sustain a habit (there was no evidence of this level; it was assumed), and that all heroin users were compelled to support their habits through crime. "If all the projected 559,000 addicts committed two or three burglaries a day, as President Nixon postulated, they would have to commit at least 365 million burglaries a year . . . two hundred times more than all the burglaries [reported] committed in 1971 in America" (Epstein, 1977:180). Other attempts at estimating the social costs of addiction are at root based on such tenuous assumptions and are likely to be self-serving to those who make them (compare DuPont, 1975).

9. DuPont defines patients or clients as anyone who makes a visit to the clinics, while at other times he uses continuing presence or residence as the criteria. At still another time, he asserts that 13,000 people (addicts it is assumed, since all treated persons are ipso facto addicts) were treated in the clinics of the National Treatment Administration between 1970–1971 (DuPont and Greene, 1973:719).

As it is repeatedly argued by DuPont that treatment is one cause of reduction in the crime rate and the addict population, these definitional changes are more than a semantic problem. DuPont and associates provided the public intellectual rationale for the effectiveness of control efforts with respect to reducing crime and use. They were the most important source of intellectual support for the political "war on drugs" during the early seventies.

10. The precise effect of treatment on the number of addicts and on the crime rate as discussed by DuPont (1971, 1972, and 1975) is somewhat difficult to discern for the definitional and political reasons discussed above (see House Testimony by DuPont, 94th Congress, 2nd Session, 9-30-76: 619–621; 631 ff.). However, DuPont and associates have nonetheless argued that as the purity of heroin decreases on the street, persons in treatment increase, street crime is also dropping, and the costs of heroin and the per milligram dosage in buys also drops. They have shown these correlations for the period 1969–1973 in Washington, D.C. (Greene and DuPont, 1974). The logic in this case would be that as the purity of the heroin available decreases (attributed by DuPont, 1975, to increases in police manpower), people go into treatment and commit fewer crimes; hence the drop in the overall crime rate and the property crime rate (DuPont, 1971, DuPont and Greene, 1973:721). Greene reported an increase in heroin prevalence in Washington, D.C. after 1974, and argued that as the purity of heroin increases, the reported number of burglaries increased (1975:245).

11. For example, Epstein (1977:174–75) reported the manipulation of figures by Nixon and Rockefeller. The debate over the number of addicts continues to the present time, as does the question of the relationship between heroin use and crime. A select house committee on drug abuse reported, on the basis of staff estimates, that "there are more than 800,000 heroin addicts in the United States at this time, more than a 100 percent increase since 1970" (Interim Report, House Select Committee, 95th Congress, 1st Session, February, 1977:66). At another point, the same committee reported that there were "400,000 to 500,000" addicts, while asserting that there were some "three to four million" occasional users (ibid., p. 54). A more precise figure, based on a survey by the U.S. Conference of Mayors, was 505,692 (ibid., p. 58). In a previous hearing of the House Committee in 1976 (94th Congress, 2nd Session, September 30–31, 1976:610, 627, 637), Robert DuPont, previous head of the Special Action Office of Drug Abuse Prevention in Nixon's administration, and at that time head of the National Institute of Drug Abuse in HEW, asserted that there were some 400,000 users. The discussion of the number of opiate users

is often confused because the high figures name anyone who has used heroin in the last year as an addict and the lower figures include only those estimated to have used it in the last week. The samples on which the figures of the Conference of Mayors were based differ from those cited by DuPont, according to testimony, but no details were given (Interim Report, February, 1977:58). At another time, a figure of "500,000 untreated daily users of heroin" was cited (ibid., p. 54). Obviously, the debate continues with little attempt to establish the actual figures. Any high level of use has a political function, and specificity is of little concern to politicians. The politicality of the figures is obviously linked to the connection that has been made in the public mind between drugs and crime. Nixon's "war on drugs" was probably the most significant factor in establishing this yet unproven assertion as a fact from the point of view of the "person in the street." A recent report issued by NIDA (the Shellow Report) was not able to prove a correlation between opiate use and crime after reviewing available research and commissioning a number of special papers and conferences on the topic. Yet, President Carter continues to make the bald and obviously not factually supported claim that ". . . as much as one-half of all street crime today is committed by drug addicts to support their habit" (speech delivered to the International Association of Chiefs of Police, quoted in Oversight Hearings, House Committee, 94th Congress, 2nd Session, September, 1976). DuPont's statements to the same committee (pp. 610–627, 637) are essentially a statement of belief in the ostensive connection between drugs and crime. No figures, studies, or research are cited to substantiate this belief. DuPont has made such unsubstantiated assertions previously (Washington *Post*, March 23, 1973:C1).

12. Drawn from interviews with command personnel and agents in two narcotics enforcement units; reviews of historic literature (King, 1971; Musto, 1973; Lindesmith, 1965); enforcement agencies documents (DEA literature; Federal White Paper, 1975); public testimony (Senate Subcommittee on Government Operations, 1975); scientific literature on drug control (writings of Levin, et al., Greene, DuPont, Moore, Hughes, et al., and Jaffe and publications of Drug Abuse Council); and sociological analyses of drug enforcement practices (Skolnick, 1966; DeFleur, 1975; Manning and Redlinger, 1977, forthcoming a, 1978).

13. See Terreberry, 1968; Bertalanffly, 1968; Thompson, 1967; Lawrence and Lorsch, 1969; Tifft, 1975.

14. This axiom would appear to be generally true in the "cops and robbers" world—the bigger the criminal, the more famous his captor becomes, for example, Billy the Kid and Pat Garrett, John Dillinger and J. Edgar Hoover.

15. It has been argued elsewhere (Manning and Redlinger, 1977) that there are other features of the illicit market that do not hold true for legitimate or licit markets and for the actions of control agencies. Several of the more important features are that the illicit sellers are unable to influence the decisions of the regulators except through "corrupt" practices being barred from legitimate

political influence on legislators, judges, regulatory boards and agencies, and the like; that they are unable to participate in the circulation of personnel between agencies and sellers, which is true of the licit market and their regulators, and that the intent of regulation of legitimate markets is to protect quality and standards and monitor production, although in the case of the illicit market, it is to suppress or eradicate the market, reduce the quality of the product, and destroy the productive capacity of the industry. Thus, an interaction effect is produced by the intent of regulation, the shape of the marketing and distribution process, and the interfacing of the two worlds of control and dealing.

16. Uncertainty permeates the ambience because one must rely on others' information; because even if the information is generally accurate (X deals in heroin) it can be situationally wrong (when a search warrant raid is mounted, X is not holding the dope); substances may not be seized, those seized may not be controlled substances or may be of insufficient quantity to prosecute; other agents may take a case (information may not be shared across squads or even with partners, and rarely with other local, state, or federal units); informants may not be able to deliver what they promise (buys, names, introductions, etc.); informants lie, etc. The information often provided by the public may be either wrong, unverifiable, an "educated guess," or, more importantly, may not be legally actionable information: that is, court-relevant information that will be credible with prosecutors, juries, and judges and will lead to conviction.

Notes to Chapter 4

1. Money is critical to drug law enforcement; many feel it is the singularly most important item required to produce effective enforcement (see Pomeroy, 1974). However, absent skills, administrative expertise, rewards to induce enforcement activity, personnel and cruisers, money alone is inadequate. It is probably overemphasized as the cause of a police department's inability to control drug traffic on putatively related crime.

2. These pressures to obstruct justice on the one hand or to "overenforce" the law on the other are both internal and external. They are logical inferences made from the synthesis of data reported in a number of studies and works on corruption and police work. We have shown elsewhere how these pressures can lead to corruption in police organizations (Manning and Redlinger, 1978). Greater pressures lead to, at least, more frequent encounters with problematic situations containing opportunities for corruption.

3. In a classic study in public administration, Kaufman (1960) describes in detail some of the kinds of pressures and inconsistencies that created variance from the formal bureaucratic map of regulations, procedures, and operating advisos so commonly found in public bureaucracies.

4. Getting at higher level dealers often involves gathering wire intercept evidence which is often excluded from court, constructing a conspiracy charge (very difficult to prove since it usually does not involve a seizure which might

permit collective possession to be established), and long and careful work. Thus the "higher" in the dealing pyramid the investigator seeks to go, the more expensive it is, the less likely to yield arrests, the more it is subject to court control and decisions, and conversely, the fewer arrests it will yield on a monthly basis.

5. This tendency to reify organizational structure has been criticized effectively by critics such as Herbert Blumer (1969), Erving Goffman (1959, 1961), Tom Burns (1958), Frederik Barth (1966), Pierre Bordieu (1977), and Anselm Strauss (1978). The most effective empirical presentation of the case is made by Edmund Leach in his brillant and innovative monograph, the *Political Systems of Highland Burma* (1965).

Notes to Chapter 5

1. Very good general treatments of the sergeant's role are found in Cain (1973:chapter 6), Rubinstein (1973:especially chapter 10), Muir (1977:235–248), and Tifft (1975). Although my experience in patrol in the United States and in England leads me to view these general descriptions of the sergeant's role as valid, I did not observe all these relations in this study. In this section on colleague and sergeant interactions with officers in the two drug units, I report only what was observed by me or told to me by informants.

2. One informant told me, "It's so rare that a specialized squad gives a uniformed officer an arrest, uniformed officers think we're trying to 'stick 'em' if we offer an arrest." They think they may be embarrassed in court, that the warrant was expired or was faulty in some other respect, that some corruption is involved, etc.

3. Day-work squads are considered by many in the branch not to be engaged in law enforcement functions: They investigate potential violations presented by complaints, do not work the streets in the same fashion as other investigators, maintain regular and unchanging day hours, and interact with higher status citizens (pharmacists, doctors, educators, etc.) where verbal skills and persuasion hold a dominant position in the skill repetoire. This is not to say that duplicity, misrepresentation, lying, verbal deception, role-playing, and the like are not essential skills for all narcs; they are. The types of verbal skills are perhaps better captured by Bernstein's distinction between the use of the elaborated versus the restricted code (1971). The day-work sections must rely more on the use of an elaborated code and pride themselves on being able to talk with "a better class of people" and being able to convince or persuade them either of violation or of the need to better control prescriptions. A restricted code is the code of the street people.

4. I have not cited the rich work on informal or small natural groups within organizational structures, such as the classic work of Shils and Janowitz (1948), Dalton (1959), Roy (1953, 1954, 1960), Gross (1953, 1955, 1961), and Burns (1955) because although I am concerned with small natural groups, I am pri-

marily focusing in this context on the bases of squad solidarity. Squads as formally designated units have differential solidarity, and their infrastructure is complex. In order to look at the organization from the level of the squad as a proximal locus of action, I needed to know what made social action possible by these acting units but did not need to know the micro-organizations that stood beneath this level of the organization; friendship pairs, informal socialization off the job, clique structures, and the like. In an important way, these are replicated in the squad groups because assignments are made to squads and partnerships on the basis of previously known friendships and compatibilities by lieutenants, because the squad places people in close proximity in many of the important and dangerous functions shared by members of the unit (search warrants, arrest warrants), and because racial and ethnic ties are reflected in the social compositions of the squads. A close analysis of squad action, decision-making at that level, and the particular choices made by squads (rather than the type of case most commonly worked), would require more systematic refinement of the above mentioned masterful analyses of microstructure.

Notes to Chapter 6

1. The Drug Enforcement Administration over the few years of its existence has tried several means of targeting. At the time of the research, they were employing the "DEA-G-DEP-Violator Classification" system shown in appendix 6A. The term "major violator" is used in Class I, although the term as it is used has expanding and contracting properties.

2. In the Metro Department, no overtime was paid for operational time (when a person accumulated more than eight hours on a turn of duty during the course of an investigation). Time off could be given in the form of "comp time" in exchange (see appendix 6B).

Notes to Chapter 7

1. Analytic induction is utilized here. See Manning, forthcoming b.

2. Thus failure or a mistake in the closing of a case is viewed as Hughes (1958) suggests all mistakes at work are viewed: in a statistical manner and with a good degree of fatalism.

3. The sergeant told me after he had seen the lieutenant that he felt the biggest problems in the unit were "personality problems" and that the officials were always "second-guessing you" and "making it difficult."

4. This information was elicited in interviews with three key informants in Metro.

5. The files are not kept up carefully in either unit because there are few controls and sanctions for not so doing and because of the negative view of pa-

perwork. Further, the pressures for success, competition between officers, the ambience of secrecy within the unit, the belief that dealers may try to obtain such information, and the danger of retaliation associated with being an informant all tend to make organizational control over informant files episodic and cyclical. This issue has been explored in more depth in Williams, Redlinger, and Manning, 1978.

6. The following paragraph is slightly modified from Williams, Manning, and Redlinger, 1977:43–46, and holds true in these two units as well as the unit studied in our pilot site.

7. Credibility is two-sided. Narcotics unit investigators may have a bad reputation among potential informants they handle. Investigators who do not keep their part of the bargain are sometimes stigmatized by the community and become known at least somewhat as untrustworthy individuals. In these instances, the investigator would have trouble making informants who would assert their willingness to inform and who also wanted to strike their bargain with some other investigator.

8. It was reiterated previously by Sergeant Smith in a meeting, which I missed, that they were not pushing the snitches hard enough and that they should get the snitch to walk them in so as to enable then to make a hand-to-hand buy. He also said that he didn't mind if the snitch got burned. They shouldn't be worried about that, either. In other words, "being burned" had two meanings. One is simply the fact that if the undercover officer is identified as a policeman at that point or subsequently by informal means, then the informant is "burned," that is, known to be associating with narcotics agents. On the other hand, it could mean that the informant is burned in the sense that he is an eyewitness to the transaction and might be called in court; although this is unlikely given the fact that it is a hand-to-hand buy and that the investigator's name would be on the warrant or on the arrest for a hand-to-hand buy.

9. This is not an entirely affluent county, but rather a county of quite marked contrast. There are lower-class areas in Vista, close to the Metro line, rural areas up toward the northern edge of the county, urban/rural fringes near Center City, and upper-class estates, mostly in and around Churchville

10. A lieutenant described to me the events leading to the murder of Officer Wilson. They had set up a buy-bust situation. Two agents and two dealers were involved. The incident took place in a motel room. The first agent who went in was Sergeant Smith, followed by the second agent, who was Wilson. One man was in the room when they entered, and one man walked in with the agents. The man in the room at the time dived quickly into the john while the man who came through the door grabbed his gun, whirled, and started to fire. He killed Wilson and shot Smith through the hand; Smith jumped on him and wrestled him to the ground. When the second dealer emerged from the restroom, he jumped on top of the two men wrestling on the floor of the room. At that time six agents who were in the adjoining motel room burst in. Apparently, as soon as

they had heard the door close and the shot, they suspected that something was happening, and they immediately rushed next door and burst in on the scene. As they broke in, there were three men on the floor and one of the officers shot the man on top of the pile. The other one was apprehended. Smith sustained permanent damage to his left arm as a result of this incident. There is a plaque to Wilson in the office. I also heard this story in Metro.

11. I had previously asked questions, for example, "How do you set up a buy-bust situation, or how do you work an informant that is under the gun or working off a beef?" And then I would get an answer. The problem with such an approach methodologically, is that if the person has never participated in a buy-bust or has never worked an informant who is under the gun, then the answers have the quality of reporting or secondary examination of what others have told them, what they think might happen in such cases. I remember this was the case with Sergeant Roy who provided very detailed information, but in fact a number of these things had not happened to him personally. I realized that for this officer, who had been working only approximately nine months, asking questions like "how do you set up a buy-bust" would tend to elicit a fairly standardized reply based on knowledge obtained from other investigators and not from personal experience.

12. Fox described this case as more of a "rip-off" than a buy-bust. It is also an example of the kind of flexible procedure that often occurs—the fear is that one will loose the arrest or control of the situation but particularly that one will loose the evidence that ties the person to the transaction.

13. I noted differences in demeanor in comparison to Metro. Uniform officers tended to be treated in a more cavalier fashion and are given less instructions as how to perform their duty and fewer thanks for their efforts, their time, and are directed much less by the young narcotics officers. A second difference is in the treatment of the prisoners in Suburban. There is less joking, less attempt to make the prisoners comfortable. The girl and boy in the Chakey case had to beg to go to the john after two-and-a-half to three hours of sitting and waiting. The boy's old man had to almost beg the officers to allow the woman to use the bathroom. Subsequently, the boy had to use the toilet under the scrutiny of a uniformed officer who went in the bathroom with him. It occurred to me that one disadvantage of not having a female officer there was they could not search her and I don't think they strip-searched him.

14. I think this was particularly true at the point when the fellow came down the stairs for the second time, would not say anything about dope one way or another. I was frustrated. Frustration could be a tipping point which could lead to violence. Furthermore, it is obviously embarrassing to come up dry. Later on, after the father had come home and been angry and ranted around, five of us were in the bedroom. They all said, "Look what you've gotten us into now, Charlie, look what you've done to us now! Yeah, look at it, Charlie." And everybody half-laughed. This kind of irony was a mode of social control, a means of

establishing his error, and of showing that they were collectively embarrassed by being there in front of the father without being able to show a major seizure.

15. Subsequently, we went out to dinner around eight o'clock with two attorney's from the state attorney's office. They chitchatted about cases and the little problems of their work, and I asked them two questions concerning working off beefs. The first was whether or not there was any policy in the state attorney's office concerning the sorts of crimes that might be worked off. One said there was no specific policy, that usually he would have the defense attorney, the prisoner, and the officer sit down with him, and they would discuss the possibilities. I then asked if the crime committed mattered with respect to whether he could work off the case. For example, I asked, did they have rules about assaults or any other types of cases. He said, "No, they didn't." I asked "Even if it were homicide?" He looked at me and said, "Well, no, there are different sorts of homicides, and it might be that he could work it off." The second attorney said that she felt that with a homicide, "You have the problem of the family." I mentioned that this might often be an issue, the objections of family and friends in the case of personal assaults, or homicides, and the objections they might raise to reduction in the charge or working off a beef. But the sense of a discussion was that this was definitely a matter of discretion by the individual state attorney, and that there was no office policy.

16. There was a similar debate in Metro, with a parallel policy being announced, then obscured by public qualification, and then rescinded. Several observers claimed that in cases involving personal possession of marijuana were not being prosecuted in Metro either. I could not verify this.

Notes to Chapter 8

1. I refer the interested reader to the recent works on decision-making in drug enforcement by chiefs-of-police (Ahern, 1972; J.V. Wilson, 1975), by critics of police actions (Gooberman, 1974; Epstein, 1977), and their own local newspapers. The "drug drive," or "heroin hunt" has been well analyzed by Redlinger (1969), Epstein (1977), and Young (1972).

2. The T.I.P. (turn in pusher) programs sponsored by the federal government and local governments were an enormous failure. A vast majority of the calls were worthless; others that had value became worthless because people would refuse to leave a number where they could be reached. The structure of this information system is similar to that encountered by the officer who answers a phone call and has to interrogate an anonymous caller. The results of T.I.P. programs, when measured in terms of arrests and/or seizures, were meager. The rewards were to be given only if the information provided led to an arrest. This was a rare event so few rewards were given. The programs have been phased out in most areas.

3. I was told later that such a call would be either referred directly to a district vice squad, or they'll say "Yes, ma'am, we'll get right on it; we'll do something

about it." According to Sergeant Long, " . . . the person might see somebody get arrested in the next ten minutes or so, anyway; drunk in the street, propositioning, prostitution, numbers, gambling, drugs—it's a pretty common thing, so you can be sure something will be happening there anyway."

4. One of the most sought dealers in the Metro area, Greasey Andrew, was apprehended when his car was stopped in a routine traffic stop for having a bent or obscured license tag. When the officer stopped him and looked in the car, he saw, according to police reports, an ounce of cocaine peeking out from under the passenger's side seat. Greasey was arrested on a possession charge, something the narcotics unit has been unable to do over the previous several years. They had been trying to arrest him since they had become aware of his activities. They viewed him as a major violator. This story was told to me on three separate occasions as evidence of "you can never tell in narcotics," the possible pay-off from chance events, and the fact that one could never match time, effort, and outcome in narcotics work.

5. Although Paul Gun was considered by many to be the best all around investigator, he was in charge of assigning the cases on the afternoon shift and kept his own case load down. Whether this was because he assigned himself very few or whether he was very efficient about clearing them, I cannot say.

Notes to Chapter 9

1. The evidence available to assess their implicit and explicit claims to be able to produce and insure order, security, protect property, and more commonly and significantly, to control crime, is not fully convincing. The data suggest that preventative patrol is only of marginal importance as a means of producing a sense of citizen satisfaction, security, increased arrest rates, or reduced crime, as independently measured by a victimization survey (Kelling, et al., 1974); that detective work is largely routine paperwork that could be handled as well by clerks and has little bearing on crime or clearance rates (Greenwood, Petersilia, and Chaiken, 1988); that resources, personnel and information do not correlate with arrest rates or reflect the level of the crime problem in the environment (Manning, 1977d; Cho, 1974; Wellford, 1975; but see Chapman, 1975; for an excellent overview of this literature see Greenberg, Kessler, and Logan, 1978); and that no evidence links the conventional police measures of performance, such as arrests, clearances, or field interrogations, with any independent measure of crime (see Manning, 1977a, chapter 8). The empirical evidence suggests an irony of extreme proportions in that they cannot be shown to measurably prevent, punish, or have an impact on crime, yet they are expected to be responsible and accept responsibility for crime control in this society.

2. Officers are routinely present in the first hour or so before and the first hour or so after a shift change, from about 7:00 to 9:00 A.M. and from 3:00 to 5:00

P.M. At these times, before roll call or a meeting which are rare in both units, officers see members of other shifts, talk about cases, friends in other units, court cases pending and in progress, and make conversation. Major topics are: hunting, fishing, cars, guns, sports, especially football, gossip about politicians and senior officers (departmental politics) and women. It is reasonable for investigators to be on the street, for they could not be raised easily on the radio even if they were riding in police vehicles. Radios were either turned off, [the force radio], malfunctioning, on the wrong channel as in Suburban where four channels were used, or were not taken along. Few officers in Metro carried a police radio when in a vehicle, relying instead, if they needed to communicate, on central communications or the telephone. In Suburban, officers usually carried a police radio in their cars, but often could not reach the communication center because they were in distant parts of the county, behind a hill or the like. The range of the hand-held radios was very limited. They do not have large two-way radios installed in their vehicles as they served both as personal cars and as "undercover" vehicles.

3. Wilson has written in *Varieties of Police Behavior* (1968), that the police do not view this mode of thought and action as the legitimating bases of their mandate. Thus it is likely that the language of bureaucracy and the formal administrative rhetoric that often issues from police administrators is a means they have of appealing for support to certain segments outside the unit or department (Manning, 1974). This behavior of strategic appeals made to different audiences in quite distinctive language results in a degree of segmentation and segregation of audiences' messages and aims that can take the form of deception and duplicity.

4. These stories tend to be either stories on one's self or stories on others and mainly are tales of errors, near-errors, and slips. From these incidents come nicknames that are often derogatory ("Space Baby" was so called because his mind was always in the clouds or spaced out). The successful instances told to me were told primarily to impress me. The more common stories are endless ones about guns that would not fire, money that was lost, persons who escaped after a long chase, complex deals that folded at the last minute, and stories about the general unpredictability of street people.

5. The arguments made here are social-psychological, but there are a number of social organizational and technological reasons why records are not well kept in either unit. In Metro the case files involving arrests other than those involving drug charges are filed in central records outside the unit. Patrol arrests and related developments are filed in the main records' offices in both units, thus creating inconvenience if one wants to retrieve information from past files. Typists and clerks are not available to file this material in either unit, and few officers in either unit are able to type. Consequently, they spent many hours typing arrest forms often with the assistance of several other members of their squads. The practical constraints on making and maintaining files are considerable in both units, and the costs associated with maintaining files are borne

directly by the individual officer. My basic contention is that if these social organizational and technological matters were changed—clerks hired, a workable filing system developed in the unit—if all officers were excellent typists and
had typewriters available, the social-psychological factors would remain, and
the same practices would continue.

6. Letter to the author from Head of the Division, Metro, October 9, 1975.

7. For example, although a sergeant can be called at home, he is not called
concerning signing overtime requests. Normally the officers proceed with the
surveillance, or the meet, or the attempted buy-bust, and then submit the request for overtime if something comes of it—generally an arrest. A verbal explanation is offered to the sergeant at the time of submission. Like the rules for
signing search warrants (they have to be approved by the captain of the Unit,
but the Lieutenant has signed when time was short), there are two sets of rules:
the official and the approved, informal rules. These two are additional instances of the potential double bind that officers find themselves in should they
be vulnerable to criticism for violating the formal rules (or the informal rules).
One can lose either way.

References

Aaronson, B., and
O. Humphrey
1970

Psychedelics. New York: Doubleday 9 co.

Agar, M.
1973

Ripping and Running. New York: Seminar Press.

Ahern, J. F.
1972

Police in Trouble. New York: Hawthorn Books, Inc.

Aldrich, H., and
J. Pfeffer
1976

"Environments of Organizations." In *Annual Review of Sociology,* eds. A. Inkeles, J. Coleman, and N. Smelser, I. Palo Alto: Annual Reviews, pp. 79–105.

Altheide, D., and
J. Johnson, eds.
1979

Modern Propaganda. Boston: Allyn and Bacon.

Arnold, T.
1935

Symbols of Government. New Haven: Yale University Press.

Ashley, R.
1976

Cocaine. New York: Warner.

Bagehot, W.
1963

The English Constitution. Introduction by R. H. S. Crossman. London: Fontana/ Collins (originally published, 1867).

Ball, J. C.
1965

"Two Patterns of Narcotic Drug Addiction in the United States." *Journal of Criminal Law, Criminology and Police Science* 56 (June):203–221.

Ball, J. C.
1967

"The Reliability and Validity of Interview Data Obtained from 59 Narcotic Drug Addicts." *American Journal of Sociology* 72 (May):650–654.

Baltimore Police
Department
1976

"DEA-Baltimore Police Education Program Enchances CDS Enforcement Efforts," *Newsletter* 10 (December 8):1–3.

Banton, Michael
1964

The Policeman in the Community. New York: Basic Books.

Barth, F.
1966

"Models of Social Organization." Royal Anthropological Institute Occasional Papers.

Becker, G.
1976

"Crime and Punishment: An Economic Approach." *Journal of Political Economy* 76 (March–April):169–217.

Becker, G. S., and
G. Stigler
1974

"Law Enforcement, Malfeasance, and Compensation of Enforcers." *Journal of Legal Studies* III (January):1–18.

Becker, H.S.
1963

Outsiders: Studies in the Sociology of Deviance.
Glencoe, IL: Free Press.

Becker, H. S.
1967

"History, Culture and Subjective Experience."
Journal of Health and Social Behavior 7
(June):163–176.

Becker, H., B. Geer,
and E. Hughes
1968

Making the Grade. New York: John Wiley and Sons.

Becker, H. S., B. Geer,
E. C. Hughes, and
A. Strauss
1961

Boys in White. Chicago: University of Chicago
Press.

Benson, J. K.
1975

"The Interorganizational Network as a Political
Economy." *Administrative Science Quarterly* 20
(June):229–249.

Benson, J. K.
1977a

"Organizations: A Dialectical View." *Administrative
Science Quarterly* 22 (March):1–21.

Benson, J. K.
1977b

"Innovation and Crisis in Organizational Analysis."
Sociological Quarterly 18 (Winter):3–16.

Berlet, C.
1976

"Inside the DEA: The Super-Agency Strikes Out."
High Times 7 (January/February):76–79, 83–89,
94–96, 105.

Bernstein, B.
1971

Class, Codes and Control, vol. I. *Theoretical Studies Towards a Sociology of Language.* London:
Routledge and Kegan Paul.

Billington, B., J. G.
Munns, G. Geis, and
J. Raner
1969

"Concerning Heroin Use and Official Records."
American Journal of Public Health 59
(October):1887–1892.

Bittner, E.
1965

"The Concept of Organization." *Social Research* 32
(Winter):230–255.

Bittner, E.
1970

The Functions of the Police in Modern Society.
Washington, D.C.: U.S. Government Printing Office.

Bittner, E.
1974

"A Theory of the Police." In *The Potential for the Reform of Criminal Justice,* ed. H. Jacob. Beverly
Hills: Sage Publications, pp. 17–44.

Blankenship, R., ed.
1977

Colleagues in Organizations. New York: John Wiley
and Sons.

Blau, P.
1977
Inequality and Heterogeneity: A Primitive Theory of Social Structure. New York: Free Press.

Blau, P., and R. W. Scott
1962
Formal Organizations. San Francisco: Chandler.

Blum, R. H., and Associates
1972
The Dream-Sellers: Perspectives on Drug Dealers. San Francisco, CA: Jossey-Bass.

Blumer, H.
1969
Symbolic Interactionism. Englewood Cliffs, NJ: Prentice-Hall.

Bonnie, R., and C. Whitebread
1974
The Marijuana Conviction. Charlottesville, VA: University of Virginia Press.

Bordua, D., ed.
1967
The Police: Six Sociological Essays. New York: John Wiley and Sons.

D. Bordua, and A. J. Reiss
1967
"Law Enforcement." In *The Uses of Sociology,* eds. P. Lazarsfeld, et al. New York: Basic Books, pp. 275–303.

Bourdieu, P.
1977
Outline of a Theory of Practice. Cambridge: Cambridge University Press.

Brecher, H. W., and the editors of *Consumer Reports*
1972
Licit and Illicit Drugs. Boston: Little, Brown.

Brown, G. F., and L. Silverman
1974
"The Retail Price of Heroin: Estimation and Applications." *Journal of the American Statistical Association.* 69 (September):595–606.

Brown, R.
1974
"Alcohol, Oligopoly and Crime." Unpublished manuscript, National Center for Alcohol Education, Washington, D.C.

Brown, R.
1975
"The Political Economy of Criminalized Drugs and their Impact on Law Enforcement Policy and Procedure." Unpublished manuscript, National Center for Alcohol Education, Washington, D.C.

Browning, F.
1976
"An American Gestapo." *Playboy* 23 (February):81–82, 86, 156–165.

Burns, T.
1955
"The Reference of Conduct in Small Groups." *Human Relations* VIII (November):467–486.

Burns, T.
1958
"The Idea of Structure in Sociology." *Human Relations* 11:217–228.

Burns, T.
1967

"The Comparative Study of Organizations." In *Methods of Organizational Research,* ed. V. Vroom. Pittsburgh: University of Pittsburgh Press, pp. 118–170.

Burns, T., and
G. M. Stalker
1961

The Management of Innovation. London: Tavistock.

Burroughs, W.
1963

Junkie. New York: Ace Books.

Cain, M.
1973

Society and the Policeman's Role. London: Routledge and Kegan Paul.

Campanis, P.
1970

"Normlessness in Management." In *Deviance and Respectability*, ed. Jack Douglas. New York: Basic Books, pp. 291–325.

Caplan, G.
1973

"Reflections on the Nationalization of Crime, 1964–1968." *Law and Social Order,* vol. 1973, no. 3:353–635.

Carey, J.
1968

The Drug Scene. Englewood Cliffs, NJ: Prentice Hall.

Carey, J., and
J. Mandel
1968

"A San Francisco Bay Area 'Speed Scene.' " *Journal of Health and Social Behavior* 9 (June):164–174.

Carter, L.
1974

The Limits of Order. Lexington, MA: Lexington Books.

Chambers, C.
1975

"Survey of Self-Reported Drug-Use in the Washington, D.C. Area." Reported in the Washington *Post*, June 6, 1975.

Chandler, A.
1962

Strategy and Structure. Cambridge, MA: The MIT Press.

Chapman, J. I.
1975

"An Economic Model of Crime and Police: Some Empirical Results." *Journal of Research in Crime and Delinquency* 13 (January):48–63.

Chein, I., D. L. Gerard,
R. S. Lee, and
E. Rosenfeld
1964

The Road to H. New York: Basic Books.

Child, J.
1972

"Organizational Structure and Performance: The Role of Strategic Choice." *Sociology* 6 (January):1–22.

Cho, Y.
1974

Public Policy and Urban Crime. Cambridge, MA:
Ballinger Publishing Company.

Cicourel, A. V.
1973

Cognitive Sociology. Harmondsworth: Penguin.

Clark, J. P., and
R. Sykes
1974

"Some Determinants of Police Organization and
Practice in a Modern Industrial Democracy." In
Handbook of Criminology, ed. D. Glaser. Chicago:
Rand McNally, pp. 455–494.

Cline, S., and
P. Goldberg
1976

*Governmental Response to Drug Abuse: The 1977
Federal Budget*. Washington, D.C.: Drug Abuse
Council.

Cohen, S.
1973

Folk Devils and Moral Panics. London: Paladin
Books.

Collins, R.
1975

Conflict Sociology. New York: Academic Press.

Crozier, M.
1964

The Bureaucratic Phenomenon. Chicago: University of Chicago Press.

Crozier, M.
1971

The World of the Office Worker, trans. D. Landau.
Chicago: University of Chicago Press.

Dai, B.
1937

Opium Addiction in Chicago. Shangai: Commercial
Press.

Dalton, M.
1959

Men Who Manage. New York: John Wiley and
Sons.

Dash, S., R. Schwartz,
and R. Knowlton
1959

The Eavesdroppers. New Brunswick, NJ: Rutgers
University Press.

Davis, F., and L. Munoz
1968

"Heads and Freaks: Patterns of Meanings of Drug
Use Among Hippies." *Journal of Health and Social
Behavior* 9 (June):156–164.

Davis, K. C.
1969

Discretionary Justice. Baton Rouge: Louisiana
State University Press.

Davis, K. C.
1975

Police Discretion. St. Paul, MN: West Publishing
Co.

Day, R., and J. V. Day
1977

"A Review of the Current State of Negotiated Order
Theory: An Appreciation and a Critique." *Sociological Quarterly* 18 (Winter):126–142.

DeFleur, L.
1975

"Biasing Influences on Drug Arrest Records: Implications for Deviance Research." *American Sociological Review* 40 (February):88–103.

Denzin, N. K.
1977
"Notes on the Criminogenic Hypothesis: A Case Study of the American Liquor Industry." *American Sociological Review* 42 (December):905–920.

Dewey, J., and
A.Bentley
1949
Knowing and the Known. Boston: Beacon Press.

Dickson, D. T.
1968
"Bureaucracy and Morality: An Organizational Perspective on a Moral Crusade." *Social Problems* 16 (Fall):143–156.

Ditton, J.
1977
Part-time Crime. London: Macmillan & Co.

Dix, G.
1975
"Undercover Investigations and Police Rule-Making." *Texas Law Review* 53 (January):202–294.

Douglas, J.
1971
American Social Order. New York: Free Press.

DuPont, R.
1971
"Profile of a Heroin Addiction Epidemic." *New England Journal of Medicine* 285 (August 5):320–324.

DuPont, R. L.
1972
"Heroin Addiction and Crime Reduction." *American Journal of Psychiatry* 128 (January):856–860.

DuPont, R. L.
1973
"Coming to Grips with an Urban Heroin Addiction Epidemic." *JAMA* 223 (January 1):46–48.

DuPont, R. L.
1975
"The Social Costs of Drug Abuse." Report of the Special Action Office for Drug Abuse Prevention. In *Hearings of Permanent Subcommittee on Investigations of Committee on Government Operations,* U.S. Senate, 94th Congress, 1st Session, June 9–11, pt. I, pp. 255–274.

DuPont, R. L.
1976
Senate Testimony. 94th Congress, 2nd Session, September 30, pp. 2–35.

DuPont, R. L.
1978
"The Drug Abuse Decade." *Journal of Drug Issues* 8 (Spring):173–187.

DuPont, R. L., and
M. Greene
1973
"The Dynamics of the Heroin Addiction Epidemic." *Science* 181 (August):716–722.

Edelman, M.
1964
The Symbolic Uses of Politics. Urbana, IL: University of Illinois Press.

Eldridge, W. B.
1967
Narcotics and the Law: A Critique of the American Experiment in Narcotic Drug Control. Chicago: University of Chicago Press.

Epstein, E.
1977

The Agency of Fear. New York: G. P. Putnam.

Erickson, E. E.
1969

"The Social Costs of the Discovery and Suppression of the Clandestine Distribution of Heroin." *Journal of Political Economy* 77 (September):484–486.

Eszterhas, J.
1974

Nark! San Francisco: Straight Arrow Books.

Farmer, D.
1978

"The Future of Law Enforcement in the United States: The Federal Role." *Police Studies* 1 (June):31–38.

Federal White Paper
(Domestic Council Drug
Abuse Task Force)
1975

White Paper on Drug Abuse. Report to the President. Washington, D.C.: U.S. Government Printing Office.

Fiddle, S.
1967

Portraits From a Shooting Gallery. New York: Harper Brothers.

Finestone, H.
1957

"Cats, Kicks and Color." *Social Problems* 5 (July):3–13.

Foucault, M.
1965

Madness and Civilization, trans. R. Howard. New York: Random House.

Foucault, M.
1972

The Archaeology of Knowledge and the Discourse on Language. New York: Harper Colophon Books.

Foucault, M.
1973

The Birth of the Clinic, trans. A. M. Sheridan-Smith. New York: Pantheon Books.

Foucault, M.
1977

Discipline and Punish: The Birth of the Prison, trans. A. Sheridan. New York: Pantheon Books.

Freidson, E.
1975

Doctoring Together. New York: Elsevier.

Gardiner, J.
1969

Traffic and the Police. Cambridge, MA: Harvard University Press.

Garfinkel, H.
1967

Studies in Ethnomethodology. Englewood Cliffs, NJ: Prentice-Hall.

Garfinkel, H., and
E. Bittner
1967

" 'Good' Organizational Reasons for 'Bad' Clinic Records." In *Studies in Ethnomethodology,* H. Garfinkel. Englewood Cliffs, NJ: Prentice-Hall, pp. 186–207.

Garza, M.
1976

A Multi-Agency Narcotics Unit Manual. LEAA/NI-LECJ: Washington: U.S. Government Printing Office.

Glaser, B., and
A. Strauss
1967

The Discovery of Grounded Theory. Chicago: Aldine.

Gluckman, M.
1971

Analysis of a Social Situation in Modern Zululand. Rhodes-Livingstone Papers, no. #28 Manchester: Manchester University Press.

Goffman, E.
1959

The Presentation of Self in Everyday Life. New York: Doubleday.

Goffman, E.
1961

Asylums. Chicago: Aldine.

Goffman, E.
1967

Interaction Ritual. Chicago: Aldine.

Goffman, E.
1969

Strategic Interaction. Philadelphia: University of Pennsylvania Press.

Goldman, A.
1975

"What Will Happen When Middle-Class America Gets the Straight Dope?" *New York* 8 (August 25): 28–36, 39–41.

Goldstein, H.
1977

Policing A Free Society. Cambridge, MA: Ballinger Publishing.

Gooberman, L. A.
1974

Operation Intercept: The Multiple Consequences of Public Policy. New York: Pergamon Press.

Goode, E.
1969a

"Marijuana and the Politics of Reality." *Journal of Health and Social Behavior* X (June):83–94.

Goode, E.
1969b

"The Marijuana Market." *Columbia Forum* 12 (Winter):4–8.

Goode, E.
1970

The Marijuana Smokers. New York: Basic Books.

Gould, L., A. L. Walker,
L. E. Crane, and
C. W. Lidz
1974

Connections: Notes From the Heroin World. New Haven: Yale University Press.

Gouldner, A. W.
1952

" 'Red Tape' As a Social Problem." In *Reader in Bureaucracy,* eds. R. K. Merton, H. Selvin, and A. Grey. Glencoe, IL: Free Press, pp 410–418.

Gouldner, A. W.
1954

Patterns of Industrial Bureaucracy. Glencoe: Free Press.

Gouldner, A. W.
1959

"Reciprocity and Autonomy in Functional Theory." In *Symposium on Sociological Theory,* ed. L. Gross. Chicago: Row, Peterson, pp. 241–270.

Greenberg, D., R. Kessler, and Charles Logan
1978

"Crime Rates and Arrest Rates: A Causal Analysis." Unpublished paper.

Greene, M.
1975

"The Resurgence of Heroin Abuse in the District of Columbia." In *Hearings of Permanent Subcommittee on Investigations of the Committee on Government Operations,* U.S. Senate, 94th Congress, 1st Session, June 9–11, pt. I, pp. 242–254.

Greene, M., B. S. Brown, and R. L. DuPont
1975

"Controlling the Abuse of Illicit Methadone in Washington, D.C." *Archives of General Psychiatry* 32 (February):221–226.

Greene, M., and R. DuPont
1974

"Heroin Addiction Trends." *American Journal of Psychiatry* 131 (May):545–550.

Greenwood, P., J. Chalken, and J. Peterislia
1977

The Criminal Investigation Process. Lexington, MA: D. C. Heath.

Grinspoon, L., and P. Hedblom
1975

The Speed Culture: Amphetamine Use and Abuse in America. Cambridge, MA: Harvard University Press.

Grinspoon, L.
1977

Marijuana Reconsidered, 2nd ed. Cambridge: Harvard University Press.

Gross, E.
1953

"Some Functional Consequences of Primary Controls in Formal Work Organizations." *American Sociological Review* 18 (August):368–373.

Gross, E.
1955

"Primary Functions of the Small Group." *American Journal of Sociology* 60 (July):24–29.

Gross, E.
1961

"Social Integration and the Control of Competition." *American Journal of Sociology* 67 (November):270–277.

Gusfield, J.
1975

"The (F)Utility of Knowledge?" The Relation of Social Science to Public Policy Toward Drugs." *Annals* 417 (January):1–15.

292   References

Haas, J., and T. Drabek
1973

Complex Organizations. New York: MacMillan.

Hall, O.
1946

"The Informal Organization of the Medical Profession." *Canadian Journal of Economics and Political Science* 12 (February):30–44.

Hall, O.
1948

"The Stages of a Medical Career." *American Journal of Sociology* 53 (March):327–336.

Hall, R.
1977

Organizations: Structure and Process, 2nd ed. Englewood Cliffs, NJ: Prentice-Hall.

Harney, M., and
L. Cross
1960

The Informer in Law Enforcement. Springfield, IL: Charles C. Thomas.

Hasenfeld, Y., and
R. English, eds.
1974

Human Service Organizations. Ann Arbor: University of Michigan Press.

Heller, J. D.
1973 a

"The Attempt to Control Illicit Drug Supply." In *Drug Use in America: The Problem in Perspective,* appendix vol. III. *Technical Papers of the Second Report of the National Commission on Marijuana and Drug Abuse.* Washington, D.C.: USGPO, pp. 383–407.

Heller, J. D.
1973b

"A Conflict of Laws: The Drug Possession Offense and the Fourth Amendment." In *Drug Use in America: The Problem in Perspective;* appendix vol. III. *Technical Papers of the National Commission on Marijuana and Drug Abuse.* Washington, D.C.: U.S. Government Printing Office, pp. 870–884.

Hellman, A.
1975

Laws Against Marijuana. Urbana, IL: University of Illinois Press.

Helmer, J.
1975

Drugs and Minority Oppression. New York: Seabury Press.

Heydebrand, W., ed.
1973

Comparative Organizations. Englewood Cliffs, NJ: Prentice-Hall.

Holahan, J.
1972

"The Economics of Heroin." In *Dealing With Drug Abuse,* ed P. Wald New York. Praeger, pp. 255–299.

Horning, D. N. M.
1970

"Blue Collar Theft: Conceptions of Property, Attitudes Toward Pilfering, and Work Group Norms in a Modern Industrial Plant," In *Crimes Against Bu-*

reaucracy, eds. E. Smigel and H. L. Ross Princeton, NJ: D. Van Hostrand, pp. 46–64.

House Select Committee on Drug Abuse
1976

Testimony. 94th Congress, 2nd Session, September 30–31, 1976.

House Select Committee on Drug Abuse
1977

Interim Report. 95th Congress, 1st Session (February). Washington: U.S. Government Printing Office.

Hughes, E. C.
1958

Men and Their Work. New York: Free Press.

Hughes, E. C.
1971

The Sociological Eye. Chicago: Aldine.

Hughes, H. M.
1961

Fantastic Lodge. New York: Fawcett Premier Books.

Hughes, P. H.
1977

Behind the Wall of Respect. Chicago: University of Chicago Press.

Hughes, P., H. W. Barker, G. A. Crawford, and J. H. Jaffee
1972

"The Natural History of a Heroin Epidemic." *American Journal of Public Health* 162 (July):995–1001.

Hunt, L. G.
1974

Recent Spread of Heroin Use in the United States: Some Unanswered Questions. Washington, D.C.: Drug Abuse Council.

Ianni, F.
1974

The Black Mafia. NY: Simon and Schuster.

Illich, Ivan
1976

Medical Nemesis. London: McClelland and Stewart.

Jehenson, R.
1973

"A Phenomenological Approach to the Study of the Formal Organization." In *Phenomenological Sociology,* ed. G. Psathas. New York: John Wiley and Sons.

Johnson, B.
1973

Marijuana Users and Drug Subcultures. New York: John Wiley and Sons.

Johnson, W. T., R. E. Peterson, and L. E. Wells
1977

"Arrest Probabilities for Marijuana Users as Indicators of Selective Law Enforcement." *American Journal of Sociology* 83 (November):681–699.

Johnson, W., and R. Bogomolny

"Selective Justice: Drug Law Enforcement in Six American Cities." In *Drug Use in America: The*

1973   *Problem in Perspective,* appendix vol. III. *Techni-
                                cal Papers of the Second Report of the National
                                Commission on Marijuana and Drug Abuse.* Wash-
                                ington: U.S. Government Printing Office, pp. 498–
                                650.

Josephson, E., and   *Drug Use.* New York: Halsted/John Wiley and Sons.
E. Carroll, eds.
1974

Kamens, D.   "Legitimating Myths and Educational
1977   Organization." *American Sociological Review* 42
                                (April):208–219.

Kamistra, J.   *Weed.* New York: Bantam Books.
1975

Kanter, R. M.   *Men and Women of the Corporation.* New York:
1977   Basic Books.

Kaplan, J.   *Marijuana: The New Prohibition.* New York: Pocket
1970   Books.

Katz, D., and R. Kahn   *The Social Psychology of Organizations.* New York:
1966   John Wiley and Sons.

Kaufman, H.   *The Forest Ranger.* Baltimore: Johns Hopkins Uni-
1960   versity Press.

Kelling, George,   *The Kansas City Preventive Patrol Experiment: A
T. Pate, D. Dieckman,   Summary Report.* Washington, D.C.: Police Foun-
and C. Brown   dation.
1974

King, R.   *America's Drug Hang-Up.* New York: W. W. Norton.
1972

King, R.   "Drug Abuse Problems and the Idioms of War."
1978   *Journal of Drug Issues* 8 (Spring):221–231.

Koch, J., and S. Grupp   "The Economies of Drug Control Policies." *The In-
1971   ternational Journal of the Addictions* 6
                                (December):571–584.

Koch, J., and S. Grupp   "Police and Illicit Drug Markets: Some Economic
1973   Considerations." *British Journal of Addictions* 68
                                (December): 351–362.

Larner, J., and   *The Addict in the Street.* New York: Grove Press.
R. Tefferteller
1964

Larson, R.
1972
Urban Police Patrol Analysis. Cambridge, MA: The MIT Press.

Laurie, P.
1972
Scotland Yard. Harmondsworth: Penguin.

Lawrence, P. R., and
J. W. Lorsch
1969
Organization and Environment. Homewood, IL: Richard D. Irwin.

LEAA
1978
"PCP — Its Rising Abuse . . . Rapid and Alarming." Interview with Peter Bensinger, Administrator, Drug Enforcement Administration. *Newsletter* 7 (September):2, 9.

Leach, E. R.
1965
The Political Systems of Highland Burma. Boston: Beacon Press.

Lemert, E.
1972
Human Deviance, Social Problems and Social Control, 2nd ed. Englewood Cliffs, NJ: Prentice-Hall.

Levine, S., and P. White
1961
"Exchange as a Conceptual Framework for the Study of Interorganizational Relationships." *Administrative Science Quarterly* 5 (March): 583–597.

Levin, G., E. Roberts,
and G. Hirsch
1975
The Persistent Poppy: A Computer-Aided Search for Heroin Policy. Cambridge: Ballinger.

Lindesmith, A.
1940a
"Dope Fiend Mythology." *Journal of Criminal Law and Criminology* 31 (2):199–208.

Lindesmith, A.
1940b
"The Drug Addict As A Psychopath." *American Sociological Review* 5 (December):914–920.

Lindesmith, A.
1947
Opiate Addiction. Bloomington, IN: Principia Press. (Republished with revisions as *Addiction and Opiates.* Chicago: Aldine, 1968.)

Lindesmith, A.
1965
The Addict and the Law. Bloomington, IN: Indiana University Press.

Lindesmith, A.
1978
"The Federal Narcotics Bureaucracy and Drug Policy." *Journal of Drug Issues* 8 (Spring):157–172.

Lupton, T.
1963
On the Shop Floor. London: Pergamon Press.

McAuliffe, W., and
R. A. Gordon
1974
"A Test of Lindesmith's Theory of Addiction: The Frequency of Euphoria Among Long-Term Addicts." *American Journal of Sociology* 79 (January):795–840.

McDonald, W. F.
1973a

"Enforcement of Narcotics Laws in the District of Columbia." In *Drug Use in America: Problem in Perspective*, appendix, vol. III *Technical Papers of the Second Report of the National Commission on Marijuana and Drug Abuse*. Washington: U.S. Government Printing Office, pp. 651–685.

McDonald, W. F.
1973b

"Administratively Choosing the Drug Criminal." *Journal of Drug Issues* 2 (Spring):123–134.

Maas, P.
1973

Serpico. New York: Dell.

Maines, D. R.
1977

"Social Organization and Social Structure in Symbolic Interactionist Thought." In *Annual Review of Sociology*, eds. A. Inkeles, J. Coleman, and N. Smelser. Palo Alto: Annual Reviews, Inc., pp. 235–259.

Mandel, J.
1969

"Problems with Official Drug Statistics." *Stanford Law Review* 21 (May):991–1040.

Mannheim, K.
1949

Man and Society in An Age of Reconstruction. New York: Harcourt, Brace.

Manning, P. K.
1971

"The Police: Mandate, Strategies and Appearances." In *Crime and Justice in American Society*, ed. Jack D. Douglas Indianapolis: Bobbs-Merrill, pp. 149–193.

Manning, P. K.
1974

"Police Lying." *Urban Life* 3 (October):283–306.

Manning, P. K.
1977a

Police Work: The Social Organization of Policing. Cambridge, MA: The MIT Press.

Manning, P. K.
1977b

"Rules in Organizational Context: Narcotics Law Enforcement in Two Settings." *Sociological Quarterly* 18 (Winter):44–61.

Manning, P. K.
1977c

"Organizational Problematics: Resolving Uncertainty." *Quaderni di Criminologia Clinica* XIX (April–June):137–196.

Manning, P. K.
1977d

"Resources, Information and Strategy: The Open Systems Perspective on Narcotics Law Enforcement." Presented to the American Society of Criminology, Atlanta, Georgia.

Manning, P. K.
forthcoming a

"Environment, Organizational Structure and the Situational Problematics of Police Work in Narcotics and Patrol." In *Work and Problematic Situations,* eds. D. Maines and N. Denzin. New York: T. Y. Crowell.

Manning, P. K.
forthcoming b

"Analytic Induction." In *Social Science Methods Qualitative Methodology,* eds. R. B. Smith and P. K. Manning, vol. I. New York: Irvington Press.

Manning, P. K., and
L. J. Redlinger
1977

"Invitational Edges of Corruption: Some Consequences of Narcotic Law Enforcement." In *Politics and Drugs,* ed. P. E. Rock. Rutgers, N.J.: E. P. Dutton/Society Books, pp. 279–310.

Manning, P. K., and
L. J. Redlinger
1978

"Observations on the Impact of Police Strategies Upon the Trade in Opiates." *IROS: The International Review of Opium Studies.* Philadelphia: Institute for the Study of Human Issues.

Manning, P. K., and
L. J. Redlinger
forthcoming

"Working Bases for Corruption: Some Consequences of Narcotic Law Enforcement." In *Drugs, Crime and Public Policy,* ed. A. Trebach. New York: Praeger. pp. 60–89.

March, J., and J. Olsen
1976

Ambiguity and Choice in Organizations. Bergen, Oslo, and Tromso, Norway: Universitetsforlaget.

March J. A., and
H. A. Simon
1958

Organizations. New York: John Wiley and Sons.

Meyer, J.
1977

"Education As An Institution." *American Journal of Sociology* 83 (July):55–77.

Meyer, J., and C.
Rowan
1977

"Institutionalized Organizations: Formal Structure as Myth and Ceremony." *American Journal of Sociology* 83 (October):340–363.

Meyer, M.
1977

Theory of Organizational Structure. Indianapolis, IN: Bobbs-Merrill Co.

Moore, R.
1971

The French Connection. New York: Bantam Books.

Moore, M.
1977

Buy and Bust. Lexington, MA: Lexington Books.

Muir, W. K., Jr.
1977

Police: Street Corner Politicians. Chicago: University of Chicago Press.

Mukerji, C.
1978

"Bullshitting: Road Lore Among Hitchhikers." *Social Problems* 25 (February):241–252.

Musto, D. F.
1973

The American Disease. New Haven: Yale University Press.

Nebeker, D.
1975

"Situational Favorability and Perceived Environmental Uncertainty: An Integrative Approach." *Administrative Science Quarterly* 20 (June):281–294.

Niederhoffer, A.
1967

Behind the Shield. New York: Doubleday Anchor.

Oaks, D.
1970

"Studying the Exclusionary Rule in Search and Seizure." *University of Chicago Law Review* 37 (Summer):665–757.

O'Donnell, J., H. L.
Voss, R. R. Clayton,
G. I. Slatin, and
R. G. W. Room
1976

Young Men and Drugs — A Nationwide Survey. Research Monograph Number 5, National Institute of Drug Abuse (NIDA). Rockville, MD: NIDA.

Packer, H. L.
1968

The Limits of the Criminal Sanction. Palo Alto: Stanford University Press.

Peabody, R. L.
1962

"Perceptions of Organizational Authority: A Comparative Analysis." *Administrative Science Quarterly* 6 (March)463–482.

Pekkanen, J.
1973

The American Drug Connection: Profiteering and Politicking in the "Ethical" Drug Industry. Chicago: Follett Publishing Co.

Pomeroy, W.
1974

Police Chiefs Discuss Drug Abuse. Washington, D.C.: Drug Abuse Council.

Preble, E., and J. Casey
1969

"Taking Care of Business: The Heroin User's Life on the Streets." *International Journal of the Addictions* 4 (March):1–24.

Preiss, J., and
H. Ehrlich
1966

An Examination of Role Theory: The Case of the State Police. Lincoln: University of Nebraska Press.

The President's Crime
Commission
1967

The Challenge of Crime. Washington, D.C.: U.S. Government Printing Office.

Ray, M.
1964

"Cycles of Abstinence and Relapse Among Heroin Addicts." In *The Other Side,* ed. H. S. Becker New York: The Free Press, pp. 281–297.

Reasons, C.
1974

"The Politics of Drugs: An Inquiry in the Sociology of Social Problems." *Sociological Quarterly* 15 (Summer):381–404.

Rebell, M. A.
1972
"The Undisclosed Informant and the Fourth Amendment." *Yale Law Review* 81 (March): 703–725.

Redlinger, L. J.
1969
Dealing in Dope: Market Mechanisms and Distribu-. tion Patterns of Illicit Narcotics. Ph.D. dissertation, Department of Sociology, Northwestern University.

Redlinger, L. J.
1975a
"Marketing and Distributing Heroin: Some Socio-logical Observations." *Journal of Psychedelic Drugs* 7 (October–December):331–353.

Redlinger, L. J.
1975b
"Notes on Heroin in Phoenix." Report to Drug Abuse Council.

Reiss, A. J., Jr.
1971
The Police and the Public. New Haven: Yale University Press.

Reiss, A. J., Jr., and
D. Bordua
1967
"Environment and Organization: A Perspective on The Police" In *The Police,* ed. D. Bordua. New York: John Wiley and Sons, pp. 25–55.

Rosengren, W. R., and
M. Lefton, eds.
1970
Organizations and Clients: Essays on the Sociology of Service. Columbus, Ohio: C.E. Merrill.

Ross, A.
1958
On Law and Justice. London: Stevens and Sons.

Rossi, P., E. Waite, C. E.
Boese, and R. E. Berk
1974
"The Seriousness of Crimes: Normative Structure and Individual Differences." *American Sociological Review* 39 (April):224–237.

Roth, J.
1963
Time Tables. Indianapolis, IN: Bobbs-Merrill.

Rottenberg, S.
1968
"The Clandestine Distribution of Heroin, Its Discov-ery and Suppression." *Journal of Political Economy* 76 (January/February):78–90.

Roy, D.
1953
"Work Satisfaction and Social Reward in Quota Achievement." *American Sociological Review* 18 (October): 507–514.

Roy, D.
1954
"Efficiency and 'The Fix': Informal InterGroup Rela-tions in a Piecework Machine Shop." *American Journal of Sociology* 60 (November):225–266.

Roy, D.
1960
" 'Banana Time': Job Satisfaction and Informal In-teraction." *Human Organization* 18 (Winter):158–168.

Rubenstein, A. H., and
C. J. Haberstroh, eds.
1966
Some Theories of Organization, revised ed. Homewood, IL: Dorsey Press.

Rubinstein, J.
1973
City Police. New York: Farrar, Straus and Giroux.

Sabbag, R.
1976
Snow-Blind. Indianapolis, IN: Bobbs-Merrill.

Schneyer, T. J.
1971
"Review" [of Kaplan, 1970]. *Stanford Law Review* 24 (November):200–216.

Schur, E.
1962
Narcotic Addiction in Britain and America: The Impact of Public Policy. Bloomington, IN: University of Indiana Press.

Schur, E.
1965
Crimes Without Victims. Englewood Cliffs, NJ: Prentice-Hall, p. 1–30.

Schutz, A.
1967
The Phenomenology of the Social World. Evanston, IL: Northwestern University Press.

Senate Testimony
1975
"Hearings" before Subcommittee on Investigations of the Committee on Government Operations, U.S. Senate 94th Congress, 1st-Session, June 9, 10, 11, pt. 1, Washington, D.C.: U.S. Government Printing Office.

Senate Testimony
1976
Interim Report on *Federal Narcotics Enforcement,* Committee on Government Operations, U.S. Senate, Subcommittee on Operations.

Shellow, R.
1976
Drug Use and Crime, Research Triangle Park, NC: National Institute on Drug Abuse and Research Triangle Institute.

Shils, E., and
M. Janowitz
1948
"Cohesion and Disintegration in the Wehrmacht in World War II." *Public Opinion Quarterly* 12 (Summer):280–315.

Silverman, D.
1971
The Theory of Organizations. New York: Basic Books.

Silverman, L., L. Spruill,
and N. Levine
1975
Heroin Supply and Urban Crime. Washington, D.C.: Drug Abuse Council.

Silverman, M.
1974
Pills, Profits and Politics. Berkeley: University of California Press.

Simon, H.
1957
Models of Man. New York: John Wiley and Sons.

Singer, M.
1971

"The Vitality of Mythical Numbers." *Public Interest* 23 (Spring):4–9.

Skolnick, J.
1966

Justice Without Trial, (2nd ed., 1975). New York: John Wiley and Sons.

Solomon, D., ed.
1966

Marijuana Papers. Indianapolis, IN: Bobbs-Merrill.

Spitzer, S., and
A. T. Scull
1977

"Privatization and Capitalist Development: The Case of the Private Police." *Social Problems* 25 (October):18–29.

Soref, M.
1975

"The Structure of Illegal Drug Markets: An Organizational Approach." Paper presented to American Sociological Association.

Steers, R.
1977

Organizational Effectiveness. Santa Monica, CA: Goodyear Publishers.

Stephens, R.
1972

"The Truthfulness of Addict Respondents in Research Projects." *International Journal of the Addictions* 7 (3):448–549.

Stigler, G.
1970

"The Optimum Enforcement of Laws." *Journal of Political Economy* 78 (May/June):526–536.

Stinchcombe, A.
1959

"Bureaucratic and Craft Administration of Production: A Comparative Study." *Administrative Science Quarterly* 4 (September):168–187.

Stoll, C. S.
1968

"Images of Man and Social Control." *Social Forces* 47 (December):119–127.

Stone, G.
1963

"Appearance and the Self." In *Human Behavior and Social Processes,* ed. A. Rose. Boston: Houghton Mifflin, pp. 86–118.

Strauss, A.
1978

Negotiations. San Francisco: Josey-Bass.

Strauss, A., L. Schatzman, R. Bucher, D. Ehrlich, and M. Sabshin
1964

Psychiatric Ideologies and Institutions. New York: Free Press.

Sudnow, D.
1965

"Normal Crimes . . . " *Social Problems* 12 (Winter):255–276.

Sykes, G.
1958

The Corruption of Authority. Princeton: Princeton University Press.

Terreberry, S.
1968
"The Evolution of Organizational Environments." *Administrative Science Quarterly* 12 (March):590–613.

Thompson, J. D.
1967
Organizations in Action. New York: McGraw-Hill.

Tifft, L.
1974
"The 'Cop Personality' Reconsidered." Journal of Police Science and Administration 2 (3):266–278.

Tifft, L.
1975
"Control Systems, Social Bases of Power, and Power Exercise in Police Organizations." *Journal of Police Science and Administration* 3, (1): 66–76.

Trist, E. L., G. W. Higgin, H. Murray, and A. B. Pollock
1963
Organizational Choice: Capabilities of Groups at the Coal Face Under Changing Technologies. London: Tavistock.

Trocchi, A.
1960
Cain's Book. New York: Grove Press.

Turk, H.
1973
Interorganizational Activation in Urban Communities: Deductions from the Concept of System. Washington, D.C.: American Sociological Association.

United States Bureau of Customs
1976
Annual Report [to Secretary of the Treasury].

von Bertalanffly, L.
1968
General System Theory. New York: George Braziller.

Waldorf, D.
1973
Careers in Dope. Englewood Cliffs, NJ: Prentice-Hall.

Washington *Post*
1973
March 23, 1973:CI

Washington *Post*
1974
November 16, 1974:AI

Weber, M.
1947
The Theory of Economic and Social Organization, ed. and introduction by Talcott Parsons, trans. A. M. Henderson. Glencoe, IL: The Free Press.

Weber, M.
1967
Max Weber on Law in Economy and Society, ed. and annotated by M. Rheinstein, trans. E. Shils and M. Rheinstein. New York: Simon and Shuster.

Webster, J.
1975
"Drug Enforcement: Have the Police Gone into Business for Themselves?" In *The Police in Society,*

eds. E. Viano and J. Reiman. Lexington, MA: D. C. Heath, pp. 189–209.

Weick, K.
1969

The Social Psychology of Organizing. Reading, MA: Addison-Wesley.

Weick, K.
1976

"Educational Organizations As Loosely Coupled Systems." *Administrative Science Quarterly* 21 (March):1–19.

Wellford, C.
1975

"Crime and the Police: A Multivariate Analysis." *Criminology* 12 (August):195–223.

Weppner, R., ed.
1977

Street Ethnography. Beverly Hills: Sage Publications.

Westley, W.
1951

"The Police: A Study in Law, Custom and Morality." Ph.D. dissertation, University of Chicago. (Published by The MIT Press as *Violence and the Police*, 1970.)

Westley, W.
1953

"Violence and the Police." *American Journal of Sociology* 51 (July):34–41.

Westley, W.
1956

"Secrecy and the Police." *Social Forces* 34 (March):254–257.

Whitebread, C., and
R. Stevens
1972

"Constructive Possession in Narcotics Cases: To Have and Have Not." *Virginia Law Review* 58 (May):751–775.

Whittemore, L. W.
1973

Super-Cops. New York: Bantam Books.

Wildavsky, A.
1974

The Politics of the Budgetary Process, 2nd ed. Boston: Little, Brown.

Williams, J. R.,
P.K. Manning, and
L. J. Redlinger
1977

The Police and Illicit Substance Control: A Preliminary Report, (March). Research Triangle Park, NC: Research Triangle Institute.

Williams, J. R.,
L. J. Redlinger, and
P. K. Manning
1978

Police Narcotics Control: Patterns and Strategies, 2 vols. Final Report submitted to National Institute of Law Enforcement and Criminal Justice, Law Enforcement Assistance Administration, Grant No. 76-N1-49-0109.

Wilson, J. Q.
1968

Varieties of Police Behavior. Cambridge, MA: Harvard University Press.

Wilson, J. Q.
1978

The Investigators. New York: Basic Books.

Wilson, J. V.   *Police Report.* Boston: Little, Brown.
1975

Winch, P.   *The Idea of a Social Science.* London: Routledge
1958   and Kegan Paul.

Woodley, R.   *Dealer.* New York: Holt, Rinehart and Winston.
1971

Young, J.   *The Drug Takers.* London: Paladin Books.
1972

Index